IN SEARCH OF MAYA SEA TRADERS

NUMBER ELEVEN:

Texas A&M University Anthropology Series

D. Gentry Steele, Series Editor

Series Advisory Board

William Irons   Eric Trinkaus

Conrad Kottak   Michael R. Waters

James. F. O'Connell   Patty Jo Watson

Harry J. Shafer

D1545986

IN SEARCH OF MAYA SEA TRADERS

HEATHER McKILLOP

TEXAS A&M UNIVERSITY PRESS *College Station*

The paper used in this book meets the minimum
requirements of the American National Standard for
Permanence of Paper for Printed Library Materials,
z39.48-1984.
Binding materials have been chosen for durability.
∞

Library of Congress Cataloging-in-Publication Data

McKillop, Heather Irene, 1953–
    In search of Maya sea traders / Heather McKillop. — 1st ed.
        p. cm. — (Texas A&M University anthropology series ;
        no. 11)
    Includes bibliographical references and index.
    ISBN 1-58544-389-1 (cloth : alk. paper)—
    ISBN 1-58544-424-3 (pbk. : alk. paper)
        1. Wild Cane Cay Site (Belize) 2. Mayas—Commerce.
    3. Mayas—Antiquities. 4. Excavations (Archaeology)—
    Belize—Punta Gorda Region. 5. Underwater archae-
    ology—Belize—Punta Gorda Region. 6. Coastwise naviga-
    tion—Belize—Punta Gorda Region. 7. Punta Gorda Region
    (Belize)—Antiquities. I. Title. II. Texas A&M
    University anthropology series ; no. 11.

    F1435.1.W6M35 2005
    972.82′401—dc22
                        2004010258

Unless otherwise indicated, all photographs and
drawings are by the author.

To Bob, Eleanor, and Gordon

CONTENTS

PREFACE

The ancient Maya civilization of Central America has fascinated and perplexed scholars and the public alike for generations. The stone temples emerging above the rainforest canopy, the rise and collapse of the civilization centuries before the sixteenth-century arrival of Europeans, and the elaborate hieroglyphs carved on stone monuments add to the appeal of this ancient culture. Less well known are the ancient Maya farmers who lived in smaller communities outside the great cities and who supported the "high culture" by food and labor taxes. Modern Maya Indians continue a traditional farming way of life perhaps little changed from ancient times. Few of them understand their ancient heritage or connection to archaeological sites that attract Western tourists, scholars, and students.

The 1839 publication of *Incidents of Travel in Central America* by John Lloyd Stephens triggered widespread interest by the educated public in America and Europe in the ancient Maya civilization. This interest has remained unabated. *National Geographic* and *Archaeology* magazines, the Discovery and History channels, public television, and the Internet have enhanced public access to Maya archaeology. A variety of volunteer organizations, notably Earthwatch, the Maya Research Program, and University Research Expedition Projects (UREP), among others, have engaged the public in fieldwork at Maya archaeological sites. Public lecture series such as the Maya weekends at the University of Pennsylvania, Tulane, and UCLA; the Maya Hieroglyphic Workshop at the University of Texas; and LSU Maya Archaeology Night bring Maya archaeologists and the interested public together to discuss the ancient Maya civilization.

In Search of Maya Sea Traders includes descriptions of my experiences carrying out fieldwork as well as the archaeology itself in order to make the processes of Maya archaeological research more accessible to the educated public and students (see Sabloff 1998). *In Search of Maya Sea Traders* is neither a comprehensive monograph on the coastal Maya archaeology of southern Belize, nor is it the definitive monograph on Wild Cane Cay aimed specifically or exclusively at academics and graduate students. Endnotes provide citations for further reading, references for interpretations, and detailed supporting information for interested readers. Much of the basic archaeological description has been published in academic journals and books but is largely unavailable to the general public. This book does include new information not published elsewhere, specifically about the stone architecture on Wild Cane Cay and Frenchman's Cay, among other findings.

This book departs from traditional publications by Maya archaeologists on their research. I contextualize fieldwork within the local communities and peoples with whom we interacted. I contextualize the excavations within the experiences of fieldwork, including food, accommodation, and travel. I contextualize the archaeology within the processes of carrying out fieldwork in order to engage the reader vicariously in the excitement and experience of fieldwork and interpretation. In these ways, I hope to bring the educated public and students closer to the experiences and processes of carrying out Maya archaeology.[1] As Jeremy Sabloff (1998, 872–73) wrote in his 1996 Distinguished Lecture to the Archaeology Division of the American Anthropological Association, "[T]he academic trend away from public communication appears to be increasing just as public interest in archaeology seems to be reaching new heights. . . . If we abandon much of the field of popular writing to the fringe, we should not be surprised at all that the public often fails to appreciate the significance of what we do. . . . I believe that we have a responsibility to give back to the public that provides us with grants, or contracts, or jobs. . . . We need to share with them our excitement in our work and our insights into how people of the past lived and how our understandings of the past can inform us about the present and future."

Some readers are familiar with Maya prehistory, but for others, I provide this brief synopsis with suggestions for further introductory reading. The ancient Maya civilization developed in the tropical rainforests of Guatemala and Belize and in parts of Mexico, Honduras, and El Salvador. The earliest evidence of human presence in the Maya area consists of isolated recoveries of stone spear points of Paleoindians who populated the Americas after the end of the last ice age, the Pleistocene. Having crossed from Siberia on the Bering Strait land bridge created by a lowering of sea level during times of maximum glaciation, the Paleoindians followed now-extinct herbivores, such as the mammoth, mastodon, giant horse, and giant armadillo, in search of food, populating the Americas by 9500 B.C. Their diagnostic chert and obsidian stone fluted points, with a gouge on each side where the point was hafted to a spear, have been found at Ladyville in Belize and at several locations in the highlands of Guatemala, notably Los Tapiales.

Following the extinction of Pleistocene megafauna in the Americas, people adapted their way of life to hunting smaller animals such as white-tailed deer and rabbits and to gathering wild plants for food. This "Archaic" way of life, in which people lived in temporary camps following the seasonal presence and abundance of wild foods in different locations, persisted until the introduction of farming and permanent settlements. Evidence for Archaic peoples in the Maya area is scarce, likely buried by rainforest vegetation and centuries of subsequent construction by the ancient Maya. The recovery of the distinctive Archaic stemmed points from various locations in northern Belize and excavation of pre-Maya occupation levels at Colha in northern Belize promise to provide information on the change from a hunting and gathering to a farming way of life.

The earliest evidence for ethnically "Maya" people dates to about 1800 B.C. along the Pacific coast of Guatemala and to about 1000 B.C. in the tropical lowlands of Belize and Guatemala. The first appearance of pottery in these areas marks the inception of the Preclassic period. Norman Hammond's excavations at Cuello in northern Belize first documented this early Maya settlement in the Maya lowlands. Cuello was a permanent village of corn farmers who had well-made pottery vessels.

The origins of Classic Maya civilization can be traced to the Late Preclassic period (300 B.C. to A.D. 300), during which time there is the elaboration of temples and other public architecture with decorated façades representing the emergence of Maya rulers. David Freidel's excavations at Cerros in northern Belize revealed a Late Preclassic community unencumbered by subsequent construction. One temple has a painted stucco façade and an offering of imported, carved, jade miniature heads at its summit.

The Classic period of Maya civilization is defined as the time when carved stone monuments called *stelae* were erected at Maya cities with dates in the Maya long count, from A.D. 300 to 900. The period begins with the earliest stela at Tikal, Guatemala, dated to A.D. 292, to the last stela, dated to A.D. 909, at Tonina, Mexico. The Classic stelae provide a dynastic record of the lives and public achievements of Maya kings and queens who governed over some eighty city-states in the lowlands of Guatemala, Belize, Honduras, El Salvador, and Mexico. Simon Martin and Nicholai Grube describe this written history in *Chronicle of Maya Kings and Queens*. Since the stunning discoveries by Tatiana Proskouriakoff, Heinrich Berlin, and others that the glyphs are historical records, much of the history of Maya royalty has been deciphered on stelae, other carved stone monuments, and painted pots. Although the Maya certainly had a sophisticated knowledge of mathematics and astronomy, these are not the themes of Classic period stelae as was the dominant view until the 1960s. Michael Coe's *Breaking the Maya Code* recounts the exciting history of the decipherment of Mayan hieroglyphs.

Travelers to Maya ruins see the sites at the height of the Late Classic (A.D. 600–900) before the collapse of the Classic period cities and their rulers. Characteristics of the Classic period include temples, palaces, and ball courts forming rectangular plazas at city centers, carved and dated stelae, and painted pictorial vases and other pots in polychrome, most commonly with red-and-black decoration on an orange background. The royal court included administrators and a variety of artisans, including scribes, masons, painters, sculptors, and traders. Although the urban character of Maya cities included tens of thousands of residents, the bulk of the Maya population lived a simpler, farming way of life in surrounding communities. Today's Maya villages of thatched palm houses provide a valuable analog for the common Maya. Both modern and ancient farmers practiced the same method of *swidden* farming, in which a plot of rainforest is burned and planted for several years until the nutrients of the soil are depleted. More intensive forms of agriculture, such as terracing hill slopes and draining swamps, as well as other food systems, such as tree cropping, are associated with the increasing population of the Late Classic period.

The ancient Maya economy consisted of the political economy, controlled by the Maya royalty to meet their needs for ritual and status paraphernalia — their badges of power — and the subsistence economy, which provided basic food and resources to elite and commoner alike. Maya researchers disagree about the degree to which the ancient Maya society and economy were centralized. Some researchers view the Maya lowlands as divided into some eighty independent city-states, while other researchers consider that alliances among city-states created larger political and economic entities. The historical focus of Mayan hieroglyphs provides little information on trade or other aspects of the ancient economy, apart from tantalizing clues that tribute in chocolate and other goods was an element of the political landscape. In *Salt, White Gold of the Ancient Maya* I describe Late Classic salt workshops located geographically distant from the power and sites of urban royal Maya. The salt produced in this coastal lagoon helped satiate the basic biological needs of the inland Maya at cities such as Lubaantun and Nim Li Punit, who likely negotiated marriage and other alliances with the coastal Maya at Wild Cane Cay and Frenchman's Cay. Other researchers describe the Maya subsistence economy as more centralized and under the control of the urban Maya elite, and this is certainly well documented by Diane Chase and Arlen Chase at Caracol, where limestone roads called *sacbes* link the downtown with other parts of the community.

The ancient Maya obtained trade goods from near their communities, as well as from elsewhere in the realm of a city-state and even farther away. Some resources from distant lands, such as obsidian — a volcanic rock used to make sharp-edged blades for ritual bloodletting and other tasks — were traded to communities of various sizes. Other exotic goods such as jade and gold, as well as highly crafted pots, had a more restricted distribution to the Maya royalty. Many goods and resources were traded at moderate distances, such as chert from northern Belize to southern Belize and granite from the Maya Mountains of southern Belize to northern Belize. *In Search of Maya Sea Traders* describes the trading port of Wild Cane Cay, where exotic obsidian and other goods were traded from distant lands, as well as the more limited, coastal-inland trade of salt, seafood, and other marine resources. Wild Cane Cay continued and even expanded after the tenth-century A.D. collapse of the lowland cities. Wild Cane Cay evidently realigned its trading alliances with the emerging polities such as Chichen Itza in the northern Yucatan of Mexico.

NOTE

1. See http://pqasb.pqarchiver.com/theadvocate/87460063.html?did=87460063&
   FMT=ABS&FMTS=FT&date=Oct+31,+2001&author=&desc=Another+
   example+of+LSU=relevance.

FURTHER INTRODUCTORY READINGS

Ashmore, Wendy, ed. *Lowland Maya Settlement Patterns.* Albuquerque: University of New Mexico Press, 1981.

Coe, Michael D. *The Maya.* New York: Thames and Hudson, 1999.

————. *Breaking the Maya Code.* New York: Thames and Hudson, 2001.

Freidel, David, Linda Schele, and Joy Parker. *Maya Cosmos.* New York: Morrow, 1993.

Harrison, Peter D., and B. L. Turner, eds. *Pre-Hispanic Maya Agriculture.* Albuquerque: University of New Mexico Press, 1978.

Martin, Simon, and Nicholai Grube. *Chronicle of Maya Kings and Queens.* New York: Thames and Hudson, 2000.

Masson, Marilyn, and David A. Freidel, eds. *Ancient Maya Political Economies.* New York: Altamira Press, 2002.

McKillop, Heather. *Salt, White Gold of the Ancient Maya.* Gainesville: University Press of Florida, 2002.

————. *The Ancient Maya.* Santa Barbara: ABC-Clio, 2004.

Sabloff, Jeremy A. "Distinguished Lecture in Archaeology: Communication and the Future of American Archaeology." *American Anthropologist* 100(4) (1998): 869–75.

Schele, Linda, and David A. Freidel. *A Forest of Kings: The Untold Story of the Ancient Maya.* New York: Morrow, 1990.

Webster, David. *The Fall of the Ancient Maya.* New York: Thames and Hudson, 2002.

ACKNOWLEDGMENTS

The archaeological fieldwork discussed in this book was made possible by permits from the Belize government Department of Archaeology and Department of Forestry and particularly by the assistance, advice, and friendship of the members of those departments, notably Archaeological Commissioners John Morris, Brian Woodeye, Jaime Awe, Alan Moore, the late Winnel Branche, and the late Harriot Topsey. The research was enabled by generous funding over the years from Earthwatch and its corps of volunteers, the Social Sciences and Humanities Research Council of Canada, National Science Foundation, Wenner-Gren Foundation, the University of California at Santa Barbara, Louisiana State University, and private donations from William Heth, M. Patricia Colquette, Cecil McCurry, among others. For their hard work and friendship, I express my thanks to all those who helped with the fieldwork: my field staff, Shannon Ascher, Mariange Beaudry, Melissa Braud, Jean Carpenter, Paul Diamond, Mai Dinh, Meredith Dreiss, Brad Ensor, Andrea Freudenberger, Laurie Jackson, Aline Magnoni, Eric Malatesta, Mirtha Martin, Maryika McKellovich, Donna Morrison, Lyra Spang, Nathaniel Spang, Ted Steiner, Laurie Stephenson, Maxine Stonecipher, Bernie Walsh, Shelly Warrington, Rachel Watson, and Ellen Whowell, among others. In particular, I gratefully acknowledge the participation of Laurie Jackson in the 1982 and 1988–1991 field seasons. My Belizean staff included Andres Ash, Catarino Cal, Reuben Cal, Sylvestre Cal, Manuel Coc, Barbara Fraser, Orlando Usher, and others.

My Earthwatch volunteers include Anne Alexander, Art Arnold, Dee Bean, Ken Benson, Martin Betcherman, Linda Bills, Russell Black, Barbara Bryant, Bob Bryant, Bob Callahan, Wayne Chatfield, Dee Christian, Kiki

Christmas, Sylvia Christmas, Linda Clark, Gerry Cole, Pat Colquette, Jim Concannon, Matthew Crampton, Michelle Cristo, Anne Daniels, Marie Dee, Chris Degraffenreid, Ellen Devine, Kate Devine, Carol Dodds, Scott Dougald, Bob Eisenberg, Lila Eisenberg, Ken Foster, Wendy Frosh, Jean Fuhr, Bob Furlong, Molly Heckscher, Cate Heneghan, Bill Heth, Anthony Holley, Eva Hurliman, Drew Ingersoll, Phil Jackubiak, Harry Jennings, Susan Kaler, Joe Kolb, Noele Krenkle, Ted Krzesowski, Eva Kulda, Claudia Lamperti, Karen Leabo, Bill Leake, Janet Liles, Jerry Lutovich, Marion Macrae, Cassie Major, Joe Mares, Cecil McCurry, Myra McFarland, Pat Merrick, Kate Mitchell, Bill Morris, Minor Myers, Jan Nevill, Todd Orland, Heather Osborn, Jack Percival, Bob Phillips, Beth Pope, Diane Powell, Julie Prodell, Pam Pulver, Cecilia Rhoades, Mike Riordan, Russell Roberts, Jack Romig, Bob Shaw, Kay Shrinker, Kimmie Sloan, Steve Stakeman, Marge Stanbury, Sally Strazdins, Gene Stroot, Frank Terwilliger, Joanne Turner, Toni Wallace, Lois Whippen, Jonathan Whitehead, Gary Whitely, Cheryl Wilson, and Darlene Yarborough. My field school students include Renny Bergeron, Mark Carpenter, Jay Cleymaet, Joel Escamilla, Sally Gaubert, Jessica Jasper, Cliff Luhn, and Fred Sunderman, as well as others who subsequently became project staff members.

I appreciate the assistance of many people in Belize, especially in Punta Gorda and the surrounding Toledo district, notably the late Adel Cabral, the late Frank Cabral, Osmond Chan, John Spang, Tanya Russ, Amber Carpenter, Robert Hangii, Paul Carpenter, Harry Gomez, Carl Gomez, Winnel Branche, Emory King Sr., Alistair King, Edna King, Max Stock, Miss Sylvia, Felix, Santiago Coc, Dr. Marenco, Brian Holland, Anne Brosier, Irene Mahung, Peter Mahung, Jack Nightingale, Barbara Fraser, Wallace Young, Felicia Young, Julio Requena, Leanor Requena, Bobbie Polonio, Lucille Johnson, Flo Johnson, Chet Schmidt, William Tate, Iris Vernon, Alejandro Vernon, Louise Ramclam, Ludwig Palacio, Thomas Mathew, Albert King Sr., the late Charlie Carson, Dr. Francis Arzu, Will Maheia, Will Heyman, Fr. Dieckmann, Joan Musa, and the late Jean Shaw, among many others.

The people of Punta Gorda and Port Honduras make the archaeological work both possible and enjoyable. I hope that we are working together to develop a coastal Maya site for tourism for the cultural and economic benefit of the people of the Port Honduras region as well as further projects that promote heritage. I appreciate Texas A&M University Press's initial and continued excitement and insights about my manuscript, as well as the enduring professional care of their editors and staff.

Many thanks go to Mary Lee Eggart, Louisiana State University, who drew most of the maps and other illustrations from my sketches or from the artifacts. Greg Stone generously set up the wave tank at LSU for an experiment described in this book. On a personal level, I appreciate the encouragement, support, and patience of my husband, Robert Tague, and our daughter, Eleanor, in my research. Of course, I will always remember Tiger, who shared these experiences, 1982–1997.

PART I
MAYA SEA TRADERS, 1981–1982

Map of Belize with inset showing location of Belize in the Maya area
(by Mary Lee Eggart).

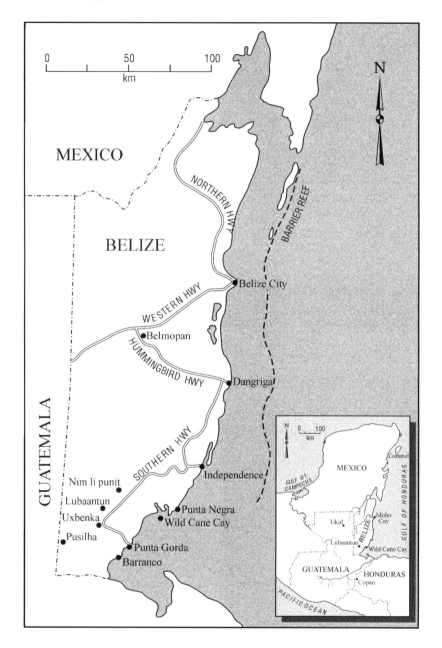

CHAPTER 1
MY FIRST VISIT TO WILD CANE CAY, 1981

I met King at the Texaco dock in Punta Gorda and hired him to take me in his small wooden boat on a reconnaissance trip to visit several archaeological sites that had been reported on the islands north of town (figure 1.1). King was middle aged, somewhat reserved, and looked better prepared to go to sea than the younger men at the Texaco dock. He had a boat and seemed to know everyone else and the sea. However, he was a stranger to me. Stepping into what was actually a dugout with a 10 horsepower engine to embark on a journey in the Caribbean worried me. Still, I could not see any other way to investigate some of the offshore islands for my proposed archaeological research on Maya sea trade. I wanted to visit some of the cays where archaeological sites had been reported in order to select a place to carry out my doctoral fieldwork.[1]

King carried no life jackets, water, food, or a radio. In fact, the dory had no basic safety equipment at all. However, I had little fear, respect, or knowledge of the sea at that time. To me, his dory was simply the available transportation.

King's black curly hair peeked out from under a navy wool cap, adding to a dark image set against the Caribbean sun. His grin revealed a flash of a gold tooth. In front of the motor was a small wooden board, where he sat as he maneuvered us through the water. I considered striking up a conversation. Since he could not hear me because of the roar of the motor, however, I relaxed on my board seat in the middle of the dory, pulled out my map of the area, and watched the sea and the patches of mangrove islands that surrounded us. The sun shimmered across ripples

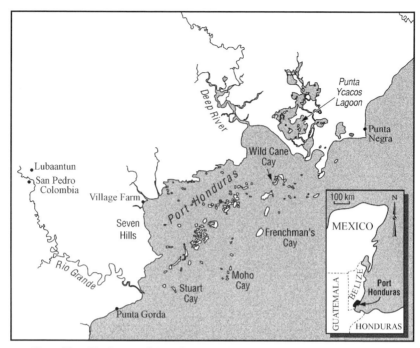

1.2 Map of Port Honduras with inset showing its location in Belize (by Mary Lee Eggart).

in the waves and provided a background for occasional dolphins that leapt in front of us. My fears of the voyage seemed unwarranted.

The coastal area north of Punta Gorda was evidently unpopulated, as the rainforest met the sea without interruption. We followed the shoreline north to a point of land that had no protection from the open sea. Once we rounded the point we traveled among small patches of mangrove islands that formed irregular shapes. Occasional coconut palms marked isolated spots of dry land. We encountered no sign of human presence in the area. The mangrove cays shielded us from the offshore breeze that was building.

With some excitement, I matched the landscape around me with my map (figure 1.2). A series of limestone hills known as the Seven Hills marked the only dramatic topography in the coastal landscape that was intermittently above sea level. The coastline formed a bight locally known as Port Honduras, into which several large rivers deposited fresh water and silt. The rivers also provided a water-transportation route in recent times from inland communities in southern Belize to Punta Gorda. In ancient times the rivers may have been trade corridors between inland Maya cities such as Lubaantun or Nim Li Punit and the offshore cays that I hoped to investigate.[2]

King threw a heavy fishing line over one side of the boat and soon caught a yellow jack. The fish lay flapping in the bottom of the boat near a coiled mass of fishing line that King had hauled, hand over hand, into the boat. He wrapped the line around a short stick and threw the hook with a shiny spoon over the side, letting the line unravel again. I began to wonder whether our fishing expedition included visiting archaeological sites.

However, King found routes around the unmarked shoals and through the clusters of mangrove islands to the various destinations I wanted to see, including "Frenchman's Cay," "Moho Cay," "Stuart Cay," and "Wild Cane Cay." As we approached Wild Cane Cay, we were greeted by a German Shepherd standing in the sea and barking at us (figures 1.3 – 1.4). A gruff, old man yelled to us from the shore, "*No* digging. *No* digging. *No* digging."

Did I look like an archaeologist? Were all foreign visitors archaeologists? The island had no telephones or radios. Was he thinking of the various archaeologists, geographers, and explorers who had visited and sometimes excavated at Wild Cane Cay and taken artifacts away since at least the turn of the century?[3]

My next memory of this initial foray is of sitting on the verandah of a dilapidated, frame house on Wild Cane Cay having fried fish and birthday cake with Frank Cabral, the man who moments before had seemed so unfriendly. We were joined by his sister, Adel Cabral — the owner of the island, and King. We were making plans for me to return in a few months to excavate on the island. Frank would locate a dory for me to buy, King would take us in his boat to procure the dory, and Adel would cook for my project. Apparently I had managed to befriend them.

Frank and I agreed that he would captain my boat with his engine — an old, six-horsepower Evinrude. In return, I would leave him my dory to use when I was not there. Although I was a graduate student on a limited budget, Frank had no other prospects for an improved lifestyle.

Even rough seas on our return voyage to Punta Gorda did not diminish my excitement about carrying out research on ancient sea trade at Wild Cane Cay. As King dropped me off at the Texaco dock, I barely considered that the sea would dominate my life for the next sixteen years.

When I returned the next year, King took Frank and me to look at a dory in Barranco, a community several miles south of Punta Gorda. Dories were scarce in Punta Gorda because so few people went to sea. Barranco was accessible only by water, so there were more dories. Both Punta Gorda and Barranco, as well as coastal towns farther north, were Garifuna communities.[4]

The Garifuna, who had recently changed their name from Black Carib, were descendants of African slaves whom the British had driven from St. Vincent's Island in the Lesser Antilles, where the British had brought them to work on the sugar plantations. The Black Caribs — a mixture of native Carib Indians and runaway African slaves — had become difficult for the British to control, so in 1797 they deported them. The Black Caribs survived a voyage to the Bay Islands off the north coast of Honduras, from where they established settlements along the Caribbean coasts of Nicaragua, Honduras, and Guatemala and had arrived in Belize perhaps as early as 1802. Their first known settlement in Belize dates to 1832 at Stann Creek Town, now called Dangriga.[5] Barranco was the most isolated and least subjected to change from outside influences.

The dory I purchased in Barranco was not meant for travel in the open seas to Wild Cane Cay. However, as a doctoral student in 1982 I had a small research grant from the University of California at Santa Barbara, where I was a student, in addition to a fellowship from the Canadian government to run a field project. The dory's price of $250 was within my budget. My concerns were to minimize expenses, which meant that I did not always do things efficiently.

In addition to foreign volunteers, I hired several men to work on the project on Wild Cane Cay.[6] The arrangements had been made with a friend of mine — Santiago Coc — who was the caretaker of the inland Maya ruin of Lubaantun. While I was in Santa Barbara, I arranged by mail for six reliable Kekchi Maya men from Santiago's village of San Pedro Colombia to take the truck-bus to Punta Gorda and to meet me at the Texaco dock on a prearranged market day for a sea journey they had never taken before.[7]

Loaded with food, Maya workers, my foreign volunteers, and me, the dory met calm waters during our first venture to sea, and for this I was thankful. The gunwales barely reached above the surface of the water, which shimmered in its stillness as we cut a trail through the sea. Clearly Frank and I were the only ones not surprised by the absence of people along the coast north of Punta Gorda.[8] Everyone sat quietly watching the landscape. While Frank steered us to Wild Cane Cay, I chatted with the Maya workers and realized that their perception of the sea was different from mine.

One of the older men, Sylvestre, admitted that he had never been to sea. I understood that, to him, the sea was just a big river. Sylvestre was comparing the Caribbean to the Rio Grande, which ran by San Pedro Colombia. Although we both spoke English, we shared little else in common. I wondered

1.3 *Oblique air view of Wild Cane Cay from the west, showing the natural harbor.*

1.4 *Wild Cane Cay from the south, showing the windward shore.*

how to start explaining the tides, oceans, or basic world geography. Since I myself had only a superficial understanding of the mechanics, I hesitated and then began to describe the effects of the moon on the tides.

Sylvestre was an intelligent man. However, I realized that he knew little about the world outside of his village. I had no idea whether I was making sense to him or to the other men, who sat paying rapt attention to my story. They smiled and accepted my words, but I never knew how they perceived this new information. I directed our conversation toward more familiar topics for me, asking them what they knew about their ancestors. I discovered that they knew virtually nothing about their heritage or their ancestors who had built the Maya cities on the mainland and ventured to the offshore islands. The Maya in the small communities of southern Belize learned British history in school, although few of them had gone beyond grade six. Fascinated to learn that they were going to uncover an old settlement of their distant relatives, they began to see this job as something more than just their only opportunity to earn a wage — although that was clearly paramount. They had no knowledge that the ancient Maya once plied the coastal waters on which we traveled. The ancient Maya world was more circumscribed than mine but was far more cosmopolitan than that of their modern descendants.

The men were happy to have the work since paid jobs in their community were scarce. They were eager to work and to please me. Unlike some Yucatec Maya Indians in northern Belize who regularly work on archaeological projects, the Kekchi Maya in southern Belize had little recent experience working with archaeologists.[9] None had done archaeological work in the south in recent years.

On the journey in my newly acquired dory, I gained an ethereal understanding of coastal trade. Wild Cane Cay was some 12 miles (20 km) north of Punta Gorda by sea. As the only coconut-palm-covered island in a sea of about 135 mangrove cays, it was easy to find during the day. I later found that travel time from Punta Gorda to Wild Cane Cay depended on a variety of factors. In my 22-foot dugout, the voyage normally took about three hours. More like a river dory, the canoe was carved from a single trunk of a local hardwood, Santa Maria, but did not have the sides built up with planks to fend off the sea like seafaring dories. We got wet on every trip, either from the rain, the sea spray, or, most commonly, simply from the waves lapping over the sides of the boat. As a consequence, trips to Punta Gorda from the field camp on Wild Cane Cay were rare.

Wild Cane Cay

1.5

*Oblique air view of the Bedford
Cays (all islands in the foreground)
from the east with other cays and
the mainland in the background.*

Our field station on Wild Cane Cay was the focus of my dissertation research on ancient Maya coastal trade. The site was incorrectly marked twice on the topographic map of the area. The actual site location was not indicated. However, local people — who did not use topographic maps — knew it was one of the Bedford Cays, a group of mangrove islands that formed a sheltered harbor (figure 1.5). Wild Cane Cay was the only dry land part of the Bedford Cays. The site covered the entire island of Wild Cane Cay, including nearly 3.5 acres of land (approximately 300 by 80 meters, or yards). Barely above sea level, the land merged into the red mangrove swamp on the eastern and western ends (figure 1.6). On the seaward side, where I had landed the previous year, the water was shallow and rocky where the sea washed against the shore. On the opposite shore, the water was protected in the quiet lagoon where we would land in the coming months.

My first impression of the island had been the dilapidated, white frame house with a verandah, all raised on wooden stilts, and the many coconut palms (figure 1.7). A closer look revealed other fruit trees, including mango, papaya, custard apple, banana, breadfruit, grapefruit, orange, lemon, guava, and tamarind. The ground was variously covered in grass, fallen palm fronds, and bare earth, the last revealing rich, dark, soil littered with ancient Maya pottery sherds, as well as broken obsidian and chert artifacts. The large

1.6 *Windward shore of Wild Cane Cay, showing the coconut palms on dry land and red mangroves in the inundated area.*

1.7 *Cabral family house on Wild Cane Cay.*

1.8 *Tent camp on western end of Wild Cane Cay.*

number of artifacts on the ground's surface was stunning in contrast to their paucity at other Maya sites I had visited. The abundance of blades made from obsidian — an imported volcanic rock — indicated that quite a bit of long-distance trade had been carried out at Wild Cane Cay. Together with its sheltered harbor located in the mouth of the Deep River (a major waterway leading into the interior of ancient Maya territory) and its location at the northern end of Port Honduras, beyond which sea travel was in open waters, Wild Cane Cay seemed like a good spot for a trading port. For my research I would focus on the age, longevity, and importance of the port in sea trade. Over the next several months, my archaeological team would dig a series of randomly selected excavations on the island to determine the relative abundance of trade goods in archaeological deposits of different ages.

If the Maya workers and students were unsettled by their dory voyage to Wild Cane Cay, they soon forgot in the excitement of setting up camp (figure 1.8). I had provided tents, which the Maya immediately recognized as a wonderful invention to keep out the rain and insects. My volunteers were overwhelmed by the idyllic island setting and the ubiquity of artifacts on its surface. We established a tent camp in the main plaza at Wild Cane Cay, avoiding the firing range of coconut palms, the holes dug by burrowing land crabs *(Cardisoma ghahumi)*, and the clumps of debris formed by fallen palm

1.9 *Frank Cabral* (center) *with Sylvestre Cal* (right) *at Wild Cane Cay.*

fronds, coconuts, and termite nests. Once everyone was set up in their tents, had swum in the lagoon, explored the island, and eaten rice and beans with chicken that we brought from town, the camp was quiet. I wandered up to the house to see Frank and Adel before retiring to my tent for the night.

Frank and Adel had returned to live on the island where they had been born and raised. Their house was a typical, Creole, one-story dwelling with a front verandah. Under the house, which was elevated on posts, was enough room for keeping chickens, baking, and general storage. The house had an ageless, weathered appearance. Adel told me that her grandparents had built it in the early part of the century.[10]

The Cabral siblings lived a Spartan life, which was somewhat improved by my project's arrival. Frank gathered coconuts and other fruits from the island. Despite arthritis, which made his movements deliberate, Frank was an imposing man. His large frame and height created an intimidating appearance, which he cultivated (figure 1.9). Adel, in contrast, exuded warmth and friendliness (figure 1.10). They referred to each other as Mr. Frank and Miss Adel. I was Miss Heather.

Frank and Adel's diet was supplemented by fresh fish, which they caught from shore or retrieved from lines that were set overnight in the shallow water. A surprising quantity of fish was caught at the edge of the bank. Adel

1.10
Adel Cabral on Wild Cane Cay.

cooked and prepared their meals. Occasionally they purchased dry goods —
coffee, sugar, rice, beans, salt, and lard — from Punta Gorda. King and other
fishermen brought them food and other supplies.

Their grandparents had settled Wild Cane Cay in the nineteenth century.
They had left their families on the barrier reef, some 25 miles out to sea, due
to insufficient land to support the expanding Cabral clan. Like their Creole
antecedents, Frank and Adel's grandparents lived by fishing and by tree cropping. Adel told me that her grandparents had cleared the native wild cane,
wild palms, and other vegetation from Wild Cane Cay in order to plant the
more productive coconut palms.[11] They had also planted trees of several introduced species, including breadfruit, citrus, banana, and several varieties of
mango.[12] Along with native papaya, guava, and calabash trees, Wild Cane Cay
was a tropical fruit paradise in 1982.

It was several years before I discovered that Adel's common-law husband
was still alive. He lived in their house in Belize City, where I happened to
meet him on one of my visits to see Adel, when she was visiting her children.

She told me that she had taken care of him for many years, but that he had become old and cranky. Adel decided their children could care for him while she returned to the cay she had left many years before. Shunning the relative material comforts of running water, electricity, and radio in Belize City, Adel seemed content to live a simple life on the cay. Charlie Chan preferred to stay in Belize City.

Frank had retired from the merchant marines and left his wife and family in Honduras to live with his sister on Wild Cane Cay. His dog Lion patrolled Wild Cane Cay and warded off intruders. I befriended both Frank and Lion — and got away with it.

Frank supported Adel and himself by selling coconuts in Punta Gorda, but until our arrival, he had no boat in which to transport his produce to town. He waited for the occasional dory to stop by in this uninhabited coastal area to hitch a ride with three or four hundred coconuts. This arrangement seemed to me to be a precarious way to survive. However, I later saw that boats stopped to transport Frank and his coconuts to Punta Gorda. Fishermen passing from the tiny Garifuna fishing village of Punta Negra to the north, on their way to sell their catch at the market in Punta Gorda, arrived to pick up Frank and his coconuts on Wednesdays or Saturdays. Anna, who lived on a nearby cay and supported herself and her family by selling fish in Punta Gorda, arrived unannounced to convey Frank and his coconuts to market. A load of several hundred coconuts was never greeted with surprise. However, Wild Cane Cay was unique in the area for its mangos, guavas, breadfruit, citrus, and other fruit trees. Frank and Adel were generous in giving them away.

People swarmed by the dory whenever Frank arrived in Punta Gorda with his wares. I suggested to him that he raise the price of his coconuts. At first, Frank was reluctant to do so since he believed that other people were poor like him, so he did not want to charge them too much. Supply and demand economics were not a consideration in Frank's life. He did, however, see the value of increasing his price for coconuts in order to break even with the groceries and rum that he bought in town.

Frank's days were spent with coconuts. My interest in mapping and collecting artifacts from the surface of the island pleased him because we cleaned the fallen coconut palm fronds and gathered the nuts. Frank never let coconuts grow where they fell. Each fallen fruit was either collected for sale in town, selected for home consumption or chicken feed, or carefully placed to space the trees apart from one another.[13] He stabbed each coconut with his machete and shook the fruit to listen for coconut water inside. Fresh coconuts were dropped into his mesh sack to eat or sell. Sprouted coconuts were carefully placed where he wanted them to grow.

Frank hauled his sack of coconuts to husking stations scattered around the island. He drove each fruit onto a sharpened wooden spear with the weight of his body and twisted the husk. The shell peeled off in three or four clean sections. He laboriously carried the small coconuts to the house, saving the best to sell in town and keeping the rest for home use. Adel's flock of chickens received a spray of grated coconut meat from the verandah each day. A mass of glistening feathers swarmed in front of the house, with Lion feverishly feeding in their midst, as Frank stood on the verandah and cast grated coconut over the railing. Coconut water was saved for drinking. Adel squeezed grated coconut for the coconut milk she used in cooking rice and stews and to prepare the coconut oil that gave our food a rich flavor. The husks were gathered later and stored under the house to keep them dry. The fibrous coconut "trash" from the husks was used to stuff cushions and mattresses or to serve as kindling for starting fires. Most of the coconut husks were used as firewood. Temperatures were moderated by allowing the hot, flaming husks to burn to coals or by moving the husks around in the fireplace. Dry coconut husks also produced a thick smoke that drove away the most determined sandflies. Even the abandoned coconut husks that became wet and soggy with the rain were used as landfill. The coconut, like its native counterparts the cohune, supa, and poknoboy, provided more than merely the palm meat.

Despite their culinary importance, coconuts were our greatest danger on the island. Every moment of the day and night we were surrounded by trees with thousands of bundles of ripening coconuts hanging above our heads as we walked underneath them. The thick, outer shell (pericarp) of the coconuts added to the size and weight of the bunches. Green coconuts, good for juice and dangerously tasty when mixed with rum, were heavier than the riper, drier fruits that contained the hard coconut meat. The temptation to relax against a coconut palm during a midday break or in the late afternoon sun had to be weighed against the potential danger of the parcel of green bombs overhead.

An intricate system of pathways and tents skirted the range of the coconut trees. By experiment, we found that the coconuts bounced off the tents. Surprisingly, no one was ever hit by a falling coconut. Frank said that the fruit fell only at night. Although I considered him an expert on coconut palm ecology, I discovered that coconuts fell whenever they were ready to fall. During the day, there were many sounds and activities to compete with the thuds of falling coconuts. At night the hollow thump of a coconut plummeting to the earth punctuated the silence. The only other noise was the swishing of rustling palm fronds that sounded like a torrential rain.

Long shafts of sunlight shone through the mangroves, across the lagoon, and into my tent. It seemed as if I hadn't slept. During the night, the eerie darkness — uninterrupted by city lights — had intensified the sounds of falling coconuts, the rustling of palm fronds, and the roar of unidentified motorboats passing the cay. I had listened intently as each boat approached — and relaxed as its engine noise dissipated in the distance. Whether the occupants were fishers or drug dealers, I was relieved that nobody was interested in stopping at our camp. I considered that Frank and Adel's presence on the island was well known and thus afforded us a buffer from visitors. Still, I had noticed Frank's rifle over the doorway in the house. The prospect of three months of sleepless nights was discouraging.

Emerging from my tent I was distracted by thousands of tiny sandflies and heard the swatting sounds and moans of my crew. We hustled to the house for breakfast, drawn by the smell of coffee and fresh bread. Adel had ignited coconut husks on the outside landing at the top of the stairs by the kitchen. The acrid smoke brought tears to my eyes but thankfully repelled the sandflies.

A smile covered Adel's face and brightened the room as she welcomed us to sit at her small mahogany table, scrubbed raw and clean, and now crowded with my crew, Frank, and Adel. In what was to become a typical breakfast, she had made fry-jacks to accompany our oatmeal and coffee. Fry-jacks are freshly made flour tortillas cut in half and deep-fried in hot oil until they puff up. They are a staple for breakfast in Belize and are often served with refried beans, stewed chicken, or scrambled eggs.[1]

17

As the months passed, I realized that Adel liked to cook for us whatever we brought her, which was basic considering my meager budget, the lack of refrigeration, limited provisions in Punta Gorda, and our infrequent expeditions to town. Supplied with flour, baking powder, yeast, and lard, Adel prepared various local breads that tremendously enhanced our diet. Even if we went to town, the only bread available there was the sliced, white variety that had withstood a punishing trek from Belize City. We had the luxury of homemade breads such as johnnycakes. They were made in a cast-iron pot with coconut-husk coals below and on top of the pot, which was placed in a metal drum under the house. The flying, flaming coconut husks constituted a slight danger because they occasionally set the house on fire. However, these fires were easily spotted and extinguished, and they cropped up only in a strong wind. Rice and beans, fried fish, land crabs, johnnycakes, fry-jacks, tortillas, eggs, hot coffee, and fresh fruit, with occasional canned meat or fresh chicken after a trip to town, were served to us with the regularity of a mother's care.

Adel stood at the kitchen window washing dishes in a plastic basin while we ate. The sun glistened against her chocolate-brown eyes, catching leathery wrinkles formed by an innate good humor. Wisps of white hair escaped from a tight bun at the nape of her neck as she emptied the water basin out the window. Her flannel shirt was tucked into a patched, green skirt. Wearing nylons and slippers, she dressed every day in expectation of visitors.

Between bites, I explained our day's objectives to my students, the Maya workers, Frank, and Adel. Our first task would be to make a map of the island using the survey equipment we'd brought. This would require clearing the ground of palm fronds and other vegetation. While we were mapping, we would set up a grid of staked squares and then collect artifacts from the surface of each square. Spatial differences in the quantity or type of artifacts on the ground surface might indicate that different activities were carried out at different places on the island. We would also set out locations for our excavations using the mapping equipment. I anticipated that mapping and establishing the excavation sites would take several weeks. After that we would begin excavating.

As I glanced past Sylvestre, he placed a handful of obsidian blades on the table (figure 2.1).[2] With straight, black hair and light brown skin the color my students would try to attain by spending long hours in the sun, Sylvestre was a proud, quiet man. The way he held himself and moved reinforced this impression. He slowly opened his hand and carefully placed the obsidian on the table. Explaining that he'd found them near his tent and that he'd also seen

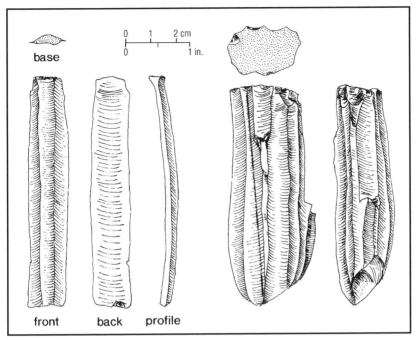

2.1 *Gray obsidian blade* (at left) *with core from which it was made* (at right) *(by Mary Lee Eggart).*

them in his village, where they were attributed to "the ancients," he asked what they were.

Of course, for me, this was the ideal opportunity to talk about obsidian, which would be key to understanding Wild Cane Cay's role in ancient Maya sea trade. I explained that, as a volcanic rock, obsidian was not naturally found in Belize but was traded from the volcanic regions of Guatemala, Mexico, and Honduras. The Maya had wanted to make blades that would be sharper than those they could fashion from locally available chert. I wanted to know when obsidian was traded to Wild Cane Cay, from what locations, and in what quantities. Our excavations would be placed to recover obsidian and other artifacts from the different time periods in which the island was inhabited in the past.

I pointed out that obsidian makes a sharp cut. I held a blade in one hand and ran my index finger gently across the edge, breaking the skin but not drawing blood. I explained that the blade had been on the ground for perhaps a thousand years — but could still cut. A freshly made obsidian blade was at least twice as sharp as surgical steel. I figured that, despite the pictures of ritual bloodletting on painted pottery vessels and on carved monuments, obsidian was probably also used for more mundane tasks like cleaning fish.[3] Hoping for a reaction, I said there was so much obsidian on the surface of the cay that one could explain the collapse of the Classic civilization by blood loss alone if obsidian were used only for ritual bloodletting. I paused, waiting for a response. I got a few chuckles, but the Maya workers, Frank, and Adel were quiet. More seriously, I continued my explanation.

Obsidian was an exotic valuable that was not normally available to the everyday, ancient Maya. Its presence at Wild Cane Cay in such quantity, even on the ground surface, was more than we would expect for a small Maya community. One explanation was that the site had been a trading port along a sea route between the highland obsidian outcrops and the ancient Maya cities in the lowlands. This was the hypothesis we were investigating — and the reason we would be excavating — at Wild Cane Cay.

Since interest in my discussion of obsidian was waning, I set my coffee mug on the table with some force and pushed my chair back while the others scurried to finish their food. When we thanked Adel for the wonderful breakfast, her smile widened. Then I stood up from the table and led a motley assortment of workers from a dimly lit room past a pile of smoking coconut husks and into the bright sunlight of a Caribbean picture-postcard scene. Some time during our meal, the wind had picked up and the sandflies were gone.

As a graduate student, I was committed to a research strategy that did not easily accommodate the realities of fieldwork. In order to form a theory of Wild Cane Cay's participation in ancient Maya sea trade, I wanted to obtain a statistically sound sample of obsidian blades and other trade goods from the different prehistoric periods during which the island was occupied. This strategy called for scientifically designed, random sampling — a concept foreign to the Maya workers and one that did not take into account the hundreds of fruit trees that covered the island.

Wild Cane Cay consists of 3.5 acres of coconut palms, as well as a variety of other economically valuable trees, none of which could be cut down in the pursuit of archaeology. Our first task was to map the site. After mixing cement to fill a four-foot hole to hold a steel rod that would serve as our permanent reference marker, or datum, for the site, I placed the survey instrument where we had a clear view from one end of the island to the other and across the island to both shores. In this way, we had an arbitrary grid with our site north, which was 27 degrees east of magnetic north. This worked since

2.2 *Using a plane-table alidade to map at Wild Cane Cay.*

we were able to set out our north-south and east-west baselines without cutting down any trees.[4]

The survey instrument we were using was a plane-table alidade, which consisted of a tripod placed over the datum maker, with a table screwed into the top of the tripod (figure 2.2). For their possible interest, I explained to the crew how the alidade worked as I set it up, although I knew I would be doing the work with the instrument. They would assist by clearing vegetation and holding the tapes and *stadia rod* — a long, wooden rod with metric measurements along one side. I placed the alidade on the table, which was covered by drafting paper. Using the plane table alidade would allow me to draw a topographic map of the site while we took measurements. I marked a point on the white paper taped to the table that would correspond to our main datum and our reference point for drawing the map. Someone would hold the stadia rod at places where I wanted to collect mapping data. By looking through the telescope barrel of the alidade at the stadia rod, I could read the measurements on the rod's location and elevation.

Over the course of several weeks, we cleared, mapped, and set out a grid for excavations and surface collection of artifacts. We started with a line of stakes every ten meters east of the datum. Then we continued west, north,

2.3 *Maya workers: Sylvestre Cal, Onessimo Chi, and Catarino Cal.*

and south and began filling in until the entire island was covered by stakes every ten meters.

The Maya workers cleared fallen vegetation and cut low palm fronds using machetes, piling and burning in advance of the mapping. I had already learned that it was best to explain the work tasks to Sylvestre, who had assumed the role of foreman, so that he could direct the other men (figure 2.3). It was difficult enough that I was a woman giving orders to adult men who were accustomed to their wives' staying at home with the children.[5] However, as a foreign female, I was regarded almost as another species. At least my unusual female behavior (from their point of view) was tolerated since not only was I their "boss," but I also paid them.[6]

We mapped the island, divided it into 10 by 10 meter squares for surface collection of artifacts, and divided it into six areas from which to randomly select excavation units (figure 2.4).[7] My goal in using random sampling was to obtain a representative sample of the site without excavating the entire island. By dividing, or *stratifying,* the island into six sampling areas, I was spreading out the coverage to ensure we sampled all parts of the cay. Although my crew suggested we just start excavating in the open area, I explained that we would have no idea whether it was representative of the entire site. If they disagreed, they remained quiet. Besides, I was in charge.

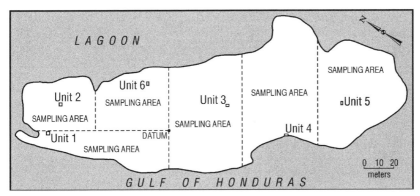

2.4 *Map of Wild Cane Cay, showing sampling areas for excavations, using site north, which is 27 degrees east of magnetic north (by Mary Lee Eggart).*

Still, they were perplexed when I pulled out a statistics book with a table of random numbers from which to select the first location. We started with Area A. On the alidade map, I'd divided Area A into 200 squares, each measuring 2 by 2 meters. I closed my eyes and pointed my finger at the page of random numbers. Then I opened them to see my finger pointing to a number. When I suggested we locate the square with that number on the ground, everyone looked truly surprised — but interested.

The students rustled around with 100 meter tapes, while I counted distances from the stakes, each marked with its location. They used two tapes to triangulate the location of the square, using the Pythagorean theorem. There was a coconut palm in the selected location. Although my students suggested just moving a bit and the Maya workers were willing to cut the tree down, I said we would go back to the table of random numbers and select another location. We picked another number, this time successful, for our first excavation. In total, we randomly selected an excavation site in each of the six sampling areas.

CHAPTER 3

TRIPS TO TOWN
AND VISITORS TO
THE CAY

Apart from an occasional visitor to the island or our infrequent trips to Punta Gorda for provisions, our only contact with the outside world was the evening news from the "Voice of America" on Frank's radio. We listened with some interest as the British military responded to the crisis in the Falkland Islands. Frank, Adel, and other local people in Punta Gorda and Punta Negra believed that if the British lost the Falklands' war, then the Guatemalans would regard the British military as weak and would invade Belize. Because Guatemala was involved in a lengthy civil war, this was an unlikely scenario, but there had been frequent border skirmishes between British and Guatemalan soldiers. With its independence from Spain in the nineteenth century, Guatemala had inherited a legitimate claim to Belize.[1] The economy of Punta Gorda was fueled by the presence of the nearby British army base at Salamanca.

An additional economic boon to Punta Gorda was provided by the Voice of America's Central American relay station, located on a 600 acre tract of land outside of Punta Gorda. Many of the town's small stores and businesses were supported by regular purchases by the British army and the Voice of America. Over the years, I learned to buy my supplies from a variety of stores around town. Initially this strategy was aimed at distributing what money I had since most of the stores carried the same, limited array of canned and dry goods. In time, moreover, I learned which stored offered interesting or different foods, and I sought them out in order to vary our rather predictable diet.

With a population of around three thousand, Punta Gorda was both the largest community in Toledo and its capital. Unfortunately, despite its regional importance on market days, Punta Gorda was a backwater in the larger Belizean economy. The Toledo district was agricultural, with Maya settlements on reservation land, as well as a medley of Creole, East Indian, Chinese, Black Carib, Confederate descendants, missionaries, and foreign-aid workers.

Although originally a Black Carib community, over the years Punta Gorda had become dominated by East Indians, who owned many of the ubiquitous, small grocery stores in the town. In 1868, after the U.S. Civil War, American Confederates from the South arrived at Cattle Landing, immediately north of Punta Gorda.[2] The Toledo and Young Company, who had purchased a tract of land in southern Belize, had offered former Confederates an opportunity to leave the United States. The company had already been logging mahogany in southern Belize, landing cattle for hauling the trees at Cattle Landing. The Confederates brought with them indentured servants from India to work the land. Faced with the daunting task of clearing the tropical rainforest to build new homes and plant crops, many of the Confederates returned to the United States after only a few years, leaving their indentured servants and their land. The government eventually reallocated the land.[3] The East Indians and Caribs had fared well in Punta Gorda.

The Texaco gas station was strategically located at the entrance to Punta Gorda from both the sea and the land (figure 3.1). With the only public dock in town, the station provided boaters the entrance to the town as well as boat gas. Otherwise, this coastal community was oriented toward land activities. The station faced north to welcome vehicular and pedestrian traffic from outside the community, either from the surrounding Toledo district or from points farther north. From the Texaco station, people follow either Front Street along the sea or Main Street, which is removed from the sea. People in town take little notice of the sea. Of course, we stood out as among the few foreigners in Punta Gorda, especially since we came by dory. Apart from foreign aid workers, foreigners usually arrive by ferry or bus and leave as soon as they can find transportation. Punta Gorda is on the tourist route but is not often a tourist destination.

Everyone arriving in Punta Gorda, leaving town, or living there comes to the Texaco station for gasoline, kerosene, car batteries, or various other services, such as air travel arrangements. Truck-buses from the outlying Maya villages stopped at the Texaco station in Punta Gorda on Wednesdays and Saturdays, bringing the Kekchi and Mopan Maya Indians to sell their produce in the Punta Gorda market and to buy dry goods from the local stores.

3.1 *Texaco PG gas station.*

The government, foreign aid agencies, and foreign religious groups brought their vehicles for gas. The various cars and trucks in town, in whatever state of disrepair, were driven to the Texaco station for gas, which was either regular or diesel, but not unleaded. The lack of unleaded gasoline was a problem only for the few newer vehicles owned by foreigners in town.

People on foot brought various containers to the gas station to fill with gas or kerosene, which, until recently, was the main cooking fuel. Kerosene was still used by the Maya Indians, the poor, and my field team. I never saw gas or kerosene cans for sale in Punta Gorda, although some people had them. I was approached at the Texaco station and asked to sell my imported, plastic, gas containers. Local stores sold empty vinegar, bleach, and cooking oil containers that were recycled for gasoline or kerosene. My experience was that you paid more for clean containers.

The Texaco station was more than the only place in Punta Gorda to buy gasoline. When I first came to Punta Gorda, variously called the "bustling hub of the Toledo district" or the "end of the road," I did not have much contact with the station. It was pronounced "TexAco," as if this English-speaking country were Spanish speaking. However, in the succeeding years, "TexAco PG" became a focal point of my life as a Maya archaeologist.

Occasionally I went to town with the fishermen from Punta Negra, who often stopped by Wild Cane Cay on their way to sell fish in Punta Gorda on market days. They had a bigger dory and motor than mine, so the voyage was faster. People from Punta Negra sometimes came by Wild Cane Cay to visit Frank and Adel, as did others. Everyone from Placencia to Barranco seemed to know Frank and Adel. Many people were apparently related to them.

Visitors who arrived on Wild Cane Cay tied their dories to a small dock on the lagoon side and went immediately to the house to see the Cabrals. When I was at the dock cleaning a fish one afternoon, I couldn't help but compare the small dory I had purchased with the visitors' larger dory, which had planks added to build up the sides. The midday sun was almost blinding as it was reflected from the sea. The inside of the visitors' boat had dried completely except for puddles under the board seats. I noticed something moving in the darkness under one of the seats. As my eyes became accustomed to the shadow, I recognized a tiny, dark puppy. Left alone, it would not have lasted much longer in the heat, so I took it.

The puppy spent the night in the tent, evidently not missed by its owners. The next day I learned that Claire, a sixteen-year-old Garifuna boy who was fishing with Anna, was taking the dog to his father. However, since Claire was more interested in my fishing rod, the trade left us both feeling we had the better deal. I named this new member of the project team "Tiger." Only several weeks later, when Frank took us to Anna's Cay for a visit, did I recognize Tiger's heritage in the half-dozen identical dogs that greeted us at the beach. Far from being a German shepherd, which I had been told, he was a Collie mix.

These healthy, although saltwater scruffy, dogs lived on fish from Anna's catch. When she returned from fishing, Anna threw a whole fish to each dog. At that point I realized the humor Anna saw when I carefully removed the bones from fish before feeding Tiger. However, none of Anna's other dogs survived more than a few years.

Although Lion was unfriendly to everyone except Frank and me, Tiger learned to be selectively friendly, depending on a person's status. Tiger's attitude had nothing to do with either my training or his alleged breed as a German shepherd, which, unlike Lion, he clearly was not. Tiger learned from his mentor to be a guard dog. However, Tiger seemed to take inventory of people who arrived with me at the cay, acknowledging their status as people to allow onshore and to protect. Nobody else was allowed to land. Dories moored offshore, kept at bay by a lunging, barking dog who ran into the shallow, near-shore waters without hesitation. He ran free, patrolling day and night. Until he was an old dog and slept in my tent, I never knew where he rested, although I often heard him outside my tent. I slept lightly with the knowledge that he rarely slept, since I would hear him growl when boats passed closer to the island than he or I liked. Although the area was virtually uninhabited, there was frequent night travelers — presumably engaged in various import-export activities for which the coast has been famous since ancient times.

During the day, Tiger met visitors in the water as they approached in their dories and kept them on board until I arrived. Nobody approached the barred teeth of snarling Tiger — until two young fishermen from Punta Negra arrived.

I saw them approaching the tent camp, where Tiger and I had returned briefly. The camp was off limits to visitors, who were given a tour of the site and visited Frank and Adel at the house. As I noticed the fishermen, Tiger ran toward them. With a rush of adrenaline and fear that Tiger would attack the strangers, I followed the dog. I ran with my eyes to the ground to avoid tripping over fallen palm fronds. When I looked up, the men were gone. Tiger had stopped running and was barking at a tree. Looking up, I saw one man hanging precariously, just above Tiger's lunging range. The other man was up another tree. When I held Tiger's collar, they jumped down from their trees.

With the wind driving from the north, Tiger had not heard either their engine or their voices as they beached their dory, tied it to the coconut tree, and walked ashore. They later were sorry that they had not called out a greeting before landing. Tiger's reputation was now well secured in Punta Negra. More importantly, the story was retold until it attained legendary proportions in Punta Gorda and the coastal waters and islands.

CHAPTER 4

HOUSEHOLD
ARCHAEOLOGY

ith their machetes, the Maya workers chopped the grass short in the area I had selected (figure 4.1).[1] The students used tape measures to set out a 2 by 2 meter square. They drove palm frond stakes into the ground and marked the perimeter with a string. I took a picture. After several weeks on the cay, we were ready to excavate *middens,* the domestic garbage from ancient Maya households. Avoiding the six mounds that contained the remains of more elaborate architecture of the island's elite, I searched for the more modest remains of households and their refuse. The artifacts in the mound would have been gathered from household garbage and other locations and used as construction fill. I wanted a more direct connection between the ancient Maya's use of obsidian and the discarded artifacts we excavated. Although we did not expect to find any traces of the houses, which were evidently made of perishable materials and had decayed, I anticipated finding discarded pottery sherds that would help us to date the occupation of the island and then to reconstruct trade patterns from the associated obsidian and other goods. Certainly the stone architecture was part of the island's history, but its excavation would have to wait for another research project. As the excavations began in unit 1, I left to help set out excavations in units 2 and 3. When I returned to check the progress on unit 1, I could see we had a problem.

Because the soil was too wet, it wouldn't pass through the excavation screens (figure 4.2). A clump of mud sat on the quarter-inch-mesh hardware cloth of the screen. The students squatted beside the screen, pushing the wet dirt around with already muddy hands. A Maya worker,

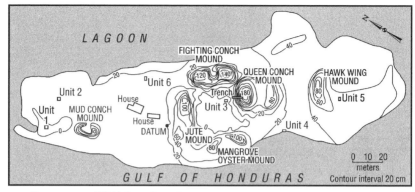

4.1 *Contour map of Wild Cane Cay, showing location of mounds and 1982 test excavation units (by Mary Lee Eggart from map by author).*

4.2 *Unit 1, with Maxine Stonecipher excavating.*

Catarino, stood nearby, his shovel stuck in the mud and his rubber boots caked in it. Nobody looked happy.

I had not expected the soil to be wet during the dry season. I could see water percolating from the ground beside Catarino's feet. He had excavated to a depth of perhaps 20 cm. I had planned to excavate in arbitrary, 10 cm levels to "sterile" soil, below all traces of ancient settlement. This strategy worked

4.3 *Water screening in the harbor by Wild Cane Cay, with Sylvestre Cal at left and Cecilio Coc at right.*

well on paper and helped me obtain necessary research funding. However, in my paper proposal, I had not taken a high water table into account.

My solution was to water-screen in the sea (figure 4.3). This tack worked surprisingly well, was easy, and revealed large quantities of artifacts. We shoveled the soil into five-gallon plastic buckets and carried them to the sea, dumped the contents onto the hardware cloth, and gently shook the screens. As the mud washed away, we were left with pottery sherds, chert, and shiny pieces of obsidian.

As I rotated among the excavation units and took my turn shoveling and screening at each one, I considered how opportunistic archaeology was — both in what we found and sometimes, as we were experiencing, the methods we used to recover artifacts. I was prepared for shoveling dry soil onto excavation screens and searching for artifacts. Instead, I was faced with the unexpected task of working in flooded conditions. Both before and during excavations we used buckets to bail the water from the units. It never occurred to me that we could stop excavating when we encountered the water table at 50 cm below the ground surface. As an archaeologist, I was accustomed to excavating to sterile soil — and then somewhat deeper — to ensure that we had found the bottom of the archaeological deposit.

The original 2 by 2 meter squares of units 1 and 2 proved to be too large

4.4 *Unit 3 in the main plaza at Wild Cane Cay with Queen Conch mound in the background.*

since the groundwater seeped in from the walls and constantly flooded those sections. I had initially planned to excavate the larger units for horizontal exposure of ancient activity areas. However, the discovery of deep, inundated deposits and the threat of wall collapse in units 1 and 2 prompted the reduction of all subsequent stratigraphic excavations to 1 by 2 meters.

As we excavated deeper and deeper in unit 1, the walls — already saturated with groundwater — appeared likely to cave in. We shored them up with pimento palms brought from the mainland. Each morning's excavations began by bailing out the units with buckets and occasionally a gas-powered water pump. The pump was less reliable than the buckets, which could be replaced when they broke. When the pump broke, it required maintenance from town and parts from Guatemala or the United States. In the meantime, the excavations continued to fill with groundwater. Despite my intentions to reach sterile soil, I decided to stop excavating unit 1 when we reached a depth of 130 cm with no diminution of cultural material. We had been digging below the water table for 80 cm, bailing, and excavating 10 cm levels in each of four 1 by 1 meter subunits. My decision encountered no resistance from the crew. Unit 2, also a 2 by 2 meter unit — was stopped at a depth of 80 cm so that we could concentrate on a smaller excavation unit, which I called unit 3, in the central plaza (figure 4.4). There, at 220 cm depth, we reached sterile

4.5 *Sorting artifacts from a 10 cm level of unit 1.*

soil but not without difficulty. To facilitate vertical excavation, we reduced this unit to 1 by 2 meters. We shored up the walls with pimento palms that were held in place with horizontal braces. As water seeped into the units, we sat nearby sorting material sieved in the screens from each 10 cm level before beginning on the next one. Sorting took hours, sometimes days, whereas we could often complete digging a 10 cm level in half an hour (figure 4.5).

As project director I rotated among the excavations, checking bags and identifying material. I was surprised to see a gallon-sized, zip-lock bag full of large pieces of charcoal, a commodity that was normally scarce at Maya sites. Picking out a large seed or nut, still fresh in appearance, with ridges along the outside, I held it up for the others to see. After much discussion in Kekchi Maya by the workmen, Catarino announced that it was a cohune nut (figure 4.6). They'd been finding them for some time but didn't realize they were of interest to me.[2] Catarino reached into the bag and pulled out a round, black seed about one inch in diameter and identified it as a coyol nut. I knew it was a palm fruit, not common in southern Belize but widely available in the northern part of the country. Also known as supa, the fresh fruit has a sweet, orange flesh around the nut. We also found the seeds of another popular tree fruit, nance, locally known as "crabbo." The seeds look like peppercorns, with the same size and a similar corrugated appearance. Crabbo is common in

Household Archaeology 33

4.6 *Cohune nuts* (Orbigyna cohune) *with prehistoric endocarps and inset showing modern fruit inside.*

markets throughout Belize, including Punta Gorda, in late June and July. Sold in small plastic bags containing perhaps twenty-five fruits covered in salt, crabbo was especially popular with children. There were no coyol, cohune, or crabbo trees on Wild Cane Cay, so their presence in our excavations was even more of a surprise.

My excitement grew as the Maya workers identified more and more plants. A large seed that was glossy on one side, with a corrugated matte appearance on the other side, was identified as the seed from mammee apple — a mango-sized fruit from a large, tropical forest tree. Sold in the Belizean markets in late May and June, they have a sandpaper-like skin and a fleshy, orange fruit with a unique and very popular flavor — perhaps a combination of pear and peach.

As I began to explain how seldom plant food remains were found at other Maya sites, the Maya workers and students began to share my excitement. I looked at three bagfuls of charcoal and other plant remains, including what looked like bark and leaves. I pulled out a small, oval seed, quickly identified as poknoboy. I'd eaten them, and the Maya workmen nodded their heads and again began talking among themselves in Kekchi. I explained to my students that the poknoboy tree had long, sharp spines on the trunk, branches, and even the small stems of leaves. Although they did not grow on Wild Cane Cay, they were in the coastal area, and I'd encountered them at a nearby site, Pork and Doughboy Point. In fact, it had been almost impossible to get on shore because of the dense underbrush of poknoboy trees.

The Kekchi stopped, and the Maya workers began telling us in English about how the British used poknoboy sticks to drive away the Spanish when they invaded St. George's Caye in 1798, after which Belize became British.[3] I added that after the Battle of St. George's Cay, the people living in what is now Belize believed that they had a rightful claim to the land since they had driven off the Spaniards. However, Spain refused to recognize this claim, as did Guatemala, who considered Belize part of the land grant from Spain when Guatemala obtained its independence in 1821. That's why the British soldiers were defending the borders with Guatemala.

As we chatted about Belizean history and prehistory, we sat in the midst of dozens of plastic bags, picking out the discarded remains of plants that had been eaten a thousand years ago. From where did the Maya on Wild Cane Cay obtain these plants, which we had not seen growing on Wild Cane Cay? Perhaps through trade, but I speculated that these trees might have actually grown here in the past if the land was drier then. Coconut palms could tolerate a shallow water table and somewhat salty soil, but I knew the other palm trees could not. The waterlogged soil had created an oxygen-free setting in which the normal decomposition of organic remains — plants and bones — did not occur. One of the poknoboy fruits still contained the white palm meat inside the hard nut, which was revealed when the nut dried and cracked after it had been removed from the anaerobic conditions of the soil.

It was not until years later, when I finally analyzed the plant remains, that I fully recognized their significance not only in the ancient diet but also for reconstructing the appearance of the ancient coastal landscape.[4] The Wild Cane Cay Maya had a diet focused on tree cropping — not unlike the modern island Maya. The ancient island Maya lived on the fruits from native tree species, especially palms. The reliance on palms at Wild Cane Cay was not surprising considering the widespread use of palms for food and other purposes by modern peoples throughout Central and South America. Three palm species in particular were used at Wild Cane Cay, including the cohune palm *(Orbigyna cohune),* the coyol, or "supa," palm *(Acrocomia mexicana),* and the poknoboy *(Bactris major)*. What was unexpected was that none of these palms grows on the cays today or are considered by botanists to be native to the area. We also recovered the remains of edible fruits from several other tree species, including mammee apple *(Calocarpum mammosum)*, hogplum *(Spondias* sp.), crabbo, or nance *(Byrsonima crassifolia)*, and sapote *(Manilkara zapota)*. Wood charcoal from avocado *(Persea americana)*, an early, domesticated species in Mesoamerica, suggested that avocados were also part of the ancient diet. We also uncovered tiny, charred corncobs from the Classic period levels.

The occurrence of flooded archaeological deposits, together with well-preserved plant remains from species that do not grow in salty or flooded soils, suggested that an environmental change had occurred since ancient times. Wild Cane Cay had once been much drier. Judging from the depth of the archaeological deposits below the modern water table, the sea level was at least one meter lower during the Classic period (A.D. 300–900). The good preservation of the Classic period plant remains indicated that the sea level had risen soon after the Classic period. Otherwise, the plant remains would have decayed as at other Maya sites.

Sitting in the sun on a small Caribbean island and picking ancient nuts and seeds from excavations provided the first exciting clues to a distant past, linking us by shared eating habits with the Maya who had lived here centuries ago. Still, the work was tedious, made more so by the massive quantities of shell, fish bones, manatee and turtle bones, pottery, and obsidian. Eventually the number of shells amassed to a point that suggested to me that it would make sense to sort and identify them on the island, keeping only a reference collection. We kept the fish and other animal bones for later identification, noting from similarities to the bones from meals we ourselves consumed that past inhabitants of Wild Cane Cay had sampled a good variety of tasty fishes. I began saving and cleaning the bones from the fish we caught and ate in order to help identify what species of fish were eaten in the past and which ones were available locally.

Animal bones and shells recovered from the stratigraphic excavations indicated that the Wild Cane Cay Maya fished and hunted from the reef to the mainland in riverine, brackish, and salt water. Deer, peccary, and paca were hunted from the mainland. Riverine species included freshwater "hicatee" turtle and "jute" shells. We recovered an abundance of bones from estuary fishes that would have been available in the coastal waters around Wild Cane Cay. The species we identified included snooks, groupers, mangrove snappers, barracudas, and yellow jacks. Manatees, still hunted in the coastal waters of Port Honduras — despite being "protected" — were also eaten by the ancient Maya at Wild Cane Cay.[5]

All in all, we identified more than forty-five species of shells, with several edible species available in the estuary waters around Wild Cane Cay.[6] These shells composed the bulk of the collection, notably the small "fighting conch," the large "queen conch" (still collected today for its tasty meat and decorative shells), the large "mud conch," and mangrove oysters. Several fish species that are absent from the coastal waters near Wild Cane Cay can be caught in saltier waters farther offshore, notably triggerfish, parrotfish, and yellowtail snappers. Fishing gear found in the excavations included a good selection of weights made from clay, reworked pottery sherds, and waterworn cobbles.[7] Standardization of the size and weight of some of the weights suggests use on nets. At least some of the weights were used for nets since parrotfish will not take a hook.

The stratigraphic test excavations consisted of prehistoric middens containing two human burials.[8] The upper excavation levels showed some historic disturbance. We uncovered local and exotic materials from different time periods, allowing me to address changes in trade over time at the island community. We unearthed pottery from different depths, which helped to assign the lower levels of units 1 and 3 to the Late Classic period (A.D. 600–900) and the upper levels of units 1 and 3 and all levels of the other units to the Postclassic period (A.D. 900–1400). Although the pottery sherds were discolored to various shades of light and dark gray, their forms and, in some cases, traces of paint provided clues to their age.

By *cross-dating,* a technique commonly used in Maya archaeology, I compared the pottery from Wild Cane Cay with similar pottery of known ages at other Maya sites and began to estimate the age of our island site. Subsequently, I sorted the pottery sherds into groups that shared characteristics of decoration and surface finish (similar to a set of Royal Doulton, Fiesta ware, or Melmac), including a variety of vessel shapes. Minor aspects of shape, including rim treatment as well as decorative features, were characteristic of several types. Based on the stratigraphic locations of the sherds in our excavations, I decided that two main time periods were represented, including the Late Classic and Early Postclassic periods. Radiocarbon dating of wood charcoal from different levels in the stratigraphic excavations supported the ceramic chronology (figure 4.7).[9]

Human burials were the only recognizable features in the stratigraphic

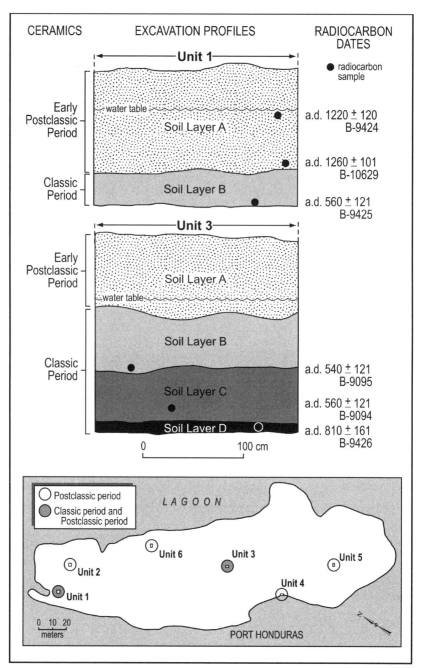

CERAMICS   EXCAVATION PROFILES   RADIOCARBON
                                                      DATES

                         ←——— Unit 1 ———→   ● radiocarbon
                                                     sample

Early   ● a.d. 1220 ± 120
Postclassic —   ~water table~   B-9424
Period   Soil Layer A

                                                   ● a.d. 1260 ± 101
                                                      B-10629

Classic   ● a.d. 560 ± 121
Period   Soil Layer B   B-9425

                         ←——— Unit 3 ———→

Early
Postclassic —   Soil Layer A
Period
                 ~water table~

                   Soil Layer B

Classic   ● a.d. 540 ± 121
Period   Soil Layer C   B-9095

                                                      a.d. 560 ± 121
                                                       B-9094
                   Soil Layer D   ○   a.d. 810 ± 161
                0   100 cm   B-9426

○ Postclassic period   LAGOON
● Classic period and
   Postclassic period

                      □ Unit 6   Unit 3
                                      ●   □ Unit 5
            ○ □ Unit 2   ●
                                            Unit 4
         ○ □ Unit 1   ●

 0 10 20   PORT HONDURAS
   meters

4.7 *Excavation profiles of units 1 and 3, with associated radiocarbon dates to two standard deviations by Beta Analytic Inc. Inset shows location and assigned ages of household middens excavated in 1982. The arrow indicates magnetic north (by Mary Lee Eggart from drawings by author).*

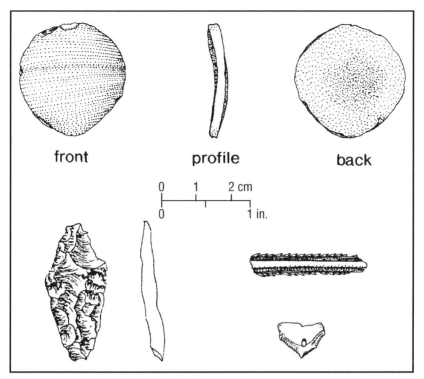

4.8 *Grave goods from unit 1 burial, including* Melongena melongena *shell disk (top row), obsidian biface (bottom left), stingray spine, and shark tooth (by Mary Lee Eggart).*

excavations. Burial 1 in unit 1 consisted of the fragmentary, disarticulated remains of two adults. Burial goods included an obsidian knife, a stingray spine, a shell disk, and a pottery incense burner (figure 4.8). Horizontal exposure of this Classic Maya burial was impossible due to the constant influx of water at the level of the burial, between 110 and 120 cm of depth in subunit 1d. Burial 2 consisted of the disarticulated, fragmentary remains of two adults recovered from Postclassic midden deposits in unit 4. Stingray spines recovered from the soil around the bones were probably placed as grave offerings. Other goods were not clearly associated with the burial. The wet soil precluded horizontal exposure of burial 2 for evidence of articulation or orientation of the interred person, who perhaps had been buried — as was often the Maya practice — under the floor of a house, in reverence to the ancestors, from whom the Maya traced both their lineage and relative importance and position in society.

Study of the stone artifacts provided evidence of trade, both long distance and more local in nature. All of the stone used for artifacts was imported. Sandstone, limestone, and mudstone were ferried from the mainland or rivers that flowed into Port Honduras. Quartz, used for temper in much of the utilitarian pottery, was carried down the adjacent Deep River from the Maya Mountains. Limestone and dolomite, also used in pottery as tempering material, was available at the base of the Seven Hills and the other karst hills near Punta Gorda or farther inland. Granite, available in the Maya Mountains, was used for grinding stones. Local sources of chert are of poor quality, but the high-quality chert from Wild Cane Cay resembles that from the chert-rich zone in northern Belize. The similarity in forms with chert artifacts from the chert-processing center of Colha (in northern Belize), particularly in the Postclassic, supports an interpretation that the chert was imported from that area. Clearly, a search for more local sources of chert in southern Belize needs to be carried out to examine this explanation.

Volcanic stone from the distant highland regions of Mesoamerica included pumice, basalt, and obsidian. The pumice was not imported by the ancient Maya but floated down the Motagua River and carried north along the Caribbean coast by coastal currents. Pumice was used as fishing floats. A surprising quantity of basalt was imported for manos and metates, including a miniature, tripod metate. The most common stone artifacts recovered at Wild Cane Cay were obsidian blades. Chemical sourcing of a sample of 105 obsidian artifacts from there revealed that the obsidian was imported to the island from six known outcrops in the volcanic, highland areas of Mesoamerica, including locations in Mexico, Guatemala, and Honduras. The recovery of obsidian in such quantities from different parts of the island and from different time periods of occupation made it possible for me to evaluate the participation of the Wild Cane Cay Maya in long-distance trade.

From February to May, 1982, we mapped, excavated six stratigraphic units, and surface collected artifacts in each of the 191 grid areas we had laid out on the island. As we carried our shovels and excavation screens back to camp for the last time, had our final swim in the lagoon, and watched the Big Dipper pointing to the mouth of the Deep River opposite Wild Cane Cay, I thought fondly of my days there and was hopeful about returning someday. The next morning I watched Adel's figure disappearing in the distance as Frank took us on the final voyage to Punta Gorda. I was thankful for another day of calm seas since the dory was overloaded with boxes of artifacts, gear, people, and my new dog, Tiger.

CHAPTER 5
OBSIDIAN TRADE

aving received a temporary export permit from the Belizean government to study the obsidian from Wild Cane Cay, I faced a daunting task. I had persuaded my dissertation committee and granting agencies that obsidian was an ideal material for me to use to study ancient Maya sea trade at Wild Cane Cay. The island was situated on a sea trade route between the highland supplies and the lowland consumers — the Maya cities in the interior of the Yucatan peninsula of Belize, Guatemala, and Mexico (figure 5.1).

How could the broken artifacts answer my questions about ancient Maya sea trade? I was specifically interested in determining how much obsidian was traded, when and from where was it traded, and whether it was possible to argue that the ancient settlement on the island served a special role as a trading port at some time in its history. Several months of measurements and observations of the obsidian provided me with information to begin to answer these questions and address Wild Cane Cay's role in obsidian sea trade.

The easiest task was to determine the origin of the obsidian used to make artifacts on the island. Since obsidian does not naturally occur in the limestone-based, Maya lowlands of Belize, Guatemala, and Yucatan of Mexico, all of the obsidian artifacts at lowland sites were imported. The exact location of this volcanic obsidian glass can be determined by matching the chemical composition of artifacts with various outcrops in the volcanic highland regions of Middle America. I discovered that the major outcrops were also visually distinctive, which allowed me to assign sources to obsidian artifacts from Wild Cane Cay.[1]

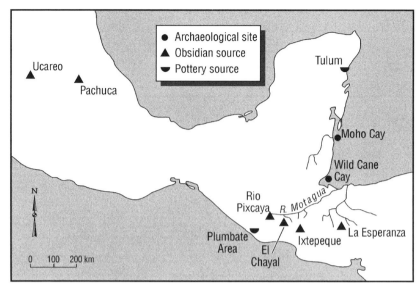

5.1 *Map of Mesoamerica with location of obsidian outcrops from which Wild Cane Cay obsidian artifacts were chemically identified (by Mary Lee Eggart).*

My next task was to determine how much obsidian was traded to Wild Cane Cay at different time periods. I counted, weighed, and measured the obsidian from different locations and depths. Ages were assigned by radiocarbon dates on charcoal from excavations that represented accumulated household garbage. In order to estimate the amount of obsidian traded, I used weights and counts. For the latter measure, I counted complete blades and the fragments with a piece of the striking platform attached, called *proximal fragments*. That count gave me a minimum number of blades traded to the island and excluded pieces of artifacts from other parts of the same blades.

It was more difficult to determine whether Wild Cane Cay was a trading port. I anticipated that a trading port would be located on a long-distance trade route and would have greater access to exotic trade goods than other Maya communities. The Spaniards disrupted a thriving sea trade along the Yucatan when they arrived in the sixteenth century. I needed evidence to argue that coastal trade had greater antiquity. Certainly the presence of a protected harbor at Wild Cane Cay would have enhanced the island's potential as a port. I decided to use the counts and weights of obsidian at Wild Cane Cay in relation to other communities to establish whether obsidian was being traded along the coast or by inland routes between the highlands and the lowlands.

A second line of evidence in building my case for Wild Cane Cay as an ancient sea port focused on how the obsidian cores were conserved in the production of blades at lowland Maya sites. I assumed that communities with regular access to obsidian — such as cities and trading ports — would not need to conserve the material since more would be arriving. Other communities, however, would conserve obsidian. The useful part of an obsidian blade is its cutting edge along both sides. A thick, wide blade can have the same cutting edge as a thin, narrow blade, which wastes less of the raw material. For my purposes, the degree of conservation could be measured by examining blade width and the length of the blade edges (the "cutting edge") relative to weight.[2]

Finally, I estimated that a trading port would have a diversity of trade goods from various locations. This should be reflected in artifacts from a range of obsidian sources and an assortment of other exotic artifacts at Wild Cane Cay.

The origin of the obsidian traded to Wild Cane Cay was determined by chemical identification of 100 obsidian artifacts that I submitted to the Lawrence Berkeley Lab for analysis. I hoped to discover the sources of obsidian traded to the island and to investigate whether there were changes in obsidian source use over time along the coast. The sample size was determined by a grant of $5,000 from the National Science Foundation. With more than four thousand obsidian items, my sample for chemical sourcing was a nonrandom selection of visually distinctive artifacts from different locations and time periods at Wild Cane Cay. The green obsidian was excluded since it originates from the Pachuca outcrop north of modern-day Mexico City.

My sample included all of the cores since they — and not blades — were transported from the source to lowland consumers (figure 5.2). Sourcing cores, or partially or "exhausted" cores, seemed a useful index of obsidian trade. In addition to blades, I included other kinds of obsidian artifacts. Some obsidian outcrops were evidently favored for making specialized tools. I know that obsidian points and knives from Tikal tended to be made from outcrops near Mexico City, whereas blades were usually made from Guatemalan sources.[3]

The results of the chemical fingerprinting indicate that most of the obsidian came from outcrops in the highlands of Guatemala (figure 5.3).[4] The El Chayal outcrop near Guatemala City, the Ixtepeque outcrop farther east, and the Rio Pixcaya (also called San Martin Jilotepeque) outcrop to the west

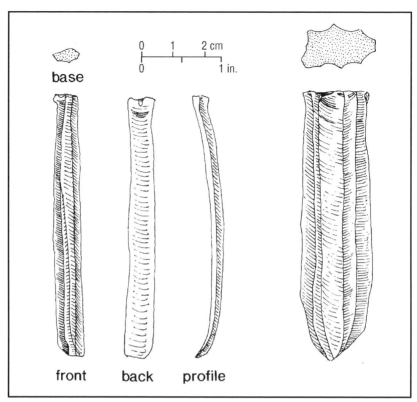

base

front   back   profile

5.2 *Narrow, thin obsidian blade from Pachuca, Mexico, with a core (compare with the wide, thick gray blade in figure 2.1) (by Mary Lee Eggart).*

accounted for all but three pieces, which were unidentified, except for the reference "unknown source Z."[5]

The Ixtepeque outcrop was the dominant source used for Wild Cane Cay artifacts during the Late Classic (A.D. 600–900) and during the Early Post-classic (A.D. 900–1200). However, use of that outcrop dramatically increased over time, from 52 percent in the Classic to 89 percent in the Postclassic. The El Chayal outcrop was an important, yet secondary, source in the Late Classic, with 41 percent. However, its role in the Postclassic was greatly diminished — to 9 percent.

The occurrence of unknown source Z prompted me to take another look at the obsidian samples returned from the lab. Sorting them on a light table into their chemically determined groups, I noticed they were visually distinctive: Those from Ixtepeque were brilliant and clear with a slight brown cast. In contrast, those from El Chayal were gray and either clear, murky, or

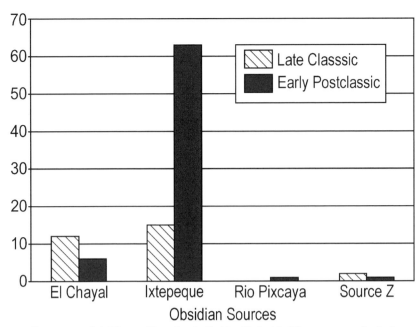

5.3 *Percentages of obsidian artifacts chemically identified with different outcrops in the Late Classic and Early Postclassic (by Mary Lee Eggart).*

slightly speckled. Some of the El Chayal and Ixtepeque obsidian had dark bands, so this was not a distinguishing trait. The three source Z artifacts were distinctive: They had a matte surface appearance and a slight bluish cast and were speckled. The samples from San Martin had a matte surface finish and had a somewhat similar, slight bluish color.

I was curious enough to test my visual identification skills to use my personal funds to chemically source a small sample of obsidian. Five blades that resembled the source Z material were sent to the lab, with my visual identifications. Of the five blades, three were from source Z. The other two blades were from other rare sources: Ucareo, north of Mexico City, and La Esperanza, in Honduras.[6] The chemists were surprised and impressed, saying that I evidently didn't need their more expensive techniques. From this and other blind tests, using visual and chemical identifications, I discovered the benefit of visually sourcing large samples for statistical analysis of trade and used chemical analysis as a verification of the groups. I have found that visual identification of the major Guatemalan outcrop material has been accurate. For the Wild Cane Cay study, this technique helped verify that obsidian from at least six, widely separated sources was traded to the island.

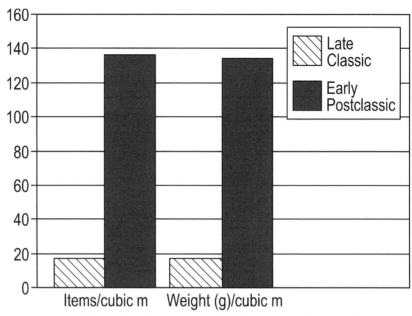

5.4 *Density of obsidian in household garbage at Wild Cane Cay (by Mary Lee Eggart).*

While visual sourcing of Maya obsidian remains controversial, lithic specialists have found it to be very accurate in blind tests.[7]

My second task was to determine how much obsidian was traded at different times in the past. The excavated collection of 4,243 obsidian items included cores, complete and fragmentary blades, other artifacts, and manu-
facturing waste. The density of obsidian was calculated by determining the
number and weight of obsidian items over time. I used a standardized volume
of one cubic meter of domestic refuse for the comparison. I found that there
was a dramatic increase in the amount of obsidian during the Postclassic
(figure 5.4).[8]

There was also a high density of obsidian on the ground surface, assigned
to the Postclassic on the basis of associated surface pottery. The highest surface density was eighty-three pieces of obsidian in a 10 by 10 meter area
(figure 5.5).[9]

In another attempt to measure the amount of obsidian traded to Wild Cane
Cay, I compared the number of blades to cores. I used only complete blades
and the proximal blade fragments to gauge the number of blades produced in
the Postclassic. Using estimates of 125 blades produced per core — which is

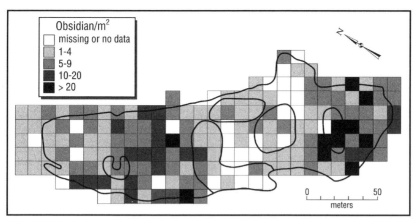

5.5 *Density of obsidian on the ground surface at Wild Cane Cay (by Mary Lee Eggart from map by author).*

a conservative estimate — I found significantly fewer blades than expected: Only 830 blades were found for the 22 Postclassic cores. These cores could have yielded at least 2,720 blades. Where were the other blades? I suggested that cores were traded to Wild Cane Cay where blades were produced, some of which were traded to other communities in the coastal region. This was a testable hypothesis that would have to wait for another project to determine whether the coastal area was even settled in the past.[10]

Evaluating the relative conservation of obsidian in blade production at Wild Cane Cay required measuring blade widths, the two cutting edges, and weights. In both blade width and the cutting edge to weight ratio, Wild Cane Cay showed a relative lack of conservation in blade production.[11] Interestingly, conservation varied according to the distance of the outcrop. Pachuca green obsidian was conserved significantly more than the gray obsidian from the closer outcrops in the highlands of Guatemala.[12]

Taken together, this evidence provides a compelling picture of Wild Cane Cay as a vibrant trading port. During the Late Classic, obsidian was traded from the highland Guatemalan outcrops of El Chayal and Ixtepeque, down the Motagua River to the Caribbean, and then north along the coast. Some of the obsidian may have been traded to Wild Cane Cay via the nearby inland city of Lubaantun, where El Chayal obsidian was found. Since no Ixtepeque obsidian was found at Lubaantun, obsidian found at Wild Cane Cay from that outcrop logically derived from a coastal transportation route.[13] It is equally likely that El Chayal obsidian was also transported along the coastal route since it is also reportedly found in other coastal Maya communities, notably Moho Cay — a Classic Maya trading port at the mouth of the Belize River.[14]

During the Classic period, Wild Cane Cay served as a coastal trading port linking the outcrops in the Guatemalan highlands with consumers in the southern Maya lowlands of Belize and Guatemala, dominated by Tikal and nearby cities. At this time, Wild Cane Cay also provided seafood, salt, and ritual items from the sea to inland cities.[15] This coastal contribution enhanced Wild Cane Cay's role as a port in that the inland Maya desired basic resources such as salt from the nearby Punta Ycacos Lagoon saltworks, fish, stingray spines, and other materials for rituals.

With the abandonment of many inland sites at the end of the Classic period, including Lubaantun and other cities in southern Belize, the Wild Cane Cay Maya reoriented their trading with emerging powers in the northern Yucatan, dominated by the Maya at Chichen Itza. This endurance, and even expansion, of trade in the Postclassic attests to the mercantile opportunism and economic and political self-reliance of the Maya on Wild Cane Cay, when its nearby Classic inland trading partners went bankrupt.[16] Other coastal trading ports emerged at this time, including Isla Cerritos near Chichen Itza, San Juan and Marco Gonzalez on Ambergris Caye, and False Cay in central Belize.[17] Their participation in coastal trade is indicated by the presence of similar trade goods such as Tohil Plumbate pottery and Mexican obsidian, particularly from Pachuca and Ucareo.[18]

Other evidence also points to Wild Cane Cay as a Postclassic trading port. A diversity of obsidian sources and other trade goods suggests traders from distant lands. Excluding unknown source Z, we found obsidian from six different outcrops represented in the artifacts at Wild Cane Cay. More importantly, these sources are distant from one another, including two sources north of Mexico City, three outcrops in the Guatemalan highlands, and one outcrop in Honduras. Some of the obsidian may have been traded with other exotics. These include Tohil Plumbate pottery from the Pacific coast of Guatemala, Tulum Red (similar to pottery from the Yucatan site of Tulum), gold, greenstone, and basalt.[19] Even more locally available goods such as granite for grinding stones, fine-ware ceramics, and volcanic ash used to temper pottery indicate distant and disparate trading partners.

High obsidian densities and low conservation of obsidian in blade production at Wild Cane Cay also indicate the island was a Postclassic trading port. Both indices demonstrate that the Wild Cane Cay Maya had regular access to obsidian. They could use and discard blades that dulled on a regular basis.

Moreover, they were wasteful of this exotic material in blade production — except for the most exotic and scarce green obsidian.

I had broken the once-daunting task of analyzing the obsidian into a logical series of questions that specific measurements of the artifacts could answer. Then, chemical and visual analysis determined the origin of the material. Measurements of the density of obsidian in the deposits and the relative conservation of obsidian cores to make blades were used to reconstruct a picture of a vibrant, coastal transportation route that increased in the Postclassic. Having built a case for Wild Cane Cay as an ancient port in coastal Maya trade based largely on obsidian, I was ready to continue my investigations.

PART II
WILD CANE CAY, 1988–1992

eturning to Wild Cane Cay was like going home. Along with a small group of student assistants, I had a day to set up camp before my first team of volunteers from an organization called Earthwatch arrived by a charter boat to live and work with us for two weeks. I would have four groups of Earthwatch volunteers over the winter from December, 1988, through March, 1989. When the first group arrived, the boat moored in the lagoon side of the cay, and the volunteers unloaded their gear by the pile of conch shells. After they set up their tents, I gave the volunteers some time to settle into their new homes and then began the site tour.

I enjoyed showing the volunteers around the island — where every part was embedded in my memory. I started at the main datum — the lightning rod set in poured concrete that was a permanent marker for the site. I explained how we had mapped the island and set out a grid system to excavate and systematically collect artifacts from the surface. The volunteers were startled by the artifacts that littered the ground surface. I explained that we did not pick up any artifacts from the ground surface unless they could be accurately connected with their grid location.

One of the volunteers reached down and picked up a painted pottery sherd. All eyes were admiring it as he held it for them to see. I mentioned that if they found something with painted decoration or a complete obsidian arrowhead, then they should call me or a staff member, and we'd find its grid reference. Otherwise, just leave it. The location of the artifacts, even their spatial distribution on the surface, indicated patterns of ancient activities on the island. If anyone picked up artifacts, we would lose that locational information. I habitually gave more information than volunteers wanted to hear. The artifact fell from his hand as all eyes watched. To assuage their loss, I told them that they would have an opportunity to participate in surface collection. The fact that we persevered in collecting artifacts from measured grid squares meant that there is a remarkable surface collection available for spatial analysis — something that I carried out years later using geographic information systems (GIS) to discover spatial patterns. Had we simply collected artifacts from the surface without pinpointing their locations, this spatial analysis would not have been possible.

I turned and led the group into the central plaza, formed by four mounds, walking through the tangled mass of tall grass and matted vines. The volunteers gingerly stepped over fallen coconut fronds, coconuts, and holes left by the giant land crabs. A canopy of palms enclosed the island in semidarkness. The new arrivals swatted mosquitoes and sandflies as I described test trenches in two of the mounds and my plans for more extensive excavation with their help (figure 6.1).

Pointing to one of the mounds, Queen Conch, on the eastern side of the central plaza, I told the group how we had excavated a trench in the center of the mound during my doctoral fieldwork. Even though my research at that time focused on finding obsidian from middens to reconstruct ancient sea trade, I knew that in order to provide a fuller picture of trade I also needed to consider the mounds' age and function, which clearly played a role in the island's ancient economy. The mounds were also a distinctive and unstudied style of architecture, using coral instead of the limestone or sandstone rocks at Maya sites on the mainland.

In order to get maximum returns on the age and use of the mound without major excavations, I followed a traditional technique that Maya archaeologists often use: center-trenching. I selected the tallest mound and excavated in the center in the hope of finding evidence of the construction from the earliest to the most recent. The trench was 1 meter wide and 7 meters from the base to the top, forming seven 1 by 1 meter units. We "peeled off" alternating layers of coral rock and finger coral. I interpreted the rock layers as foundations for buildings of perishable materials — an interpretation that would need further investigation by more extensive mound excavations.

The volunteers followed me to the adjacent mound, Fighting Conch, on the northeast side of the plaza. Their eyes wandered across the grass-covered mound with a trench in the center as I explained how the owners of the cay had dug a pit into the center of the mound for a pigpen, which was no longer

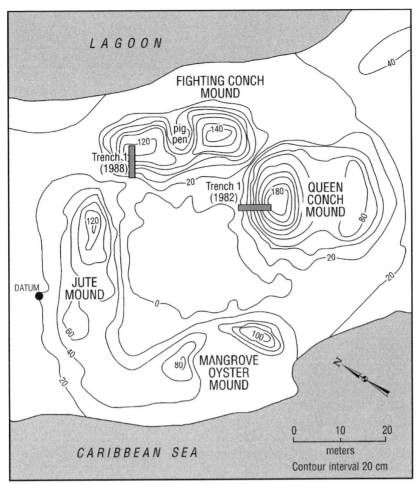

6.1 *Central plaza mound group on Wild Cane Cay, showing location of initial trenches in Queen Conch and Fighting Conch mounds (by Mary Lee Eggart from map by author).*

in use, although Frank and Adel remembered its use in their youth. The pig-pen was marked on Junius Bird's 1931 map of the island, made during his brief visit with the Boekelmann shell-heap expedition to Central America, so it was at least that old.[1]

I pointed to the western side of the mound. There was no trace of the trench excavation, now backfilled, that I began to describe to the volunteers. I explained that before undertaking major excavations, I wanted to know whether there were intact buildings buried inside the mound. Unlike Queen Conch, which had an enormous pit in the center, Fighting Conch appeared

6.2 *Alternating layers of coral and dirt in Fighting Conch trench.*

little disturbed, apart from the pigpen. Several people volunteered to accompany me for ten days to make an initial, exploratory excavation in Fighting Conch earlier in 1988. The results were so exciting and promising to me that I submitted a major grant proposal to Earthwatch for extensive mound excavations.

The exploratory trench extended 7 meters from the top to the base of the mound and was 1 meter wide. As with Queen Conch, the trench was divided into 1 by 1 meter units. Not knowing what we were going to find, we excavated by arbitrary 25 cm levels, which was the length of the biggest coral rocks protruding from the mound. Once we encountered differences in formation, we followed the construction layers, which varied in thickness. The trench revealed what appeared to be three dirt floors, each resting on coral foundations consisting of alternating layers of coral rock and finger coral (figures 6.2 and 6.3). The walls and roofs of the structures had collapsed or been torn down in antiquity for subsequent building renovations. The only remaining evidence of walls was clay with impressions of thatch. We water-screened the floors through fine-mesh window screen to recover charcoal for radiocarbon dating. I hoped to find small inclusions that could indicate activities that had taken place in the buildings. We screened the soil mixed in

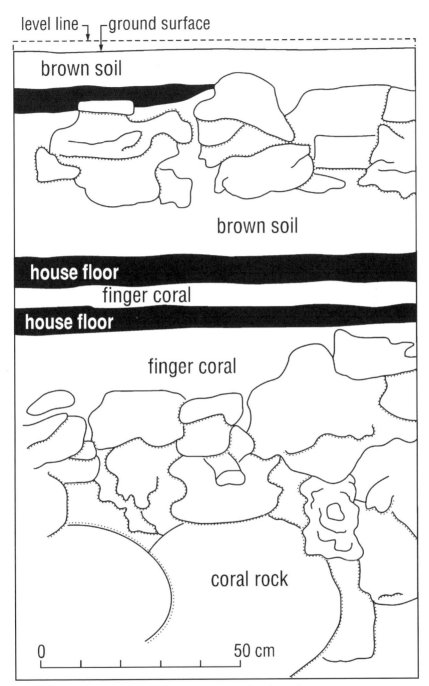

level line — ┌ground surface

brown soil

brown soil

house floor

finger coral

house floor

finger coral

coral rock

0   50 cm

6.3 *Floors and coral foundations in wall of Fighting Conch trench.*

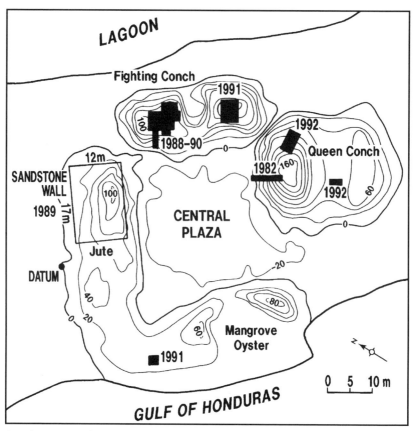

6.4 *Area excavated in Fighting Conch and other mounds of central plaza mound group (by Mary Lee Eggart from map by author).*

the coral rock foundations through quarter-inch excavation mesh. Unfortunately, the trench was too narrow to expose and excavate the large coral rocks that extended across the width of the trench at its base. To excavate deeper would require larger excavations.

The trench excavation indicated that despite the disturbance of the pig-pen, the mound still contained undisturbed structural remains. I explained to the volunteers how they would be helping to find out whether the mound contained the remains of three ancient Maya buildings, as the alternating layers of hard-packed dirt and coral rock exposed in the test trench suggested. To test this interpretation, we would horizontally expose each of the construction layers (figure 6.4). We would start the next day, but in the meantime I wanted to show them the rest of the ancient site.

We continued our tour past the tamarind tree and the calabash trees with their gourds hanging awkwardly from the limbs. I stopped at Hawk Wing mound, pointing out the cement crypts that were the only remaining visible evidence of the many historic graves dug into the ancient Maya mound by the Cabral family. The croton bushes marked the grave site, although my volunteers may not have realized this mortuary symbol. We continued through overgrown coconut sprouts and fallen palm fronds and stopped by the modern edge of the cay. I looked beyond, into the arched prop roots of the red mangroves. The volunteers followed my gaze into the swamp as I explained that the site continued in that direction, but a rise in sea level has inundated much of it. I'm not sure they believed me when I said that part of our fieldwork would be to determine the ancient size of the site by digging in the swamp and the shallow, offshore area at the other end of the cay.

How far did the site once extend into the offshore area at the other end of the island and into the mangrove swamp at this end? Since I knew some of the volunteers might be surprised by this approach to Maya archaeology, I continued my discussion. Because of the water-logged soil, the preservation of ancient plant foods and animal bones was incredible. The kind of material we found at Wild Cane Cay simply was not found at other Maya sites. Looking at the volunteers' bewildered faces, hot and sweaty and pestered by sandflies, I realized it was time to wrap up the tour. I smiled at the group and suggested we head back to camp for a swim or to get settled in before supper at 6 P.M. As I led the group back along the trail, I realized they were probably overloaded and exhausted. Most of them would rest in their tents until mealtime.

The next morning everyone was up with the sun and ready to begin work. We had set up a kitchen under the house — which termites had rendered no longer habitable. After coffee, oatmeal porridge, and toast, I assigned volunteers to each staff member to begin the day's mapping and excavation. Enthusiasm and curiosity kept the volunteers working through the heat and humidity that shocks a North American's system for the first few days in the tropics. By day four, most of the volunteers had acclimatized. They were fitting into the schedule of working hard and playing hard that characterized most of the time on Wild Cane Cay.

Over the weeks and months that followed, I spent each day rotating around the island, checking on the fieldwork in the mound and offshore, but most of my time was occupied with the mound excavations. With a backpack slung over my shoulder and a machete in my hand, I followed the path from my tent to our excavations in Fighting Conch mound. My mind was

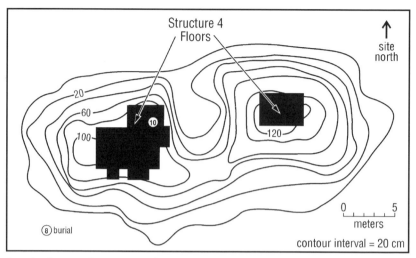

6.5 *Areal extent of excavations of structure 4 in Fighting Conch mound showing location of burial 10 (by Mary Lee Eggart from map by author).*

focused on the mound that had been home to a group of Maya traders and their ancestors.

As I approached the excavation, I noticed two of my staff members carefully exposing human skeletal material from burial 10 (figure 6.5). One crouched beside the skull, flicking dirt from the fragmentary cranial bones with the large blade on a Swiss army knife. The other was cleaning dirt from the area near the lower limbs with a trowel and dustpan, gradually exposing the tibia and fibula (figures 6.6 and 6.7). A pottery vessel was exposed near the right shoulder. The vessel surface was obscured by a thick crust of cemented coral, so we couldn't tell whether the vessel was decorated. It would first have to be cleaned in the lab.

I stood silently watching them expose the skeleton, trying to figure out where the burial had been placed in the sequence of building foundations and floors. The bones were embedded in the reddish clay material of a floor. I followed the floor to the east wall of the excavation. The bones rested on the floor of structure 3. The body had been buried after the use of the building since the bones were in the foundation for the construction of structure four.

I turned to look at the burial once again, more visible now as the bones were exposed with delicate brushes, dental picks, and the Swiss army knife. Although excited about the possible interpretations of this unusual burial, I felt more comfortable reconstructing building sequences and testing ideas about the economy and subsistence and thus found it more difficult to evaluate the

6.6 *Burial 10 person in prone position with legs folded and hand and foot bones commingled behind person's back (photo by author).*

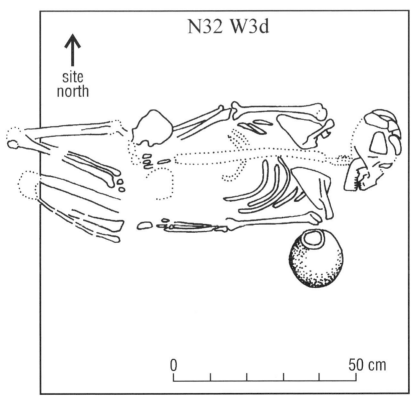

6.7 *Drawing of burial 10 showing pottery vessel and human interment (by Mary Lee Eggart from map by author).*

ritual implications of this burial. The person was buried face down, with legs folded back and arms behind the back in the bound-captive style typical of conquest scenes on Classic Maya vases. This may have been a sacrificial victim, perhaps a dedication to a new building. Of the burials we found in Fighting Conch mound, this person was the only one buried face down. Otherwise, this burial fit the pattern of the others in Fighting Conch, which were recovered in structural fill and were probably interred during building renovation. Burial 10, along with the pottery vessel, could have been a dedicatory offering associated with the building of structure four. Alternatively, it could have been an acceptable interment style of the times, like at Baking Pot Site, west of Belize City, or Marco Gonzalez on Ambergris Cay, where Maya were buried face down.[2] Otherwise, the Maya might simply have been minimizing space. I tended toward the sacrificial-victim interpretation.

The students had stopped excavating and were looking at the skeleton, now fully exposed on the floor. After some discussion about interpreting sex from skeletal remains, we concluded that the person was likely female — an interpretation that the lab later verified. The angle of the mandible was quite sloped, which was a female characteristic, contrasting with the sharper angle for males. Several traits of the hip bones also supported this interpretation. Related to the larger size of the opening of the hip bones for human birth, the sciatic notch and the subpubic angle seemed wide.[3] Also, the blade of the hip bone flared out, which would have provided a large pelvic cavity.

The three of us later worked together to complete the excavation and drawing of the burial. We took detailed, close-up photos of the bones and the pottery vessel in case they deteriorated when we took them from the ground, which in fact occurred. We removed the burial, bone by bone, and placed each bone in a bag with a number corresponding to a number on a drawing. The vessel was chiseled from the coral encrustation that concealed painted decoration (figure 6.8). In order to remove the encrusted coral, I later soaked the vessel in warm water and gently removed the coral with my bare hands. A Maya pot, elaborately painted in black, red, and orange on cream, was exposed (figure 6.9). A mythical creature was depicted on two sides of the vessel, and abstract motifs separating the panels formed a decorated panel below the vessel's rim.

The discovery and excavation of burials in Fighting Conch mound extended from field seasons in 1988 through 1992. Two large areas of the mound were excavated, revealing the remains of six buildings and fifteen

6.8 *Burial 10 pottery vessel encrusted with coral before conservation (photo by author).*

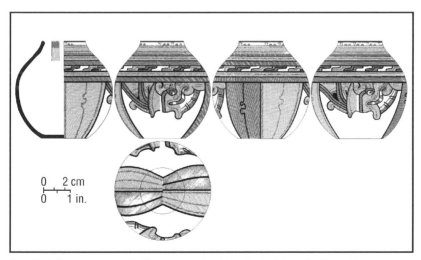

6.9 *Burial 10 pottery vessel after conservation (drawing by Mary Lee Eggart).*

6.10 *Earthwatch volunteers shoveling soil into rocker screen.*

burials (figures 6.10 and 6.11). The earliest structure, structure 1, was built on Classic period domestic refuse. Over the course of several hundred years, five additional buildings were constructed over the demolished remains of previous structures (figure 6.12). During each renovation, coral was added as a foundation, raising each building in turn higher than the previous one. The buildings had coral foundations that supported perishable pole-and-thatch structures. The platforms were faced with cut limestone and in some cases sandstone from the mainland. Perhaps the façades were plastered and painted

6.11 *Earthwatch volunteers excavating and recording Fighting Conch mound.*

as were public buildings at inland communities. Only the dirt floors and thatch-impressed clay that had once covered the stick walls remained from the structures (figure 6.13).

The Maya had no separate cemeteries or churchyard burial grounds as in modern Western cultures. They buried their dead relatives below house or temple floors.[4] High-status Maya were buried in temples dedicated by carved monuments with hieroglyphic texts in front of the buildings. Some people were buried in the foundations of new buildings that marked the beginning of a sovereign's reign. The burials in Fighting Conch likely marked the deaths of members of the ruling lineage at the island trading port. Most of the Wild Cane Cay burials were placed in the coral foundations during structural rebuilding. In some cases, burial pits had been dug through floors for interments. Since it was imported, the construction material represented considerable labor investment. The coral rock and finger coral that formed the foundations of the buildings were dredged from the sea or gathered from storm beaches and transported to the island. Slabs of sandstone, limestone, and mud stone were ferried from the adjacent mainland or rivers for use in tombs and building façades.

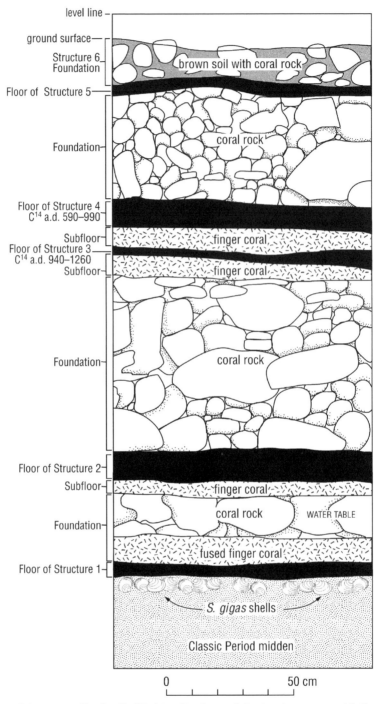

level line —

ground surface—

Structure 6
Foundation

brown soil with coral rock

Floor of Structure 5—

Foundation—

coral rock

Floor of Structure 4
C^{14} a.d. 590–990

Subfloor—

finger coral

Floor of Structure 3
C^{14} a.d. 940–1260

Subfloor—

finger coral

Foundation—

coral rock

Floor of Structure 2—

Subfloor—

finger coral

Foundation—

coral rock

WATER TABLE

fused finger coral

Floor of Structure 1—

S. gigas shells

Classic Period midden

0   50 cm

6.12 *Schematic profile of wall of Fighting Conch mound showing six structures with dirt floors resting on coral foundations (by Mary Lee Eggart from drawing by author).*

6.13 *Western part of Fighting Conch mound showing dirt floor exposed in excavations, with coral rock backfill of trench 1 visible in left rear of photo.*

The Wild Cane Cay Maya buried offerings with the dead — not in any great quantity, but reflecting the diversity of origins of trade goods and marine resources that were brought to the island. A variety of exotic and valuable goods was associated with the burials, notably obsidian, gold, and pottery. Semicircular, obsidian, lunate blades from the highlands of Guatemala were found with burial 1. More unusual green obsidian from the Pachuca source north of Mexico City was found in several burials. Both complete and ritually smashed or fragmentary pottery vessels were found in burials, including some in the Tulum Red style, named after the site of Tulum on the eastern coast of Mexico.[5]

At the end of each field season, we filled in our excavations, partly to deter looters and partly to protect the sides of our excavations from collapse. Neither the filling of excavations nor their reexcavation the next year was ever considered pleasurable; this work required sheer physical endurance (figure 6.14). Ultimately, I reconstructed the years of work from drawings, photographs, and notes. Although our excavations necessarily followed a top-to-bottom approach, my reconstruction began with the earliest, modest construction discovered at the base of our excavations.

6.14 *Backfilling eastern part of Fighting Conch mound, 1991.*

STRUCTURE 1

The earliest construction activity in Fighting Conch mound was discovered in a small excavation below the water table in the mound's eastern part (figures 6.15 and 6.16). In the quest to discover the base of the mound construction, we chiseled through a layer of finger coral that had solidified below the water table. The remains of the earliest building were discovered below. All that was left was a layer of hard-packed, red, clayey soil overlying a layer of queen conch *(Strombus gigas)* shells. The floor rested on Classic period domestic refuse, indicating a date for the initial construction in the Late Classic (A.D. 600–900) or more recently. The fact that the floor was 20 cm below the modern water table indicated the building was submerged during or after the Classic period. Of course, the sea may have continued to rise during the Postclassic period.

STRUCTURE 2

The remains of the next building, structure 2, were exposed in an excavation area of 20 square meters. Presumably the first building had been torn down, leaving only the foundation. Structure 1 may have been torn down when the roof thatching rotted, when an important family member died and

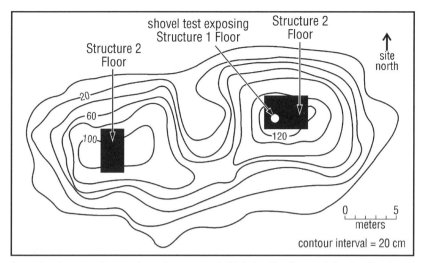

6.15 *Areal extent of excavations of structure 2 in Fighting Conch mound showing location of shovel test exposing structure 1 floor (by Mary Lee Eggart from map by author).*

was buried, or when the next generation in a family inherited the property. Although conjectural in the case of Fighting Conch mound, these interpretations are consistent with building renovations at inland Maya communities.

The structure 2 remains consisted of a red clay floor placed on a coral rock foundation. The foundation was below the modern water table, suggesting either that structure 2 was built as a response to rising seas or perhaps that the sea covered the building at a later date. First exposed in the 1989 excavations in the western part of Fighting Conch, structure 2 was later also found in the 1991 excavations in the eastern part of the mound. On the eastern side, the coral rock foundation was overlain by a layer of finger coral. No burials or dedicatory caches were discovered. However, they may lie in an unexcavated area of the mound.

STRUCTURE 3

At some point, structure 2 was demolished, and a thick layer of coral rock was placed over its floor, raising the foundation 70 cm for the construction of the next building, structure 3 (figure 6.17). Next, a layer of finger coral was added, which leveled the foundation for the placement of a hard-packed, red soil floor. The finger coral subfloor varied in thickness, filling spaces between coral rocks. It was thickest where burials had been placed in the foundation during the construction of building 3.

6.16 *Excavation of eastern part of Fighting Conch mound from the south, showing floor 2, with a shovel test to floor 1 visible below water table in foreground.*

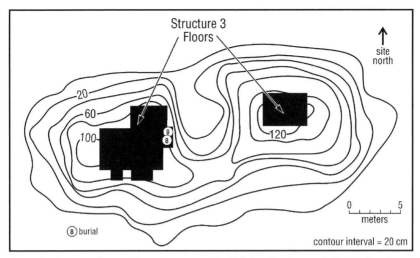

6.17 *Areal extent of excavations of structure 3 in Fighting Conch mound showing location of associated burials (by Mary Lee Eggart from map by author).*

Structure 3 was first exposed in trench 2 — my first, exploratory excavation in the western part of Fighting Conch. My identification of alternating layers of red soil and coral in the first trench as the remains of floors and their foundations, respectively, was met with surprise by others. With horizontal exposure of the layers, I felt not only vindicated but also somewhat surprised at the outstanding preservation of these structural remains over a millennium.

Charcoal from the floor of structure 3 dates the use of the building between A.D. 940 and 1260 (Beta 25741), which is during the Early Postclassic.[6] During the 1989 and 1990 field seasons, the floor and foundation of structure 3 were exposed over an area of 36 square meters, extending on both sides of the 1988 test trench. An additional 12 square meters of structure 3 was exposed in the 1991 excavations of that size in the eastern part of Fighting Conch, on the other side of the modern pigpen.

Two burials were discovered associated with the construction of structure 3 (figure 6.18). Burial 8 was a tomb made from sandstone, limestone, and mud stone slabs. The tomb was set within the finger coral that formed the foundation of structure 3. The tomb's size reflected its contents — a pedestal-based, orange-slipped vase, with a gouge-incised panel decorating one side of the vessel (figure 6.19). The tomb was not large enough for the associated human bones of two adult females that extruded from the capstone into the surrounding coral construction fill. Nearby, the skeletal remains of

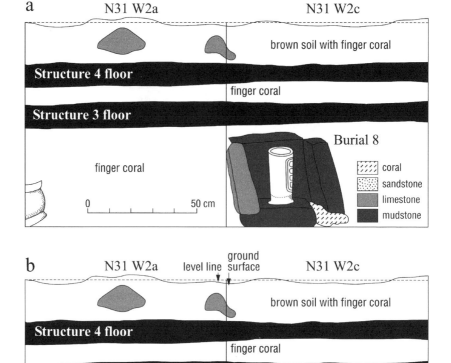

6.18 *Profile of burials 8 (on right, unit N31W2C) and 9 under structure 3 floor in Fighting Conch mound: (a) pottery vessel in burial 8 stone tomb; (b) skeletal remains from burials 8 and 9, with stone tomb of burial 8 prior to excavation (by Mary Lee Eggart from drawing by author).*

three people — an adult male, an adult female, and a child (burial 9), associated with another vessel and two bone awls — were chiseled from the cemented finger coral foundation (figure 6.20). Flecks of gold foil were recovered from the loose finger coral fill around both burials. The dispersal of the gold indicates that the burial ceremony was not restricted to the tomb itself, but instead was ritually associated with the dedication or construction of the building.

| 0 | | 2 | | 4 | | 6 | | 8 | | 10 cm |
| 0 | | | | 2 | | | | | | 4 in. |

6.19 *Pedestal-based, orange-slipped vase with a gouge-incised panel decorating one side of the vessel, from burial 8 (by Mary Lee Eggart).*

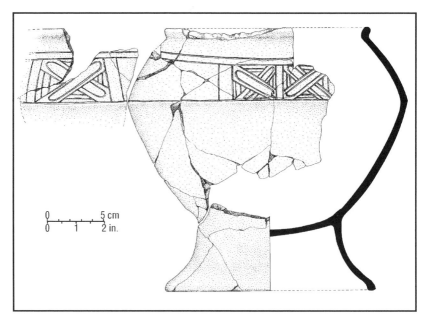

6.20 *Pedestal-based, orange-slipped bowl with gouge-incised decoration in panel around vessel circumference, from burial 9 (by Mary Lee Eggart).*

STRUCTURE 4

The next building discovered in Fighting Conch mound was structure 4, which consisted of a finger coral foundation on the demolished remains of structure 3. Burial 10, the female buried in a bound-captive position, likely as an offering or dedication to the renovation of the building, was found on the floor of structure 3, within structure 4's foundation.

In contrast to the thick foundations for structure 3, relatively little material was quarried for the structure 4 foundation. A radiocarbon date of A.D. 590 to 990 (Beta 25740) on charcoal from the floor of structure 4 overlapped the radiocarbon date for structure 3 in the Early Postclassic. This overlap means that the dates are statistically indistinguishable.

STRUCTURE 5

A layer of coral rocks up to a half-meter in thickness was placed over the remains of demolished structure 4 as a foundation for structure 5 (figure 6.21). Stone burial chambers were discovered in the foundation, placed on the floor of structure 4. Structure 5, first discovered in the 1988 test

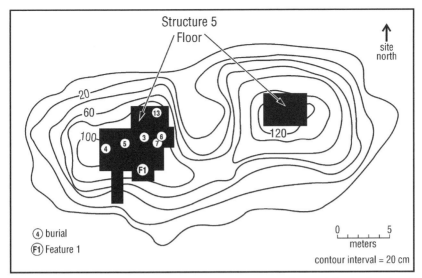

6.21 *Areal extent of excavations of structure 5 in Fighting Conch mound showing location of associated burials (by Mary Lee Eggart from map by author).*

trench, was exposed in a large area of the eastern and western parts of Fighting Conch mound between 1989 and 1990.

A total of six burials and one rock pile that may once have marked a burial were discovered. People had been interred in flexed, supine, and seated positions. Most of the burials were in stone tombs. Other burials were marked by thirty to forty cut sandstone and limestone rocks placed above the buried people. Grave offerings were made from obsidian, chert, ground stone, pottery, and shell. Taken together, the burials document a tight cluster of people interred over a relatively short period of time during the construction and use of structure 5.

Burial 3, located in the western part of Fighting Conch, consisted of the articulated skeletal remains of an adult male interred in a sandstone tomb placed on the floor of structure 4 (figure 6.22). The body had been placed on its left side in a flexed position, with the head facing west. A jade bead below the chin suggested that the man had worn a necklace (figure 6.23). Several deciduous teeth were all that remained of a child.

Burial 4 included the fragmentary skeletal remains of an adult male buried in a seated position inside a circular stone tomb. The tomb consisted of coral rock and slabs of limestone, sandstone, and mud stone. A fragmentary pottery vessel was recovered by the head — either smashed during the interment ritual or broken by the weight of a millennium of coral rock and building use

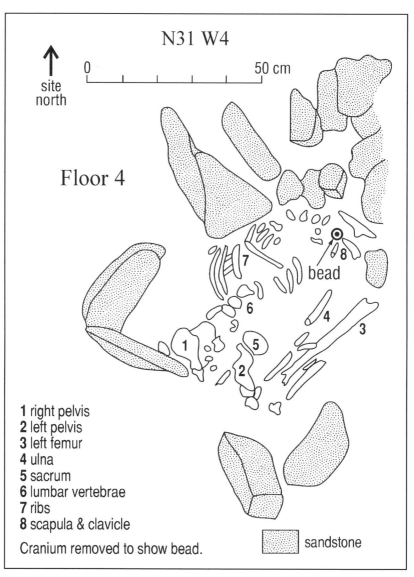

N31 W4

site north

0   50 cm

Floor 4

bead

7
6
8
4
3
1
5
2

1 right pelvis
2 left pelvis
3 left femur
4 ulna
5 sacrum
6 lumbar vertebrae
7 ribs
8 scapula & clavicle

Cranium removed to show bead.

sandstone

6.22 *Burial 3 consisting of sandstone tomb with adult male on floor of structure 4 (by Mary Lee Eggart from drawing by author).*

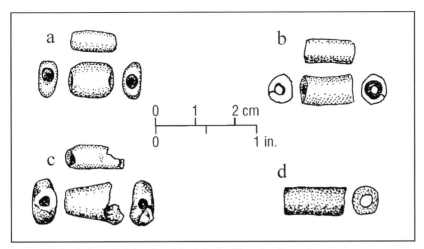

6.23 *Jade beads from Fighting Conch burials (by Mary Lee Eggart).*

above the grave (figure 6.24). The man was seated on a bed of charcoal but was not burned. There were three trade goods buried in the ashes underneath the charcoal, including an obsidian blade, a chert biface, and a ground stone axe (figure 6.25). None of the burial offerings was burned.

The person in burial 4 may have been interred in a hearth associated with structure 4. The hearth contained ash and charcoal encircled by rocks. During the burial ceremony, the three trade goods were placed in the base of the hearth. A bed of charcoal was placed on the offerings. The hearth was built with more rocks. Then the body was placed inside, in a seated position on the bed of charcoal. Before the tomb was capped, a pottery vessel was placed or smashed on the head of the deceased. Subsequently, the coral rock foundation was added around the burial chamber.

Burial 5 consisted of fragmentary human bones recovered from beneath a pile of coral rock and slabs of sandstone and limestone that rested on the floor of demolished structure 4.

Burials 6 and 7 were discovered in the western part of Fighting Conch mound resting on the floor of demolished structure 4 in the foundation for structure 5 (figure 6.26). The burial complex includes four adults. The bones of two of the adults were articulated, with the people lying in extended positions. The other two adults were identified from additional, fragmentary remains. At the neck of the person in burial 6 was a bead. The person in burial 7 had filed teeth, a popular decorative practice among the ancient Maya

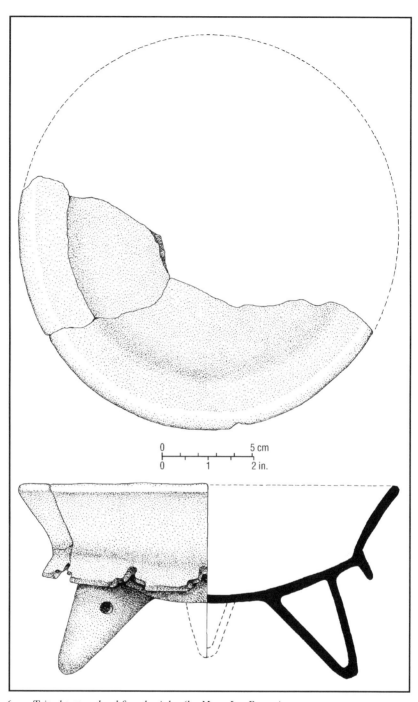

6.24 *Tripod pottery bowl from burial 4 (by Mary Lee Eggart).*

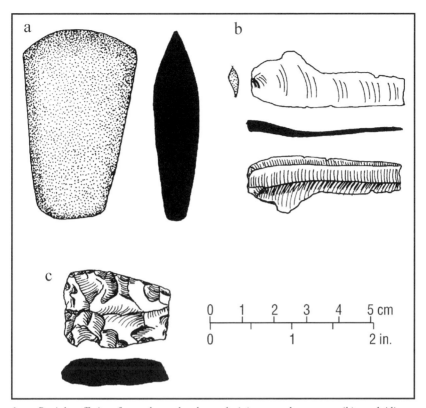

6.25 *Burial 4 offerings from ashes under charcoal: (a) a ground stone axe, (b) an obsidian blade, and (c) a chert biface (by Mary Lee Eggart).*

6.26 *Oblique view from south of burials 6 and 7 with associated limestone rock memorial resting on Fighting Conch structure 4.*

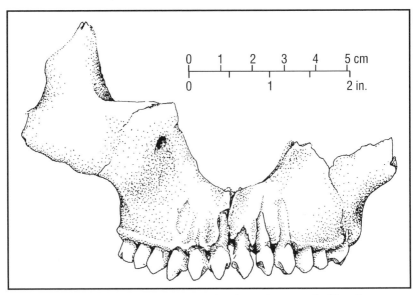

6.27 *Filed teeth of upper dentition of Fighting Conch burial 7 person (by Mary Lee Eggart).*

(figure 6.27). There were two females, a male, and an adult of undetermined sex. A pile composed of coral rocks and slabs of limestone and sandstone was placed above the burials. Perhaps the rocks had originally formed a tomb that had collapsed from the weight of foundations above. The heads and shoulders of the deceased individuals protruded from beneath the rock pile to the north and west respectively. Coral rock for the foundation of structure 5 was placed over the deceased and the rock memorial.

Burial 13 consisted of the fragmentary skeletal remains of an adult of undetermined sex with a partial Tulum Red pottery vessel in the western part of Fighting Conch mound (figure 6.28). A scalloped-edge, flanged bowl sherd was nested inside the burial vessel.

Feature 1 consisted of a rock pile at the southern edge of the floor of structure 4. The feature is similar to the rock pile associated with nearby burials 6 and 7. I attribute the lack of skeletal remains in feature 1 to poorer bone preservation in the abutting soil, in contrast to the coral matrix that formed the buildings in Fighting Conch. Similarly, the preservation of skeletal material was poor in the soil-filled tomb discovered in the trench 1 excavations in Queen Conch mound in 1982.

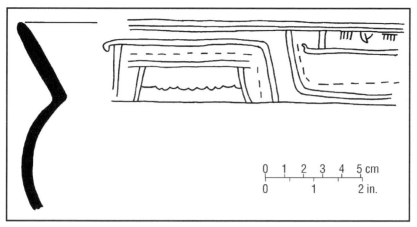

0 1 2 3 4 5 cm
0 1 2 in.

6.28 *Tulum Red pottery vessel from burial 13 (by Mary Lee Eggart).*

STRUCTURE 6

The most recent building discovered in Fighting Conch mound is structure 6, which was eroded from hurricanes and other weathering and disturbed by historic use of the area (figure 6.29). The foundation was the only remaining evidence that a structure had once stood at the site. Five burials are associated with the construction of the structure.

Burial 1 consisted of the fragmentary, human skeletal remains of an adult male accompanied by obsidian and shell artifacts. There were seven lunate, obsidian eccentrics, including three visually identifiable to the Ixtepeque obsidian outcrop and four visually identifiable to the El Chayal obsidian outcrop (figure 6.30). Ten gray obsidian blades were visually identified to the Ixtepeque obsidian outcrop. The shell artifacts included two lunate carvings similar in size and shape to the obsidian lunate eccentrics, as well as a polished shell shaped as an incisor tooth. Tulum Red pottery sherds were recovered from the burial fill, indicating an age at least in the Middle-to-Late Postclassic for the interment.

Burials 11 and 12 were discovered near the modern ground surface adjacent to the pigpen in the western part of Fighting Conch. A Tulum Red bowl was reconstructed from a cluster of pottery sherds (figure 6.31). Obsidian, fish bones, cohune *(Orbignya cohune)* palm fruit shells (endocarps), and fragmentary and commingled human skeletal remains consisting of two adult males, two adult females, and a child or teenager compose the other findings.

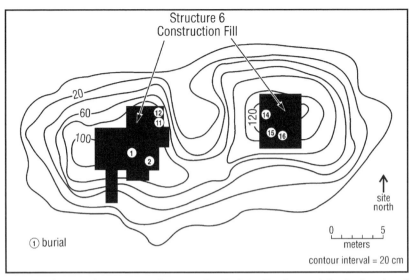

6.29 *Areal extent of excavations of structure 6 in Fighting Conch mound showing location of associated burials (by Mary Lee Eggart from map by author).*

Burial 14 was discovered close to the modern ground surface adjacent to the pigpen on the eastern part of Fighting Conch mound. Demarcated on the ground surface by sandstone slabs, the burial includes the fragmentary skeletal remains of a child under the age of three in a seated position. The burial position was not discovered during excavation of the fragmentary skeletal remains, but only later reconstructed from the drawings of successive layers of excavated bones. Obsidian and shell grave offerings accompanied the child (figure 6.32). Visual inspection indicated that two of the complete obsidian blades derive from the Ixtepeque obsidian outcrop, whereas the remaining, complete obsidian blade is from the El Chayal outcrop. Four other obsidian blade fragments include two each from Ixtepeque and El Chayal, by visual identification. A *Spondylus* sp. shell disk with two holes drilled for suspension was also recovered from the grave. Too young to have achieved wealth or status, this child would have been buried with exotic items in a mound because of the family's status on the cay.

Burials 15 and 16 were discovered eroding from the surface on the eastern part of Fighting Conch mound to the south of our excavations. These burials were partially excavated when they were discovered on the last day of excavations in 1991, but we had to cover them again for more careful excavation in the following field season. The placement and alignment of the identifiable

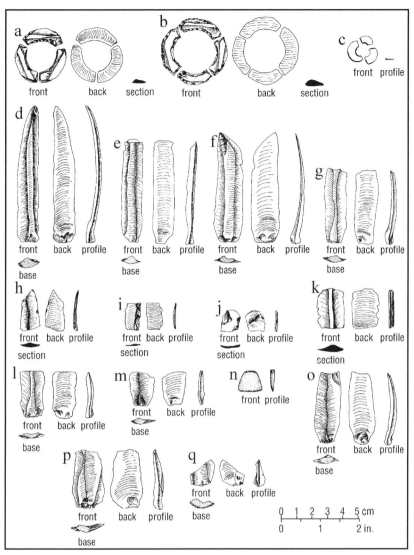

6.30 *Obsidian and shell artifacts from burial 1: (a–b) obsidian lunates; (c) shell lunate; (d–m) and (o–q) obsidian blade fragments; and (n) incisor-shaped shell (by Mary Lee Eggart).*

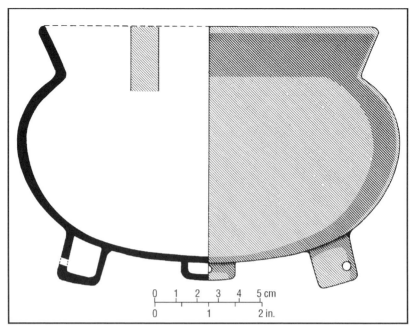

6.31 *Tulum Red bowl associated with burials 12 and 13 (by Mary Lee Eggart).*

long bones, vertebrae, ribs, and teeth in burial 15 indicate that the remains include those of an adult buried in a seated position. The skeletal remains in burial 16 were also disarticulated and fragmentary, and unfortunately no burial position was evident. The remains of two adult males and two adult females were included in commingled burials 15 and 16. Grave offerings that may have been placed with the deceased in burials 15 and 16 may have disintegrated since the skeletal remains were discovered eroding from the ground surface.

STATUS AMONG THE DEAD

The coral construction with associated human burials exposed in Fighting Conch mound helps to define the place of Wild Cane Cay in the Maya world (figure 6.33). The use of coral for building construction was previously unreported for other Maya sites. More recently we have excavated similar buildings at Frenchman's Cay and Green Vine Snake in Port Honduras.[7]

The bulk of the population on Wild Cane Cay lived in houses made from perishable materials without stone foundations. Although the materials were

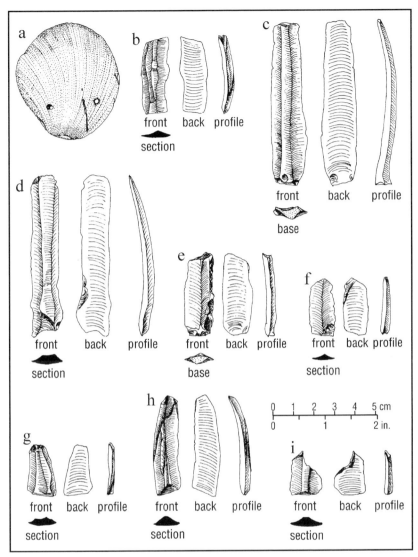

6.32 *Burial 14 grave offerings: (a)* Spondylus *sp. shell disk with two perforations for suspension, and (b–i) obsidian blade fragments (by Mary Lee Eggart).*

not imported from great distances, the quarrying and transport of coral from the sea and slabs of limestone, sandstone, and mud stone from the adjacent mainland represented considerable labor investment. Coral rock and finger coral were dredged from deposits in the sea or from storm beaches. Sandstone may have been extracted from the mainland rivers, notably several kilometers up Deep River.

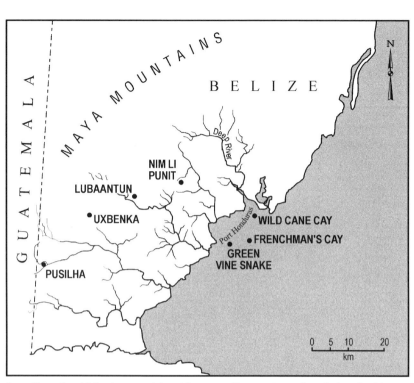

6.33 *Coastal and inland communities with stone architecture in southern Belize (by Mary Lee Eggart).*

Grave goods placed with Maya ancestors in Fighting Conch structures denote their trading ties throughout the Maya world during the Early Post-classic. Tulum Red pottery vessels mark trade ties to the north. Ixtepeque and El Chayal obsidian, traded to the island as cores and formed into blades and eccentrics for the Fighting Conch grave offerings, mark the trade ties to the southern Maya highlands. The green obsidian blades from Pachuca tie the Wild Cane Cay Maya through trade with central Mexico. Gold foil from graves extend the trade ties toward the lower Central American sources. A polychrome heirloom vessel associated with burial 10 links Wild Cane Cay with the abandoned, Classic-period inland cities of southern Belize and Guatemala.

The juxtaposition of grave offerings from the sea with exotic materials from distant lands reinforces the importance of the sea in the life and death of the ancient Maya. In life, the sea was important as an avenue for traders and as a supply zone for ritual objects, food, salt, and religious ideology. Carved *Spondylus* and other mollusks from burials, sea-urchin spines embedded in the structure floors, and the coral foundations themselves point to the significance of the sea in culture of the Wild Cane Cay Maya.[8]

Late at night in my tent, in that hazy state between waking and sleeping, I wondered about the possible sacrificial victim. It seemed like a disrespectful way to bury someone. Even for the Maya, this was the bound-captive position, but I wondered what kind of evidence was needed to say for sure that she was a sacrificial victim. The skull, although fragmentary, looked distorted from cranial deformation. It seemed it would remain speculation that she was an elite Maya woman offered in sacrifice to the final remodeling of Fighting Conch.

I watched the sun setting over the sea and remembered the imagery of death and rebirth associated with the sea for the ancient Maya. The sea was a portal to the underworld. In Maya art and in reality, the sea was full of dangerous creatures: Barracudas, sharks, and stingrays must have been formidable threats in the past just as they are today. Stingray spines were used for ritual bloodletting. I remembered the stingray spines in the Classic Period burial at Moho Cay.[9] That island site near Belize City had been destroyed to build a marina — a week before my second field season.[10] There were two stingray spines and three obsidian blades found beside the skull of an adult. Maya traders brought obsidian blades from highland Guatemala, Mexico, and Honduras. This combination of trade goods and ritual paraphernalia, exotic trade goods, and sea resources seemed to signify the dual significance of trade and ritual of Maya trading sites. Moho Cay was a major trading port in the mouth of the Belize River that led into the interior heartland of large Maya cities like Tikal. Wild Cane Cay was located at the northern terminus of the sheltered Port Honduras coastal bight. The island was also located in the mouth of Deep River, a major river providing access to the interior Maya lowlands and adjacent Maya Mountains.

Death and rebirth were both associated with the sea.[11] The setting sun was a daily reminder of death. It was difficult to ignore the setting sun on the vast expanse of sea — unlike at Maya cities in the forest. Was this volcanic glass for ritual bloodletting perhaps like the Aztec — to coax the sun to rise again each day? Were obsidian and stingray spines mainly used for ritual bloodletting? How common was this practice? Was it important to the daily life of the ancient Maya as it was at the time of the conquest of the Aztecs?

The ancient Maya goddess of childbirth, Ix Chel, had her shrine at a sea trading site on Cozumel Island farther north.[12] Cozumel and Tulum had been described as ritual pilgrimage centers. David Freidel had proposed that pilgrimage fairs may have provided the main exchange opportunity at lowland Maya cities.[13] Both local and exotic commodities and resources could have been exchanged at these events. By way of contrast, various coastal communities with shrines farther north along the Yucatan coast had been described as coastal shrines, with more religious than economic roles.[14] The religious orientation of some coastal sites, according to Arthur Miller, for example, may have stabilized the economy of small trading communities in poor economic times. The Wild Cane Cay Maya seemed instead to have reoriented their trading ties from the southern Maya lowlands during the Classic period to the northern Maya lowlands during the Postclassic period, as the economic focus of the inland cities shifted from Tikal to Chichen Itza.[15] They may have couched their lifestyle and buried their dead within a symbolism submerged in the sea and its associated ideology, but their livelihood reflected their status as opportunistic and successful traders who survived the collapse of cities in the southern Maya lowlands. Wild Cane Cay was, in fact, at the center of serious Maya beliefs. I closed my eyes and drifted off to sleep, dreaming of the ritual sacrificial victim and the other burials in Fighting Conch mound, of the dangers of the sea, and of living on the cay.

n my drowsy state just before 5:30 A.M., I dressed quickly. I was attentive to covering my body to protect myself from the sandflies that waited outside my tent in the early morning calm. I dressed in long pants, long-sleeved shirt, boots, and rain coat, with the draw-string hood snugly wrapped around my head to minimize exposure of my face. Quickly leaving the tent, taking care to completely close its zipper, I ran along the path toward the outhouse. Watching my footing as I walked on the boards suspended over the sea, I pointed the radio antenna in the direction of Punta Gorda to make my morning call there.

In 1988 the limited communication I had with Punta Gorda by CB radio when I returned for fieldwork at Wild Cane Cay was a tremendous improvement over my first field season in 1982. In 1982 we had no contact with town once we left the dock by the Texaco station. Unfortunately, communication from Wild Cane Cay to Punta Gorda in 1988 was reliable only at 5:30 A.M., so that's when I called Leonore Requena — every day. I chatted with her for awhile. Everyone on the island who was still asleep before my radio call was awakened by our conversation. In the tents around me, I knew that my students and volunteers cringed in their sleeping bags. I peered at their tent screens blackened by swarms of sandflies sheltering from the morning wind that was just beginning to pick up. The reception was variable with my handheld CB, but it was best when I talked from the shore facing Punta Gorda.

I stood still on the wooden planks, listening for a response and ignoring the swarming sandflies around my face and hands. I waited again for a response, realizing as

I looked ahead to the person seated at the outhouse in front of me that I wasn't the first one up that morning. One of the volunteers sat covered by a gray rain poncho on the wooden seat over the sea at the end of the walkway. When I heard Leonore on the radio, my attention was thankfully diverted.

She spoke in a careful, straightforward manner, knowing that communication with my CB radios was unlikely during the day and rarely possible at night because of interference from more powerful radios from outside the area. I turned off the radio and ran from the outhouse to the other side of the cay, where a slight breeze was driving away the sandflies. The morning radio calls became more pleasant for me when we raised an antenna on a wooden pole outside my tent. The new antenna allowed me to call from the relative comfort of my tent, without the irritation of thousands of sandflies. Everyone in camp still awoke to what sounded to them as inconsequential conversation — even gossip, but was in fact our only tie to the outside world.

Leonore's husband, Julio, had found a dory in Guatemala for me to purchase. According to Leonore, it was large and reasonably priced, the equivalent of $800 in U.S. funds. The boat had been used to haul vegetables twice a week to Punta Gorda from Puerto Barrios in Guatemala and for fishing. It was mahogany with the sides built up with planks.

Dories were scarce. People were buying skiffs made of molded fiberglass. They were often called "Mexican boats" because they were imported from Mexico. By 1988 they were available in Belize City, or "across" in Guatemala, either in Puerto Barrios or Livingston. However, a skiff cost about $6,000, whereas a dory cost much less. The problem was finding one. Before returning to Belize, I had written to Julio in Punta Gorda, asking him to find one for me to buy. Few people were still making dories — especially big ones — in 1988, so I felt pleased with this used one. I also was pleased with the price.

I needed a new dory because I had no idea where my old one was. Frank had died, so I had lost both a friend and my boat captain. Until I found the new boat and hired a new dory driver, I had been relying on charters — perhaps an exaggerated use of the term for hiring someone to take us between Punta Gorda and Wild Cane Cay in a dory. That field season, as we had approached Wild Cane Cay in a dory whose driver I barely knew and who I was sure carried no safety gear, I was reminded of the precarious lifestyle the local people lived on the sea. I remembered a day in 1982 when, while returning to Wild Cane Cay with Frank, our dory loaded with provisions from Punta Gorda, the engine stopped. After we drifted for some time, I realized that we had a serious problem. The shear pin had broken on the propeller. Frank had no replacement and in fact not even a tool kit. As we drifted, I looked at my companions. I realized that I was no longer in a tropical paradise.

Herbert was of mixed American and Belizean stock, a good mechanic, and once a skilled dory builder — when he was not drinking, a pastime of many adult males in Punta Gorda. Herbert and his son, Sammy, had arrived to stay on Wild Cane Cay during our fieldwork. I hired them intermittently as my funds and their interest and skills permitted.

The four of us were drifting at sea. Since I had no solution and would have said only the obvious, like "I guess we don't have a repair kit" or "So, what are we going to do?" I remained quiet.

Suddenly Frank pointed to a nondescript piece of swamp, not evidently different from the mangrove cays we had been passing for the last hour and said that Anna had once lived there. We landed and walked around. While no clear evidence of human settlement was obvious to me, even as an archaeologist, Frank picked up what he referred to as "part of the old rabbit cage," broke off a nail, and replaced the shear pin in the propeller. He started the engine without difficulty, and we continued our journey. Frank did not take a "spare" nail. He handled the situation the way he and many other Belizean fishermen routinely dealt with the sea. They had little choice, given the low income of most of the people who lived day by day selling fish or coconuts in Punta Gorda. Given the choice of a precarious life on the sea or a relatively safer life on land, Frank had gambled and chosen the life he loved. Sooner or later, most of the local people lose.

Frank used my dory until his death in 1985. He had wanted to be buried in the Cabral family cemetery on Wild Cane Cay, but his relatives buried him in town. Mystery still surrounds his death, just as it did much of his life. Since poor health had forced Adel to return to her family in Belize City, Frank had been living alone on the cay. Of course, people came by to visit him quite frequently. In addition, it was arranged for Herbert to live on the cay with Frank. However, Herbert had gone to town and stayed to drink — one of his many forays that occasionally landed him in the hospital and will contribute to his own death someday. Frank was essentially alone, except for Lion.

Anna had found Frank facedown by his dory, loaded with fruits and flowers, ready to set off, probably to see her. Old and crippled with arthritis, he had probably tripped on the coral pathway and hit his head. Everything of value was gone from the house — his rifle, the china dishes, the pots and pans. Rumors that he was murdered are still recounted, perhaps to displace memories of an unwanted, unwarranted death. For me, I will always wonder whether he would have survived had he not been alone on the cay.

This feeling was carved in my memory when we arrived at Wild Cane Cay in 1988 and found Lion's bones scattered on the conch shell pile by the dory landing. I knew instantly the skull was that of a German Shepherd. Identifying animal bones is one of my skills as an archaeologist. I gathered the bones and imagined Lion waiting by the landing for Frank to return, slowly starving to death.

I later found my dory had been stolen from Wild Cane Cay by a man who used it to pinch coconuts from the cays to sell in Punta Gorda. When I recovered the boat, it had begun to rot. The man who took it had repaired rotten areas with patches of wood and fiberglass — crude repairs for which he wanted me to pay him! Frank's motor had disappeared. It was time to purchase a new dory and to find a new captain. In addition to getting food, supplies, and my volunteers from Punta Gorda, I liked the idea of not being stranded without a boat on a remote Caribbean island. I was pleased to have a new dory and driver. Julio and his son Pepito — or Julio Jr., as he preferred to be addressed — brought me the new dory, an engine, and a man from town to drive it. Although the boat gave me the ability to get to town once again, the driver did not work out.

I hired a series of drivers from Punta Gorda who were unreliable because they drank, beat their wives, or were unfamiliar with the sea — until I met Orlando. He arrived at Wild Cane Cay and set up his tent, fishing lines, nets, and equipment, evidently to stay for a while. He had paddled to the cay in a small dory. Orlando's whole life was carefully set out in sections along the length of this small, unpainted dory. As he stepped into the boat, he took a rag from the back and wiped off the cushion on the seat. The dory was long and sleek, just like Orlando. This was no desperate man seeking shelter, but a fisherman always in control and comfortable with his life and the sea. It had not occurred to him that we did not want him to stay. After all, he told me when I asked him to leave, he was just going to do some fishing in the area. Although it was clear that his behavior was a little odd, only later did I discover he had schizophrenia.

However, from talking to him, I realized that he knew more about the sea than the others I had hired — and certainly than I knew at the time. I persuaded my volunteers to take advantage of his knowledge of fishing and hunting and to ask him questions as he wandered along the shoreline whistling and watching for places to set his nets or lines. When I discovered he could drive a dory, I hired him to be our driver. With a bottle of beer, Adel christened the new boat, which we had freshly painted blue and white, laughing when I asked her to call it the *Adel 2*.

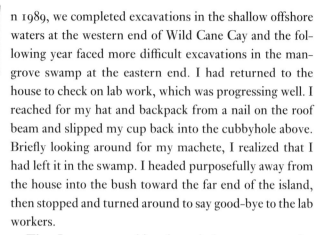

n 1989, we completed excavations in the shallow offshore waters at the western end of Wild Cane Cay and the following year faced more difficult excavations in the mangrove swamp at the eastern end. I had returned to the house to check on lab work, which was progressing well. I reached for my hat and backpack from a nail on the roof beam and slipped my cup back into the cubbyhole above. Briefly looking around for my machete, I realized that I had left it in the swamp. I headed purposefully away from the house into the bush toward the far end of the island, then stopped and turned around to say good-bye to the lab workers.

Then I was gone, rushing through the overgrown palm fronds, past the graves on Hawkwing mound marked by crimson and yellow crotons, emerging at the edge of the cay on a scene that a few minutes later centered on Andrea, who was at the transit. She was sighting the locations for a new line of excavations from the edge of the cay into the mangroves beyond. She was wet and muddy to her thighs. I could see the mud line. I had one, too. Strands of wispy, blond hair peeked out from her bandana and stuck to the mud across her left cheek. Reaching her upper arm around to expose a section of relatively clean shirt, she wiped the sweat that glistened on her forehead with her shirt sleeve. In other circumstances, one would say that she was attractive. Nice blue eyes, blond hair, tall, and slender. But the acrid, almost sulfurous, smell of mangrove mud oozing from her rubber boots and dripping off her pants indicated she was at work. She resembled the group of similarly clad men standing nearby who were waiting for her instructions — or mine, now

8.1 *Shallow area offshore in leeward, harbor side of Wild Cane Cay, where artifacts were exposed at low tide.*

that I had returned. I wasn't sure that they understood why we were excavating in the offshore area, but they relished the hard work — the *real* digging. Furthermore, they were not going to quit and be shown up by two women. I got a lot of work done with female staff, especially when I participated in the hardest labor. Did they simply want a thorough, physical workout? Did they want the opportunity to tell a grueling story later? I hoped that perhaps they had listened to me earlier when I had explained why we were digging in the sea and the swamp instead of on the island.

On my first visit to the cay in 1981 I had noticed artifacts on the seafloor. When I returned for my first field season in 1982, we noticed artifacts in the shallow, offshore area, both on the lagoon side and the seaward side of the island. At full moon, when the tides are most exaggerated, there was a broad, shallow, exposed area that was littered with artifacts (figure 8.1). Had they eroded from the shore and been spread across the seafloor? Or were they

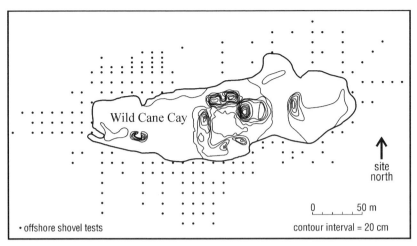

8.2 *Location of offshore shovel tests at Wild Cane Cay (by Mary Lee Eggart from map by author).*

eroding from the seafloor and in fact in situ? If the latter scenario, then the sea level must have risen and covered the objects. The waterlogged deposits we had encountered on the island supported that interpretation. The way to test these alternative hypotheses was to excavate in the offshore area. Neither my student staff members nor the volunteers knew that this offshore shovel testing was not standard archaeological procedure.

We set up the transit at our main datum marker on Wild Cane Cay and extended the 10 by 10 meter grid that was on the island into the offshore area around the cay. We placed a stake every 10 meters out to sea, as far as was possible while walking in water with a stadia rod and a hundred-meter tape (figure 8.2). Generally we stopped about 50 to 70 m from shore when the depth dropped precipitously. Then we took shovels, screens, and bags and excavated at each marked location (figure 8.3).[1] We excavated in arbitrary 20 cm levels, screening the sediment in the excavation screens that floated with the hardware mesh slightly submerged. We continued each unit until no artifacts were found — the typical procedure of excavating to sterile soil. We continued out to sea until we excavated shovel tests devoid of artifacts. The work was popular since standing in the Caribbean in a bathing suit was a good way to stay cool, get a tan, and escape from the sandflies. A typical scene included two teams of excavators, each with a shoveler and a screener. Tiger was attentive to our whereabouts, following us in the sea and wading between teams.

Offshore transect excavations were less popular at the eastern end of the cay, where tangled webs of mangrove roots extended into the water. It was

8.3 *Offshore excavations on windward, southern side of Wild Cane Cay.*

also more difficult to imagine that this area was also part of the ancient site. It seemed possible that the open lagoon waters and the shallow coastal waters at the other end of the cay had once been dry land. However, we recovered abundant artifacts in deeply buried deposits up to 50 meters offshore all around the island.

We were working in the worst conditions — the loosely consolidated soil of a red mangrove forest at the far end of the cay where nobody normally walks. We were beyond the Cabral family cemetery. We set out a line of excavations going into the mangroves off the eastern end of the island, first walking in the mud and then wading in water among mangrove stilts. The eerie silence of the mangrove forest was interrupted by the sound of our machete cuts bouncing off the hard roots. In 1982, the Maya workers said they heard strange noises from the mangroves. Regardless of whether crocodiles or iguanas lived in the mangroves, the heavy shovels full of pottery sherds embedded in mangrove mud focused our attention on excavating. We recovered material to 100 cm depth, although it was hard to dig among the mangrove roots. Some of the volunteers and students had broken their shovels when they used a shovel like a crowbar to pry the earth. Apparently I was fond of saying that shovels don't break; people break shovels. I acknowledged that some shovels may have rusted from the salt, despite our careful oiling and greasing of the equipment. The depth of the excavations reminded me of the time we were digging in the open area in the lagoon near the tents and only the tallest volunteer could reach the deepest shovel test locations. When it got too deep even for him, he offered to tie his leg to a cement block to weight himself down as he dived with a trowel and bucket. Despite his dedication to science and the project, we stopped.

At the end of each day Andrea and I plotted the location of "positive" excavation locations (those with artifacts). The mapping gave further incentive to our crew, who saw that with each excavation they were extending the ancient boundary of the site. In total, we excavated 186 shovel tests over two field seasons.

The offshore transect excavations revealed artifacts in stratified deposits below the seafloor down to a depth of 100 cm. We found tremendous quantities of pottery sherds, chert, obsidian, and plant and animal remains in the submerged deposits — all discolored a uniform dark gray from the salty water. Some 20 cm levels had three large bags — each about 6 by 12 inches — full of material. This discovery meant that the island had previously extended into the offshore area and that a rise in sea level had submerged a large part of the site, which was now still underwater. In fact, the offshore excavations revealed that the ancient site extended about ten acres, making it a sizable village.

CHAPTER 9
VOLUNTEERS

I n addition to providing archaeological experience, participating in my project was often a turning point — even a catalyst for change — in the lives of many of the volunteers. Being thrown together with strangers on a remote island in rustic conditions challenged some of the volunteers' preconceived self-limits. Some actively looked for ways to prove themselves. Quite a few looked to the project to put new meaning in their lives or to find new people to do so. Sadly for others, their experience meant a final acceptance of their own limitations when they noticed that advancing age and declining health had an impact on their lifestyle. At least one man was "in hiding" while on my project.

Many dreamed of a life in Maya archaeology. For two weeks they lived that life and in so doing made my fieldwork both possible and enjoyable. My field staff and I tried to provide safe surroundings for the volunteers who suspended their normal lives and living conditions for two weeks to participate in my project. They were vulnerable in their new environment since everything was new and unfamiliar to them, and they were dependent on us to provide for them. We carefully controlled the physical and social setting of the project in order to enable them to assist in the fieldwork.

My single requirement for volunteers — or students on my project — was that they be able to swim. After that, flexibility, enthusiasm, and an ability to survive in the rustic conditions of our tent camp characterized my ideal volunteer. I found that some basic health and age considerations were also necessary to live in a tent in the swamp, without running water, electricity, or proximity to a hospital.

When I picked up the last-minute fax applications from Earthwatch at the Texaco station before picking up a team at the airstrip, the first thing I checked was the age and health status of the members of the next team. Occasionally elderly people told Earthwatch that they would be able to live in the primitive conditions of my field camp, and some were able to do so successfully. I noticed from one application that Arthur Maclean, an eighty-six-year-old man with back trouble, was on his way. His application stated that he had trouble with his coccyx that would not interfere in his participation. My knowledge of human osteology was useful in that I realized that problems with his tailbone might cause him difficulty on Wild Cane Cay.

The charming older gentleman I met later that morning at the airstrip was distinguishable only by his advanced age and the vinyl cushion he carried with a wedge cut out for his tailbone. He and the other volunteers were outfitted in expensive-looking safari wear for the expedition. They looked clean, eager, and friendly. In my boots, wide-brimmed dirty-white hat, and old red pack slung across my right shoulder, I think I scared them. My zip-off pant legs didn't even match the shorts, which were more heavily worn. However, as the plane taxied down the runway and we heard the roar of the plane's engine, I knew it was too late for them to escape. For the next two weeks their lives would be in my hands.

Slowly, Arthur's activities had been restricted to sitting under the house on a bench, washing artifacts, and placing them on trays to dry. He had traveled extensively as a foreign diplomat and visited many archaeological sites. This project fulfilled a lifelong dream to actually participate in an archaeological project. It also made him realize that he could no longer do everything he wanted to do. He hadn't really realized that at age eighty-six he was getting old and that declining health should deter him from living in a tent on a mangrove swamp island and carrying out hard labor. Arthur had begun excavating on Fighting Conch mound, sitting on the excavation wall propped up by his special cushion, but when I saw a piece of bone flying through the air, I moved him to screening. However, his eyes weren't good enough to distinguish the artifacts in the screen. Although it was sad for me to provide the circumstances for self-realizations such as Arthur's, he was not devastated. After all, he had found a charming older woman, Marie, with whom he spent every day washing artifacts on a tropical island in the Caribbean. He had fulfilled a dream of excavating at a Maya site. In the evening, while the moon rose and sent sparkles dancing on the waves, he read Gaelic poetry to us that he had written from his travels. A palm tree draped its fronds across the seascape. Even for a senior citizen, archaeology wasn't that bad. After all, Marie couldn't get away.

I knew that Arthur had a crush on Marie despite the difference in their ages: She was only seventy-four. She complained that he talked too much, which wasn't surprising since he removed his hearing aids, which were not working well in the high humidity. One day I saw Marie wandering toward the camp through the thicket of lime trees on mound 2. I was surprised she had not taken the path from the excavations that skirted the edge of mound 2 but discovered that she had tunnel vision and could not see well. In fact, she had no peripheral vision and was virtually blind at night. That explained to me how she had recently stepped on the dog who lay sleeping on the ground between us as she walked toward me. I realized that she may not have seen the path. I walked toward her, took her arm, and guided her to the house — or rather under the house — where lunch was displayed on the table. I made sure that someone took Marie to her tent at night. Whether a romance with Arthur ever developed I don't know.

What a contrast to the romance novelist who had come looking for a setting for a new novel or perhaps a story. She said there was nothing in my project that could be turned into a romance novel. That summed up her experience after two weeks on Wild Cane Cay. She never met Arthur and Marie or the others who flirted, made long-lasting friendships, or pursed one another after the project was over.

For some people my project marked a turning point. Simply to choose to live for two weeks with a group of people whom you do not know, isolated on a small Caribbean island, and doing archaeology that you have never done before takes courage and a hope for new directions. One volunteer had apparently never lived outside a city and was looking for a gentler Outward Bound experience. Cheryl had not even been in a tent before. The Outward Bound guide on another team said my project was perhaps more difficult than some of their trips. Cheryl encountered so many new challenges — like bathing in the sea, cooking over an open fire, and working with swarms of sandflies — that it was difficult for her to cope. However, she survived. Part of the attraction of my project — for volunteers, for my staff, and for me — is facing tests every day. I returned a few to Punta Gorda before their two-week stay was over. Many of those who survived their remote island experience told me they gained confidence in themselves and were surprised by my ability to test their endurance. I think this was mainly the men trying to keep pace with a female archaeologist who could wield a shovel better than they could.

I met interesting people who brought energy and enthusiasm to the project and broadened my horizons. While I was so narrowly focused in Maya archaeology, my volunteers exposed me to their diverse careers. A few people were reluctant to talk about themselves, but none was as secretive as "John Smith" (not his real name), who arrived without even luggage. Apparently from New Jersey, John had paid Earthwatch to participate in my project but had not completed an application. His lack of clothes was remedied by loans from other volunteers and from purchases from the street vendors in Punta Gorda. That he would not talk about his job, together with his attachment to Tiger, suggested to me that he worked as an animal control officer. It was therefore a surprise when he casually announced at an Earthwatch conference some years later that he worked for the U.S. government, had been "underground" on a drug case, and had been told to "get lost." My project evidently filled the bill.

Occasionally I met someone with odd ideas that eventually surfaced in the close quarters of our field camp. As we stood gazing up at the stars one night, a computer programmer announced that he could ride light beams. Perhaps unfairly, I asked why he had paid to travel to Belize by plane. When he didn't answer, I asked him whether it was because he couldn't take luggage on a light beam. Nobody pursued this discussion. My objective was not only to survive one another's company for two weeks but also to enjoy it in the process of doing archaeology.

The romance novelist should have been on team 2 (I'll keep the year to myself to protect the volunteers' anonymity). No matter how hard I worked them, they stayed up drinking rum, talking, and dancing under the stars until 2 A.M. Nobody was rowdy or obnoxious. They were simply having a good time. They worked hard. They played hard. They drank a case of rum between each trip to town. We went to Punta Gorda on market days — Wednesdays and Saturdays — to buy food. The team was gaining quite a reputation in town, so much so that Charlie Carson, our closest neighbor on the mainland, came to borrow some rum from us on Wild Cane Cay. He also came to sell us his "hard-luck Charlie" T-shirts, perhaps aptly named since he subsequently drank away the profits and tragically died in a boating accident some years later while returning home alone from Punta Gorda, having spent the afternoon in a local bar. I was afraid we might run out of coffee or that the team would run out of cigarettes. I did not view my project as a time for volunteers to quit bad habits.

For the most part, it was just good fun. The problem was that I was getting tired. Although I could pour the volunteers into the plane to leave at the end of their stay, I still had to prepare for team 3's arrival. Fortunately, by day ten, when I was about to impose an 8 P.M. curfew so the rest of us could get some sleep, the volunteers were exhausted. They went to their tents at a reasonable hour for the duration of the project. When the volunteers on that team retired to their tents about 8 P.M. each evening, I fondly remembered the excitement of the previous team. I still keep in touch with many of them.

The volunteers had helped me explore Wild Cane Cay's coral architecture, revealing the elite lineage history of the Maya traders entombed there in their houses, immortalized by their living descendants' homes above. Similar to the mortuary practice at mainland cities, both the use of coral as a building material in the stone foundations and the exotic, marine origins of many of the grave goods set the Wild Cane Cay mounds apart from others in the Maya world.

The underwater excavations in the offshore area around the island were a clear departure from Maya archaeology as practiced at other sites in the lowlands. Nonetheless, the inundated context of the site called for innovative techniques to help answer questions about ancient sea-level rise and its impact on the coastal Maya in general and at Wild Cane Cay in particular. The results were astounding in that we established that there had been a sea-level rise that had impacted the ancient settlement on Wild Cane Cay. This discovery — as documented by endless days, weeks, and months of excavations in the mangroves and the sea — set in motion a multiyear project to investigate sea-level rise throughout Port Honduras and the ancient Maya's response to the rising seas. The years of fieldwork on Wild Cane Cay had helped me answer many questions about ancient Maya trading ports but left me wondering about their importance locally.

PART III
IN SEARCH OF OTHER MAYA SITES

CHAPTER 10

IN SEARCH OF
THE COASTAL
MAYA

y doctoral committee had asked me whether Wild Cane
Cay was an isolated trading port for long-distance sea
traders. In other words, was the coastal area north of
Punta Gorda, which was virtually devoid of modern
settlement, also virtually uninhabited in ancient times?
Or were there other sites in the area? If there were other
sites in the Port Honduras coastal region, did the Maya at
those communities have access — by trade — to the exotic artifacts and raw materials that were traded to Wild
Cane Cay? Once my dissertation was completed, I was
able to address those questions.

We had already found a few sites while traveling to and
from Wild Cane Cay or going up Deep River to get drinking water. Nevertheless, I wanted to more comprehen-
sively and systematically search the coast and cays for archaeological sites. Initially this task seemed quite small
since there was little dry land in the region apart from our
tent camp on Wild Cane Cay. I was surprised to find that
sites were not restricted to dry land. We discovered ancient Maya sites in the mangrove swamps on the mainland
and on the cays that were currently uninhabited and inhospitable. As at Wild Cane Cay, several of the sites continued into the shallow water around other cays. Some
sites were even completely underwater with no dry land.
Fortunately, neither the volunteers nor my student field
assistants had other archaeological experience, so they did
not realize that my project was in any way unusual.[1]

Evidently the landscape and seascape of Port Honduras was quite different in ancient times. There must
have been more dry land to support human settlement.
There had been either a widespread rise in sea level that

had affected the region, a subsidence of the land, or a combination of sea-level rise and subsidence. The alternate hypothesis, that the ancient Maya lived underwater, provided comic relief and produced chuckles from the students and volunteers.

Once we found a site, we inspected the ground surface and collected artifacts with decoration or a shape that I recognized as characteristic of a particular time period. If there were no distinctive artifacts on the ground surface, we often excavated a 1 by 1 m test unit. Where there was no dry land or when we found no artifacts on the ground surface, we sometimes did shovel tests. In fact, in many instances there was no surface evidence of an ancient site or even the likelihood of an ancient site (no dry land), but we found deeply buried archaeological deposits. My suspicion was that almost anywhere we excavated we would find buried sites, and this speculation was borne out by the sites we found. We mapped the sites and backfilled the excavations, returning to some sites for further excavations if they were large or I had other reasons to return, such as finding trade goods in datable deposits or documenting changes in sea level. When we excavated submerged sites, we recorded the depth of the ancient deposits below the current sea level and the age of the artifacts, based either on their styles or on radiocarbon dates of associated organic remains. Even though I couldn't tell whether the sea had actually risen or the land had sunk, I could document the dates of sites at particular depths below the current sea level.

Obsidian continued to be a useful gauge of external trading ties.[2] Nevertheless, we increasingly found resources and artifacts from nearby that indicated active trade locally between the coast and the adjacent, inland Maya communities. Local goods from the coast included sea urchin spines, stingray spines, salt, coral, manatee and shell carvings, and seafood. (We didn't actually find salt but instead the pots that were used to boil brine to make salt.) Inland trade goods at coastal sites included the freshwater river shell "jute," limestone, chert, and pottery, including figurine whistles and jars with distinctive, stamped impressions. A growing body of evidence contributed to a view of a vibrant coastal-inland trade in Port Honduras that linked with the long-distance trading port at Wild Cane Cay.

Having a base camp on Wild Cane Cay allowed me to explore the coastal waters when the sea was relatively calm while continuing to excavate on the island. With big teams of Earthwatch volunteers arriving every couple of weeks, I had an enthusiastic crew. Fortunately, the project offered enough activities to match the skills, interests, and abilities of the volunteers with my research objectives. When I accepted a faculty position at LSU in 1990, my fieldwork included students who helped me supervise the volunteers. However, with the academic appointment, fieldwork was limited to the summers and other holidays. We were able to complete the offshore transect excavations at Wild Cane Cay in the 1990 field season, which prompted me to explore the coastal area. Mound excavations continued through the 1992 field season, with small areas excavated and backfilled each year that ultimately uncovered a large section of the burials and buried buildings.

My goal for the 1991 summer field season was to make a good map of each of the sites we had found. I planned to spend a couple of days at each site. We'd start off at a nice open site on the savannah up the Deep River, but with each successive site, the field conditions would deteriorate since we would be working in the mangroves, in the mud, and in the sea. To get a good map of each site meant using the transit instead of the pace-and-compass or tape-and-compass method that archaeologists often use for a preliminary sketch map while on reconnaissance. The sites were difficult to access, so I figured we might as well produce an accurate map since we might not visit the locations again. My list included Clearwater on the savannah up a branch of the Deep River, Ping Wing in a swamp along the eastern branch of Punta Ycacos Lagoon, and several offshore island sites, including Tiger Mound, Madre Cacao, and Frenchman's Cay. We'd take the measurements during the day and draw the maps in the evening. What I didn't realize at the time was that the field conditions would be even worse than I had anticipated and that we would encounter environmental hazards at two sites that would lead me to rename them Killer Bee and Green Vine Snake.

I had purchased a second dory, named *Seirrita*, from a fisherman from the Temash River, south of Barranco. I decided I would learn to drive a dory. I had previously rented one from a man who said he needed it back to "haul leaf," which for some time I erroneously thought referred to palm fronds to thatch a roof. Apart from Anna Ramirez, the only fisher in Port Honduras, and Tanya Russ, the expatriate American woman who lived with her family on the mainland in Port Honduras, no other women drove dories. Although I was an experienced canoeist and sailor, I was aware that driving a motorized boat would be very different. Basically, it involved steering a 32 foot, hollowed-out tree trunk from the back. With practice, I became the third female dory driver in the area.

The mapping and excavation began with a site with a natural well that we'd found up Deep River. Deep River was of particular interest to me since it was opposite Wild Cane Cay and was a major waterway that provided access far inland. Perhaps Deep River was a major trade route between Wild Cane Cay and inland communities.

Leaving Wild Cane Cay on the north side, I pointed the *Adel 2* to the mouth of Deep River. I scanned the sea and the sky and kept an eye on my crew. Always alert for danger, I relaxed somewhat with the rolling waves hitting the bow. I reached for a stick wrapped with some heavy fishing line and a big hook and spoon stuck into the rail beside my boots. The *Adel 2* glided through the waves, with an occasional wave splashing against the starboard side of the bow and spraying saltwater into the boat and on the crew. I loosened some line and let it unravel over the side of the boat.

The seas became choppier as we approached the open sea between Wild Cane Cay and the mouth of the Deep River. With the bow pointed into the wind and waves, the dory rose on a big wave and then crashed down on the sea as the wave disappeared. Was the force of the impact strong enough to crack the dory? Certainly my crew felt the impact on their backs. Looking for a smoother and possibly safer ride, I let the wind and waves push the bow to port, out of the wind, and we glided broadside on the crest of a wave, surfing, or "riding the wave," as the crew remarked. When the wave dissipated, the dory slipped broadside into the trough between the waves. I held the tiller firmly, fighting the weather helm, and directed the *Adel 2* into the wind, looking for another big wave. With a big dory such as the *Adel 2,* a driver has a lot of wood to control. I played the sea, catching big waves, until we reached the constriction in the mouth of Deep River, where the wind died, and we entered another world.

The mangroves crept into the sea on either side of the dory. In the calm waters of the river mouth I hauled in a big barracuda that would provide our evening meal. I'd clean and store it in our ice chest when we made our first stop. The river was about 30 meters across at the entrance, narrowing as we approached the right turn up Muschamp Creek. We had passed sites already, including Butterfly Wing — a shell midden with distinctive pottery that made it the earliest site in southern Belize. Butterfly Wing dated to the Late Preclassic (300 B.C. to A.D. 300) or possibly earlier. On the right we passed Pineapple Grove, a small historic camp marked by nineteenth-century china. The site was on a hummock in a swamp.

10.1 *Excavations at Clearwater site.*

The water in the creek was opaque brown — a dramatic change since the rainy season had started, bringing silt from upriver. An occasional heron or egret flew from the bush, startled by our arrival. Whatever lurked in the water was protected from our vision. We turned up the creek, following the meandering, winding waters into an open savannah to the north, on the right side of the boat, with scattered clumps of palmettos and pines. On the left, the mangroves had given way to tropical rainforest, which I knew grew more luxuriant farther up the main channel of Deep River. We passed a nineteenth-century camp on the savannah, marked only by china and glass. The Muschamp family in Punta Gorda said their family had lived somewhere on the creek. Perhaps this was the location.

We stopped the dory by a cut-bank and brought our gear onto the open savannah. Our mission was to map and excavate a small, ancient hunting camp adjacent to a natural spring. We excavated three 1 by 1 m units in the shallow, sandy soil of the savannah, locating evidence of a temporary fishing and hunting camp we called Clearwater (figure 10.1). The artifact inventory included a few nondescript pottery sherds, a small, Postclassic chert arrowhead, and a couple of pottery fishing weights — formed clay pellets with notches at the ends in the distinctive style of the Postclassic. The excavation team rested by the freshwater spring, savoring the cold water emerging from the ground.

One of my staff members, Melissa, and a volunteer, Scott, labored with the transit, taking detailed measurements of the flat savannah — the only topography being the cut-bank and gully by the spring. The map they produced later that evening reflected the same level of detail, with contours marked at every 1 cm of change in elevation. I later reduced the contour interval to 10 cm to more accurately reflect the limited change in topography at the site. Their careful mapping and drawing prepared them well for the week ahead. As I introduced yet another challenging site for them to plot each day, they grew more confident in their map-making skills and their jungle trekking. I myself added a solid week of boating to my experience as one of the few women dory drivers in southern Belize — and likely beyond.

Green Vine Snake, one of the three Maya island sites with the distinctive coral architecture, is the least damaged by looters but the most inhospitable (figure 10.2). Transect excavations in the nonmound area revealed that artifacts were deeply buried below the ground surface in the mangrove swamp. Except for the mounds, the site is slightly below sea level. The location of the island and preliminary excavations suggest the island formed the near-shore connection in the triad of coastal trading ports, along with Wild Cane Cay and Frenchman's Cay, whose inhabitants controlled travel through the coastal waters of Port Honduras in ancient times.[3]

I named the site after a couple of 7 foot long green vine snakes fell from the trees on our heads while we were mapping the mounds (figure 10.3). This experience also changed my views about the absence of snakes on the cays. The snakes were dead before I saw them. Orlando had noticed them and killed them. He was excavating a test unit in the mound we were mapping. In a loud, firm voice, Orlando told his excavation partner to stay still. She froze in the pose of holding the trowel against the soil she was scraping. She later told me she felt the reverberation from the machete slashing through the air behind her. The machete hit the ground and revealed a coiled mass of vivid green snakes.

I asked Orlando whether they were poisonous. When he answered that they were semipoisonous, I was more than a little anxious. I realized that to many Belizeans all snakes are potentially poisonous, so you kill them first and then discuss them. However, I really wanted to know what he meant by semipoisonous. Did they kill some of the people? Did they kill the weak and infirm? Did they kill the young and the elderly? Or did they "sort of" kill you

10.2 *Oblique air view of Green Vine Snake showing a natural harbor and site in the mangrove swamp in the foreground.*

but not quite? "Semipoisonous" was a term I didn't like when presented by a new species of occupants of the cays.

My students pointed out that I had told them there were no poisonous snakes on the cays. I told them that was what I had thought, but evidently I was wrong. One of the students, Eric, was distressed to the point that he believed we were going to die when I suggested we continue mapping. Minimally he didn't want his professor to die, so he volunteered to map instead of me. Even though I was worried, he seemed to be taking this incident too seriously.

In the meantime, Scott had walked over from the transit and was looking down at the dead snakes on the ground. By his description we took him to be

10.3
*Mapping at Green Vine Snake,
with student holding a
stadia rod.*

a snake lover. He explained that the shape of their heads showed that they weren't poisonous and in fact were harmless. Although he seemed to know about snakes, I was not disappointed that Orlando had killed them. Only later did I discover that they were indeed harmless.

I stayed close to the students as they stretched the 100 meter tape from the transit to measure the distance to new points — occasionally walking back to check on Scott at the transit (figure 10.4). I helped clear vegetation so that the stadia rod could be held vertically and he could read the numbers indicating elevation. I recorded the elevation, distance, angle, and any commentary in the transit book. Either I had been recording wrong numbers — they were diminishing — or there was a mound. I was about 25 meters away but could see that the stadia looked higher even through the mangroves. The vegetation was different, too. The mangroves had stopped, and there was a clump of madre cacao trees, just like on Caribbean Oyster mound. In the dense mangrove vegetation the crew had not realized they had walked up a low coral rock mound.

I had visited the site at least four times before and had not noticed the mound, which I named Flat Tree Oyster. Now I knew there were three

10.4 *Earthwatch volunteer standing beside transit in mangroves at Green Vine Snake.*

mounds, as on Frenchman's Cay (figure 10.5). The entire site was hidden in a thick, red mangrove swamp. Slightly below water table, we cut a trail from the lagoon side, being careful to make it barely visible from the water. We mainly walked over mangrove stilts and cut as little as possible. After about 100 meters, we saw the first mound, Caribbean Oyster — a large, coral-rock-faced heap rising out of the mangroves and covered with madre cacao trees. Beyond the mass was a clearing with the short stems of black mangroves rising through the water. We could see another, lower coral mound beyond. That was Lion's Paw, where we had later come across the green vine snakes. Of course, the snakes were on all of the mounds, and later we saw them on other cays as well. I called the site Green Vine Snake for obvious reasons. Beautiful to watch, an iridescent green, not unlike green moray eels, the green

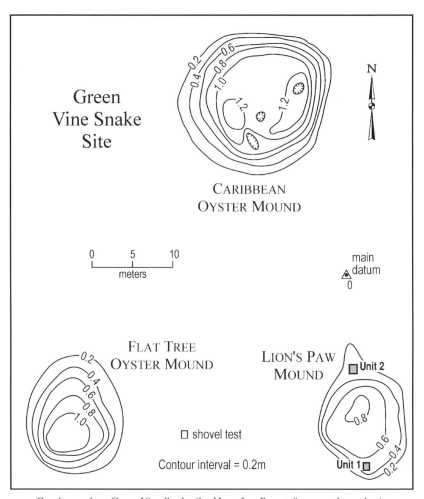

Green
Vine Snake
Site

CARIBBEAN
OYSTER MOUND

0   5   10
meters

main
△datum
0

FLAT TREE
OYSTER MOUND

LION'S PAW
MOUND

▣Unit 2

□ shovel test

Contour interval = 0.2m

Unit 1▣

10.5 *Coral mounds at Green Vine Snake (by Mary Lee Eggart from map by author).*

vine snake was nonpoisonous. Figuring out the age of the settlement and when the community had participated in coastal Maya trade would have to wait for another field season.

Not so harmless, however, were the killer bees who visited us one afternoon deep in the mangroves. We were on survey at a site in Punta Ycacos Lagoon (figure 10.6).[4] I was at the transit, waiting for Melissa and an Earthwatch volunteer, Ted, to place the tape and stadia rod at a new location so I could take a reading through the telescope barrel. They were gazing off into space. When I asked what was going on, the only word that came out was "bees!" I

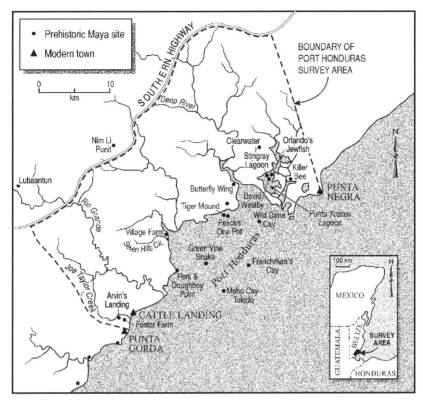

10.6 *Port Honduras survey region, with Punta Ycacos Lagoon forming the northern boundary (drawing by Mary Lee Eggart).*

looked up and saw a haze of dark flecks in the sky coming toward us, following the path we had taken from the dory. Then I heard the bees — a loud drone like a jet engine — as they came closer to the clearing where we stood. The sky was dark with the moving mass of bees following our path cut through the mangrove swamp from the dory to the site — a distance of at least 500 meters and a 10 minute walk — if along the cleared pathway. I was terrified.

I looked around. Our only easy exit was back along the path to the dory where the bees were advancing. The site, the low earthen mound covered in the prickly "ping wing" vegetation and surrounded by red mangroves with artifacts on the surface, was on the edge of the mangrove swamp and the higher ground. Our best escape — where we might eventually return to the dory — was to head 90 degrees away from the path into the swamp and then

10.7 *Red mangroves* (Rhizophora mangle) *at the Killer Bee site.*

make a loop back to the boat (figure 10.7). Mainly I just wanted to get as far away as possible — immediately. Our bee-sting kits were useless against a swarm of bees.

We abandoned the equipment, and I led the crew into the red mangrove swamp. We took our raincoats. If the bees caught up with us, we could lie down and cover ourselves if necessary.

I led a motley group of archaeologists into the red mangrove swamp and away from the bees. Were they killer bees? We weren't going to stick around to find out. Later that week I read an account of an elderly woman in Punta Gorda who had been killed by a swarm of killer bees, and in fact years later I saw killer bees in Punta Gorda near the post office. A drove of any kind of bees could kill us. I'd never seen anything like this moving mass, so I believed they were killer bees.

To maneuver through the red mangrove stilts, we either had to swing our legs over the roots or crawl under them. Ann, a teacher from Texas, went under more than the rest of us, who were taller. She seemed to be a good sport about it and even asked later if we minded if she embellished the story a bit to tell her students. I personally didn't think the story needed embellishing.

The mangroves were becoming thick and virtually impenetrable. I considered a circuitous route away from the site, then parallel to the path toward the water, and then walking along the "shoreline" back to the dory. However, the mangroves were too dense to walk through this close to the shore, so I decided we'd walk along the shore in the water. I walked along the root systems of the mangroves and carefully lowered myself into the water. The others were prepared to follow, except Melissa. Her voice seemed to suggest what I was thinking but dared not mention: crocodiles. She pleaded with me to get out of the water, although she eventually followed me into the opaque lagoon. By this time I had walked perhaps 25 yards along the water's edge. I had made substantial progress in the water compared to walking in the swamp. It was a test of my nerves how long I could stay in the water, measuring the greater distance traveled there against the possibility of a crocodile attack. When the crew caught up with me, I got out of the water and headed inland, where the mangroves were not so dense. The others virtually lunged out of the water. Danger was all around us, and I didn't want to die by bees or crocodiles or snakes. By the time we arrived at the dory, the bees had departed. We returned to the site up our pathway, picked up the equipment, filled in the excavation in the small, earthen mound, and left. I have never returned. We call it Killer Bee Site.

We had excavated a 1 by 1 m unit on the mound at the Killer Bee site and made a shovel test off the mound in 20 cm levels to 100 cm. The artifacts indicate it was a small, salt-making site similar to the underwater sites we would subsequently discover in Punta Ycacos Lagoon.[5] In fact, I have spent a lot of time searching for underwater sites in the lagoon itself, and although I know there are crocodiles, we've fortunately never encountered any. Perhaps they are well fed. I have seen a lot of stingrays in the lagoon, but they are not aggressive and have so far left us alone. The stingrays are attracted to the silt we stir up walking through the lagoon. I put aside any fears of crocodiles, stingrays, or other sea creatures with the anticipation of being the first person to see a new site in thirteen hundred years when the sea level was lower.

The clay cylinders, vessel supports, thick-walled pottery vessel sherds, and lumps of fired clay on the ground surface and in our shovel test all point to a specialized activity. The earthen mound was a slag heap where seawater had been enriched in salinity by pouring it through salt-saturated soil. The resulting concentrated brine was boiled in pots over fires. This process has been identified prehistorically and historically at various sites around the world, including the modern Maya village of Sacapulas in the Guatemalan highlands. The site's modern location at the edge of the red mangrove swamp and the dry land, with deposits extending below the water table, suggest a different environmental setting in the ancient past. If the sea level were a meter lower a thousand years ago, when Killer Bee was occupied, then the site might have been in a dry location several hundred meters inland. Although we found no evidence of salt-making artifacts or indeed other objects in the mangroves between the modern shoreline and the site, that area might have been dry land.

Alternatively, the area might have been covered by water, with an expansion of mangroves in recent times, putting the site at the edge of the lagoon. Sediment cores into the mangroves might help resolve the question, with identification of pollen and small animals such as foraminifera and ostracods, which are sensitive indicators of sea level and salinity changes, but coring would require us to return to Killer Bee. If we do, it will be a measure of my curiosity about the site.

By comparison with Green Vine Snake and Killer Bee, Tiger Mound site was relatively free of hazards. We set out to map the site that we had found on what turned out to be a memorable Sunday in 1988. We left in the dories for a day at the beach on Snake Cay, a white sand cay in crystal blue water several miles out to sea from Wild Cane Cay. Storm clouds had appeared on the horizon on our way to Snake Cay, however, so we turned back. Realizing that spending a day in the rain in our tents would not be much fun, we went on boat survey, trying to outrun the rain. This is sometimes possible since the sky is dome shaped on the open water and you can see storms moving from great distances across the sky. Whether you can outrun a storm depends, in part, on the size of your engine. Obviously, you can't outrun much with a 20 horsepower motor on a 32 foot dory.

Cautiously keeping close to land and far from the dark clouds on the south horizon, we approached a small, mangrove-covered island south of Deep

10.8 *Grass-covered earthen mound in clearing surrounded by mangrove swamp at Tiger Mound site.*

River. Since it was my turn to check out the land, Tiger followed me out of the dory, past Adel, who was seated in the bow. She laughed as the dog leapt past her, springing into the water and climbing over the mangrove prop roots to keep up with me. Machete in my right hand, I cut mangroves only when it was otherwise impossible to walk. The ground surface was slightly below the water table. This was not a great place to camp.

I wandered about 100 meters across the small spit of a cay and started west to look systematically over the island for obtrusive evidence of ancient settlement (mounds) or less visible evidence (pottery sherds on the surface). The near silence of individual rustling leaves had replaced the rushing noise of the sea in the background. I looked around, realizing that few people had likely ventured on this cay. I tightened my grip on the machete. I'd never encountered a crocodile, but I knew they were in the area. A boa constrictor could grow to quite a size on an uninhabited island. Then a sharp bark alerted me to possible danger.

I turned in the direction of the bark, climbing quickly over red mangrove roots. Tiger was standing, alone, in a clearing. Dead trunks of black-and-white mangroves glistened gray in the bright sun. A small, grassy mound was in the center of the clearing (figure 10.8). I looked down and saw pottery sherds on the ground surface a couple of centimeters below the water table. My dog had found a site. I later called it Tiger Mound site.

Tiger Mound provided solid evidence for a rise in sea level. Apart from the small earthen mound, the site was below sea level. A 2 by 2 meter excavation unit, as well as four transects of excavations, indicated deeply buried cultural deposits consisting of household garbage. A radiocarbon date placed the site in the Late Classic period. Both El Chayal and Ixtepeque obsidian were recovered, based on chemical identification. Tiger Mound had once been a small, thriving fishing community that was eventually abandoned, possibly as rising seas submerged it. Now the site was virtually invisible from the ground surface and buried in a mangrove swamp.

Difficult to excavate because of the mud and perilously hard to map because of the hot weather, even the government archaeologists had turned back part way along the path — itself submerged — when I took them to visit the site in 1991. They waited in the dory while we set up the transit to take some missing measurements. A bit disappointed that the government archaeologists, George Thompson and Brian Woodeye, were not interested in some of my best sites, I considered that they had assisted with a day's excavation at Green Vine Snake and perhaps were ready to return to the drier sites that some of my colleagues were studying. Would these visits be as memorable and physically challenging? For some reason, none of the government archaeologists has been interested in visiting my project since that time.

CHAPTER 11
RETURNING TO WILD CANE CAY IN 1992

I met the first team of volunteers of the 1992 field season at the Punta Gorda airstrip and led them along a path north of town to Joe Taylor Creek, where I stored my equipment and supplies and where my field staff were awaiting our arrival before setting off for Wild Cane Cay. The wind caught my hair, sweeping a braid across my neck. With a toss of my hand, I pushed the braid back over my shoulder. With my other hand I swung the machete at a vine that stretched across the pathway. My boots oozed in the mud, but I did not slow down. I checked over my shoulder again to make sure that the volunteers were still there. Tired but determined to keep pace with me, they followed quietly behind me, taking in the scenery. My self-imposed march through the bush ended abruptly. We emerged in the clearing by the storage shed where my project staff members were retrieving our equipment and loading the dories. They had finished and were filling five-gallon plastic containers with drinking water. They had about thirty bags. Orlando was checking the engines, which seemed fine.

As the volunteers dropped their backpacks and assorted gear in a cluster nearby, I turned around once more. They looked to me for direction. Clearly they knew I had a plan. I explained that I paid storage fees for a local man and his family to keep my dories and equipment when I was in the United States. I gave them a few minutes to rest from our trek and then asked them to load their gear into the dories, packing some of the things they had bought in town, unless they needed them in the next couple of hours, in the boats. Since I realized they probably wouldn't know what they might need, I suggested they keep life jackets, raincoats, sun hats, and any soda pop they had bought in town. Although I knew they wouldn't really understand or believe me, I suggested that if they weren't wearing long pants and long- sleeved shirts, they should get them from their packs before we left since there would be biting insects on the cay. I realized I was giving them a lot of information but saw no reason to slow down. They'd have time to relax on the trip to Wild Cane Cay. We'd have lunch in the boats. I turned my head toward Joe Taylor Creek and the dories.

Orlando was eager to work for me again after his small dory and engine sank. Although this event may not seem like a good recommendation for his seamanship, there were in fact few men both available to captain a dory and capable of doing so.[1] I had given him my old, unpainted dory after I purchased the *Adel 2*. The income he earned from fieldwork on my project was sporadic. He used the dory to supplement his income from fishing and hunting by taking tourists out to sea. Once, while he was out boating with a group of tourists, the sea became rough. Orlando said that he ordered his three passengers to put on their life jackets — ones that I had donated to him as they were evidently not for sale in Punta Gorda. The real problem was the distribution of weight in the dory. According to Orlando, the "fat lady" was in the bow and refused to move. I suggested to him that perhaps if he had called her by her name instead of calling her "fat lady," she might have followed his instructions. Orlando lacked any semblance of tact.

As he told the story to me later, the waves lapped over the bow deck and along the gunwales, slowly filling the dory. Orlando held his course with a firm grip of the left hand on the tiller, eyes focused straight ahead, picking a course and changing speed to match the waves. His right hand held a cutdown bleach container, which rhythmically scooped water from the dory near his feet and emptied it over the side of the boat. A series of waves seemed to crescendo across the bow deck, filling the dory faster than he could bail. Suddenly the bow disappeared into a wave, followed by the entire twenty-foot length of the boat. Although Orlando yelled at his passengers to hold on to the dory while they drifted to nearby Moho Cay, the fat lady didn't pay any attention. She was floating near the dory and made no attempt to get closer to the boat.

The three remaining boaters hung on to the dory and soon drifted to Moho Cay, where they sheltered in the army pagoda — a palm-thatched, oval structure with a cement floor and a wooden bar along one side. Bobbie Polonio picked them up the next day when he brought a group of soldiers from

Punta Gorda to spend their day off on the cays. When they returned to Punta Gorda — which is about three miles offshore — they found the fat lady recounting her adventures to a small audience of tourists and locals at the ice cream store. Not even embellishment would have detracted from the truth of the story. They had picked her up in Punta Gorda at the Texaco dock the next morning, apparently unperturbed by her long swim from Moho Cay. The others had stayed near the dory when it sank, and they had floated less than 100 meters to the cay. They all thought it was great fun except for Orlando, who owned the boat and motor that now lie at the bottom of the sea. He was ready to work for me again when I returned to explore the cays in Port Honduras.

Orlando and my students had loaded the food, equipment, and gear in the *Adel 2* and the *Seirrita* by the time I arrived with the volunteers. Tiger waited for me in the *Adel 2*. The volunteers were excited and easily encouraged to help load their gear and get into the boats. After checking the storage shed for any items we may have inadvertently left behind, I waded into the shallow water alongside the *Adel 2* and climbed over the side by the stern.

I pulled off my boots and placed them upside down between a board and the hull, more for easy retrieval than in the expectation that they might get dry inside. I turned to face the engine, placed a foot on the stern seat, and concentrated. I made sure that the engine was secured to the stern, pumped the gas, turned the knob to start, and pulled out the choke. I reached for the throttle and held the plastic handle firmly and pulled with purpose. I'd done this many times, but still I was relieved when the engine started. I pushed in the choke, looked around, and hauled in the lines that had moored us to the shore.

I put the engine in reverse, holding on to it to keep the propeller in the water as the waves rushed against the stern. We slowly moved backward away from the shore. I put the engine in forward gear, cranked up the throttle, and headed down the creek and out to sea. I looked around and saw Orlando behind me. He was sitting back in the *Seirrita* with a soda pop in his right hand and his left arm bent back holding the tiller. I reached down for my own soda and sat back with the solitude of a roaring engine.

In the silence I thought about Adel Cabral, who had accompanied me so many times to her island and home on Wild Cane Cay. She had recently died from gangrene poisoning. Adel had stubbed her toe on a loose floorboard in the house on Wild Cane Cay during my first field season in 1982 and had only reluctantly agreed to let me take her to Punta Gorda to see a doctor. In her

11.1 *Returning to Wild Cane Cay in the* Adel 2.

singsong voice, she had assured me that it would be all right since she was cleaning it with peroxide. She correctly feared that the doctor would keep her in town and she wouldn't be able to return with us to the cay. After many appeals and polite requests were rebuffed, I insisted she go with me to see the doctor in Punta Gorda. She did not return that field season. The infection spread from the toenail, aggravated by her newly diagnosed diabetes and the tropical environment, where wounds often heal poorly. Gradually, over the years, gangrene spread throughout her foot, and she underwent a series of operations to amputate pieces of her foot. Gangrene finally took her life nine years later in the Belize City hospital. It was no consolation to me that the dory I was driving to her island bore her name (figure 11.1).

CHAPTER 12

PROVISIONS FROM
PUNTA GORDA

ieldwork was interrupted by trips to Punta Gorda to pick up and deliver volunteers, which provided an opportunity to procure food, supplies, and drinking water. At other times we obtained some supplies from the Texaco station where we bought boat gas for survey work, especially early in the morning.

Because there were no public docks, the best time to arrive in Punta Gorda, either for gas, food, or mail or to pick up or deliver passengers was when the sea was calm. Normally this was early in the morning, so we arrived when the Texaco station opened at 6 A.M. As the day wore on the sea became progressively rougher. By noon, when the stores closed for lunch, the sea was usually choppy. If we had to stay in town until the stores reopened at 2 P.M., the sea was sometimes even rough. So, it was better to be early or avoid traveling in the "evening," which meant anytime after 12 noon — confusing at first when you ask when the stores will open and they say "this evening," which could mean 2 P.M. When you passed someone on the street after 6 P.M. and they said "Good night," they were not about to go to sleep. They were just giving you the appropriate greeting for that time of day. These were abbreviated as "Morning," "Evening," and "Good night." There was no afternoon.

Punta Gorda appeared to the unsuspecting visitor or geographer like a coastal community, but it was not. It was a town at the edge of the sea, which most townspeople viewed as an iron curtain, precipice, or, as the ancient Maya might have viewed the ocean, the "underworld," full of danger, death, and destruction. The sea met the land abruptly with a seawall.

Because the town had no dock, we approached the land with caution, cut the engine, and threw the rear anchor seaward to hold the dory and keep the waves from rushing against the sides of the boat. Then we secured the bow to a stable object on shore to hold the dory in a more or less immobile position. Passengers stepped over the side into the water, wearing rubber boots to protect their feet and ankles. Returning to the dory, we emptied the water from our boots after we climbed into the boat. The stores that carried boots in Punta Gorda sold dozens of pairs of rubber boots to my project volunteers and staff over the years. Apart from the "Indians," as the townsfolk referred to the Maya, the archaeologists were the only people who wore boots in town. We had the distinction of having audibly wet feet.

When I first came to Punta Gorda, the Texaco station had a wooden dock, which made it the friendliest place in town for dories to arrive. Until it warped, bent, and finally fell into the sea, we used the Texaco dock as a staging area for gas, water, food, and supplies, hauled from all over town to the dory, held in place, and guarded at the dock. We returned to town to buy gas or hoarded it in gas cans on the island. Everything becomes scarce from time to time and is hoarded, or things become scarce because they are hoarded. I never seemed to have enough viable plastic gas containers to horde enough gas to stay at sea for very long.

When the rainwater storage tank collapsed on Wild Cane Cay, a quest for fresh water brought us to town until we found sources on the mainland, such as Big Pond near Punta Negra or a freshwater well at Punta Ycacos, or up one of the nearby rivers. Even with bathing in the sea and washing clothes and dishes in seawater, we consumed 18 to 20 bags of water every few days. I encouraged people both to drink lots of water and to conserve water for any other purpose. We hauled five-gallon, plastic water bags with hard plastic handles that bit into our hands as the weight of the water increased on the walk from the town water tank or a store or friend's house toward the boat. It was with great relief that we arranged to get water from Village Farm in the survey area, where we could fill the water bags in the dories using a hose.

Ice for the coolers was a luxury that we experienced for several years until I decided it tied us to trips to town every three or four days. Sometimes the gas station carried ice. The standard price for a small bag of ice in town was one dollar. Ten bags filled a regular cooler, but our big, white ice chests needed 18 to 20 bags. The search for ice was an ordeal. Reserving 18 bags from the ice lady, Mrs. Ramclam, who had a tiny store opposite the market, usually worked. She sold ice only to regulars, however. Money on hand was not the main criterion, nor was reserving ahead of time. Getting to town early and becoming a regular provided access to ice, if she had any.

The gas station even carried ice cream for a short time, but it was only the soft drink cooler that lasted. A cold Coke in the early morning was an experience that my volunteers did not initially appreciate. Along with the containers for mixed gas for the boats and kerosene for the pressure lanterns, the ritual of early morning gas trips to Texaco included two Cokes each for the staff — a cold drink immediately and another saved for the return boat trip out to sea. I never drank sodas before coming to Belize but acquired a taste for Coke, orange soda, red Fanta, or Sprite from the red-and-silver metal case just inside the Texaco station.

A major objective of the scheduled trips to Punta Gorda was procuring food, supplies, and volunteers quickly enough to return to sea before the water began to get rough. Occasionally we forgot something important on a shopping list. The day we forgot the fresh and frozen food stands out in my memory.

On that particular trip the sea was choppy by the time we left Punta Gorda with a new group of volunteers, their gear, coolers, boxes of food, and bags of water. We traveled along the mainland coast to relax and fish in the more-sheltered waters. From Orlando I learned that if we wanted to catch a fish while trolling, we might have to detour from the most direct route. Traveling with him at the helm was frequently a fight between catching fish or arriving at our destination in a timely fashion. We could reach Wild Cane Cay from Punta Gorda on a direct line of sight through open seas that we named the "Straits of Magellan." If the seas were rough, we had to stay closer to shore. Regardless of the weather, traveling with Orlando meant fishing. The barracudas and other fish were concentrated along the mangrove cays.

Orlando had driven close to shore to shelter from the sea when something pulled the line. Hand over hand, I pulled the heavy line into the dory, planning where the fish was going to land in the boat. My mind was focused on keeping the pressure on the line to haul the fish toward the dory. One moment of relaxation would allow this fish to loosen its mouth from the hook and be on his way. I had seen too many fish laugh at us to loosen my grip. A mass of loosely coiled line was gathered in the dory, so I knew the fish was close. I stood up and gathered all my strength to drag the yellow jack into the dory. On its side, it lunged and snapped its jaws until I hit it with the paddle.

When I opened the cooler to put in the fish, I realized that, while shopping at various places in town, we had neglected to pick up the fresh and frozen food order after we filled the cooler with ice. This was not a great loss, though, because now we had enough ice to keep all the fish we caught that day. We picked up the forgotten food order on our next trip to town. The magnificent fish we caught off Pork and Doughboy Point that day provided a wonderful meal and a memorable story.

ith the realization that sea-level rise had submerged Classic Maya sites, we began looking not just in shallow water around known sites such as Wild Cane Cay, but also in shallow water elsewhere in Port Honduras. We found three sites in a coastal lagoon north of Deep River and opposite Wild Cane Cay. While slowly traversing the lagoon in the dory, we looked over the gunwales for artifacts on the seafloor. My strategy was for whoever saw artifacts to immediately jump overboard to mark the spot and determine whether it was in fact a site. The rule was that someone had to stay on board, preferably the driver. Since Orlando liked to cut the engine and jump overboard in search of possible sites, I normally stayed in the dory. I had images of the dory motoring away while we stood in the water.

In 1991 we found three underwater sites in Punta Ycacos Lagoon.[1] Although it was difficult to describe their locations, I always found them once I was immersed in the landscape of red mangroves that fringed the lagoon shores and formed ephemeral islands. My system broke down, however, after Hurricane Iris whipped across the land on October 8, 2001, at 140 mph, uprooting trees and defoliating the mangroves. By that time I had begun to record the location of sites with a global positioning system (GPS), which had become critical to relocating the underwater sites once the landscape markers were destroyed (figure 13.1).

Stingray Lagoon was the first underwater site we found, and we excavated it in 1991.[2] The site wasn't really underwater in the sense of our having to wear scuba gear. However, it was about 300 meters offshore in the center of

13.1 *Using a global positioning system (GPS) to record location of underwater site in Punta Ycacos Lagoon.*

Punta Ycacos Lagoon — just north of Deep River (figure 13.2). The site lay under about a meter of water, which meant that the sea level had risen more than that for the spot to have once been dry land. Even with a microtidal variation of about 50 cm between high and low tides, the living surface of an ancient community had to be enough above sea level to be permanently dry, including accommodating tidal variations. When I first reported Stingray Lagoon at the Society for American Archaeology annual conference, some members of the audience chuckled at the sight of transit mapping in the water and people standing in waist-high water with shovels and excavation screens. Now my colleagues simply accept that my slides will be wet and muddy, and the only outbursts of laughter are from newcomers. Neither my students nor the volunteers knew that setting up the transit in the sea to make a map with a stadia rod and hundred-meter tape was unusual.

I know the site was 310 meters offshore because Melissa took the stadia rod to the north shore, stopping each 10 meters to take an elevation — or perhaps we should have called it a depth reading. We had set up a protective net around the main part of the site where we were mapping and excavating. The net protected us from stingrays that were attracted to the silt that we stirred

13.2 *Air view of Punta Ycacos Lagoon, where saltwork sites were discovered in the water.*

up as we walked. Melissa was mapping beyond the net, so I sent a volunteer to be a lookout for stingrays and other creatures. Partway across, I noticed that the volunteer was simply snorkeling — not much of a lookout. Melissa, as she reminds me from time to time, was well aware of the potential danger to which the volunteer seemed oblivious. They made it back safely, and fortunately the mapping had to be done only once.

Our excavations at Stingray Lagoon called for innovative techniques in order to locate and recover the evidence from the inundated setting. One of the appeals of field archaeology is figuring out what methods are appropriate in different situations. Fortunately, at Stingray Lagoon and the other underwater sites in Punta Ycacos Lagoon we have excavated, the sites are shallow enough to allow us to stand in the water (figure 13.3).

We set up the transit in the water, established a datum, and mapped the surface distribution of artifacts on the seafloor. Then we set out an excavation unit with red mangrove poles forming the outlines instead of string. Whereas other wood might have floated away, fresh red mangrove wood sinks, so it stayed in place. Another advantage of using the mangrove frame was that we could feel the location of the excavation units even in the low-visibility

13.3 *Fieldwork in Punta Ycacos Lagoon at a submerged saltwork site, Eleanor Betty, discovered and excavated in 2003.*

conditions we created when we started excavating and disturbed the silt on the lagoon floor. We excavated with shovels and screens as if we were on land. Because a thin veneer of silt covered the artifacts, we had staked out protective nets around the area we were excavating.

The artifacts were embedded in a conglomerate of charcoal and fired clay that represented the remains of fires for making salt by the "sal cocida" method of boiling brine in pots. We had a standardized collection of thick jar and bowl pottery sherds from large vessels, as well as the ubiquitous clay cylinder, vessel supports, which always raised alternative interpretations as coprolites or phallic symbols (figure 13.4). Instead, they were props to hold the pots over the fires during the boiling of brine to produce the salt. The vessels appeared crude and unattractive (figure 13.5) when compared with the beautiful painted pots for which the Late Classic Maya are known from other sites or indeed the burial vessels from Wild Cane Cay.

However, the pottery from Stingray Lagoon and other salt sites was well crafted for its intended purpose. The large pieces of quartz that were quite apparent throughout the clay — both in the vessels and in the supports — would have absorbed and dissipated much of the heat and prevented the pots

13.4 *Solid clay cylinders from Stingray Lagoon site used as vessel supports for salt pots.*

13.5 *Jar sherds from salt pots from Stingray Lagoon site.*

from breaking during repeated uses. The thin walls of the pots and their rounded sides were well suited to cooking and distributing the heat to the vessels' contents. By way of contrast, the thick, outward-curving rims would have been useful for placing and removing the jars on the supports for cooking. Brine boiling in pots to produce salt cakes was a common occurrence elsewhere in prehistory and even historical times. The modern Maya at the highland Guatemalan community of Sacapulas use this technique, only with metal pots, but place up to two dozen pots on a fire at a time to boil. At Sacapulas, the first evaporation removes the moisture and produces loose salt. Then the salt is gathered into open bowls and hardened over the fires to produce salt cakes. If this technique were followed at Stingray Lagoon and the other saltwork shops in Punta Ycacos Lagoon, the salt cakes may have been traded inland as cakes, with no archaeological traces of their export.

I was excited about these saltworks, whose existence and location addressed several research areas of interest even to my colleagues excavating at large Maya cities in the interior. Could enough salt have been produced to reduce or eliminate the need for bulk import of this daily necessity from places farther away from the salt flats along the northern coast of the Yucatan? Was this an example of workshop production that suggested economic specialization near the source of the raw material (salt) and away from the control of the big Maya cities? If so, then the ancient Maya economy and trading system was not as centrally controlled as previously believed. And blatantly obvious, how could we explain the present underwater location of these salt sites and many other submerged sites in the coastal area? Some, like the saltwork shops, were abandoned at the end of the Classic period, about A.D. 900, which may have resulted from changing demands for salt, but the sites may not have been flooded until later.

With the abandonment of many large Maya cities at the end of the Classic and the revitalization of sea trade with the rise of the Postclassic city of Chichen Itza in the northern Yucatan, the trading port at Wild Cane Cay expanded: In the Postclassic, the density of obsidian and the variety of imported pottery and copper increased dramatically. We also found visible evidence of increased wealth in the form of the coral architecture. Perhaps the focus of the coastal area was reoriented from the production of salt and other marine resources for the inland Maya in the south to participation in the long-distance canoe trade around the Yucatan.

Although Stingray Lagoon and the other flooded sites were more difficult to excavate than dry land sites, they yielded an abundance of information on the ancient environment and diet.[1] Of course the submerged location of these sites was good evidence that the modern landscape of Port Honduras was different from its ancient counterpart. What did this ancient landscape look like? Clearly it was drier since it had supported human settlements as well as the saltwork shops in Punta Ycacos Lagoon, which would have been islands in a salt flat that was periodically inundated during the rainy season. The organic material, such as ancient palm fruits, corncobs, and mamey apple pits, also attest to a drier landscape. These food remains point to a diet rich in tree crops, which was a good strategy for the limited land on island communities.[2]

The plants we recovered in our excavations did not grow in the salty or flooded conditions of the mangrove swamps along the coast and offshore islands. More compelling perhaps was that the sites we discovered and excavated were consistently submerged below the modern water level. This explains the modern absence of settlement and our difficulty in finding ancient sites. With the documentation of the rising sea level, one of the projects goals was to address the ancient Maya's responses to rising sea levels. I believed that our findings could help us learn about modern environmental problems associated with global warming and rising sea levels.

The ancient Maya's response to the rising seas at Stingray Lagoon seemed clear since the site, which dates (on the basis of ceramics styles and radiocarbon dating) to the Late and Terminal Classic period (A.D. 800–900), lay under about a meter of water. The lack of subsequent settlement evidence dating to the Postclassic period and the inundated nature of the site indicates it was abandoned. The Maya abandoned Stingray Lagoon because the market for the salt they produced was greatly reduced with the abandonment of nearby, inland Maya cities at the end of the Classic period. Although I think the site was abandoned for economic rather than environmental reasons, Stingray Lagoon would not have been habitable or usable as a saltwork shop during the Postclassic since it was submerged. The exact timing of the inundation in relation to the departure of the Maya is unknown.

In addition to the discovery and excavation of archaeological sites in Port Honduras, we documented a sea-level rise of one meter or more since the end of the Late Classic period, about A.D. 900.[3] The submergence of Late Classic communities is compelling evidence for sea-level rise — either an actual rise in sea levels, subsidence of the land, or a combination of both. Some of the sites, such as the underwater locations in Punta Ycacos Lagoon, are completely submerged with no dry land component. A second category of sites, such as Tiger Mound and Pork and Doughboy Point, are located on land, but their lower reaches are below the water table, and they also often have offshore areas that are inundated. Some of these sites, such as Wild Cane Cay and Frenchman's Cay, are sizable communities with stone architectural remains. Pelican Cay representing a third category of inundated sites, is buried under mangrove peat and has no dry land on the island, which consists of red mangroves.

I created a model of the relationship between sea-level rise and ancient Maya settlement in the area.[4] Several factors were important in the continued settlement or abandonment of communities in Port Honduras, all of which were threatened by a rising sea level. Although the immediate reason for the abandonment of particular saltwork shops in Punta Ycacos Lagoon may have been rising seas, the Maya could have relocated the workshops to drier locations had there been a market for salt: The Punta Ycacos saltworks were abandoned because the inland market for salt ended when the nearby inland cities were deserted at the end of the Late Classic. Wild Cane Cay benefited from centuries of human settlement on the island in that the accumulation of garbage helped to build up the island and ward off the effects of rising seas. This anthropogenic effect was further enhanced by the Postclassic construction of stone building platforms upon which houses were constructed. Since the island's historic occupants left in the late-twentieth century, rising seas have been more effectively submerging the cay. Smaller communities, such as

Pelican, which were abandoned at the end of the Late Classic and reclaimed by the rising seas, are now buried under mangrove peat, living mangroves, and seawater.

I consider Port Honduras as a laboratory for investigating ancient Maya economy, particularly sea trade and its relationship to a local economy. Apart from my interest in working and living on small Caribbean islands and experiencing the excitement of traveling in small boats in the open seas, there are more pragmatic features that make Port Honduras especially valuable archaeologically: There is virtually no modern historic settlement covering the ancient Maya sites. Many of these places, in fact, are buried in mangrove peat or otherwise submerged, which has afforded them unusually good preservation of organic food remains compared to other Maya sites. However, the relative smallness of the Maya communities and workshops makes it possible to figure out their age, size, and nature in a reasonable time. Compared with most large, ancient Maya cities that require a team of archaeologists working for many years to learn part of the site's history, it is possible for me to learn much about the Port Honduras sites.

People along the coast of Belize have long provided import-export services, and the ancient Maya were no exception.[5] My coastal survey in Port Honduras, including excavations at various sites, was aimed at investigating the ancient coastal Maya systems of import, export, and regional distribution of goods and resources. In the first phase of the research I was able to identify Wild Cane Cay as a major trading port during both the Classic and Postclassic periods, with radiocarbon-dated settlement from about A.D. 300 to 1400. The high population density on this ten-acre island was made possible by the abundant seafood and the specialized tree cropping evident from the fish bones and plant remains in our household excavations in 1982. Of the six mounds on the island, intensive excavations in Fighting Conch revealed that it shrouded a series of six successive structures built with coral dredged from the sea or gathered from storm beaches and with limestone and sandstone slabs ferried from the nearby mainland and rivers. The labor necessary to obtain and construct the coral foundations demarcated Wild Cane Cay from most of the other sites in Port Honduras that we had found and investigated.

Once I had established the role of Wild Cane Cay as a coastal trading port, it was logical to investigate the community's place in the surrounding Port Honduras region. I wanted to discover whether there were sites and, if so, how they compared in age with Wild Cane Cay and whether they had obsidian and other trade goods. In particular, I was interested in finding out whether obsidian and other trade goods brought to Wild Cane Cay were distributed within the Port Honduras region. An alternative was that Wild Cane Cay was a stopover on a coastal trade route for bringing exotic goods for the lowland Maya elite at large cities, but that goods were not distributed locally to small communities. The regional search for sites in Port Honduras addressed these questions by locating and dating sites and estimating their access to exotic goods relative to Wild Cane Cay. The swamps of Port Honduras revealed a surprising number of ancient Maya sites.

That Port Honduras virtually lacks modern settlement in favor of widespread mangrove swamps was not a deterrent to the ancient Maya. A significant rise in sea level since the Classic period had transformed the land form and vegetation of what was once a more hospitable environment. The existence of waterlogged coastal deposits is no surprise to archaeologists who have ventured along the coast of Belize, but few projects have systematically pursued archaeology below the water table and in the sea. The first clues to the extent of the transformation of the coastal landscape emerged with the offshore excavations at Wild Cane Cay. The distribution of buried archaeological deposits more than doubled the size of the ancient site.

Since the time of the offshore excavations at Wild Cane Cay, two other kinds of sites were added to the inventory of inhospitable settlement locations. Some places, such as Tiger Mound, Green Vine Snake, Killer Bee, and Pelican Cay, are deeply buried beneath modern red mangrove peat and (apart from occasional mounds at some sites) invisible from the ground surface. The ground surface at Pelican Cay, for example, is slightly below the water table. A search for tent sites revealed no dry land on the island and no artifacts on the ground surface. However, there are Classic Maya midden deposits buried under 40 cm of mangrove peat. Other sites, such as Stingray Lagoon, David Westby, and Orlando's Jewfish, are underwater sites with no dry land components. It was neither the ancient Maya's unlikely propensity for underwater living nor my project's desire to work in inundated settings that focused my fieldwork at these places. Instead, it was the realization that a rise in sea level had submerged substantial portions of Port Honduras, dramatically reduced the land available for ancient settlement, and transformed the vegetation patterns. A search for sites in well-drained upland soils, where it was clear from my colleagues' research that the ancient Maya preferred to live, would have resulted in a diminished view of the ancient settlement in the Port Honduras area. Still more sites remain submerged and hidden even from my deliberate search, which has not yet covered all of the inundated locations.

Our hunt for coastal sites revealed that settlement in Port Honduras spanned more than two millennia. The earliest settlement is on the banks of Deep River and consists of a small shell midden that we called Butterfly Wing. Based on my comparison of the pottery sherds with collections at Harvard's Peabody Museum, I conclude that the site is the earliest in the region, dating to as early as 300 B.C., at the beginning of the Late Preclassic. Butterfly Wing was a camp where local shellfish were eaten and discarded. The community marks the beginning of coastal trade in Port Honduras, with obsidian flakes imported from the El Chayal outcrop near modern Guatemala City.

Although the Early Classic, between A.D. 300 and 600, is poorly known in Port Honduras, it is represented by radiocarbon-dated, domestic middens at Wild Cane Cay and Pelican Cay. By way of contrast, there is ample evidence of Late Classic settlement, mirroring settlement farther inland in southern Belize. A number of offshore island, coastal, and river sites were occupied during the Late Classic, between A.D. 600 and 900, at the same time as a substantial settlement at Wild Cane Cay. Several sites (notably Arvin's Landing and Foster Farm on Joe Taylor Creek north of Punta Gorda as well as Village Farm) located on the mainland near river mouths participated in obsidian trade.

In addition to the regional distribution of obsidian within Port Honduras, we also found evidence of a thriving exchange between the coast and inland cities. Lubaantun, located some 25 km up the Rio Grande, which formed the southern terminus of Port Honduras, was evidently exclusively occupied during the Late Classic. Its presence was felt on the coast in the form of figurine whistles made in molds in a style distinctive to Lubaantun. Pottery jars with animal and geometric designs stamped around the vessel shoulder found at Wild Cane Cay and the underwater sites in Punta Ycacos Lagoon were distributed in southern Belize and the adjacent Pasion and Petexbatun area of Guatemala during the Late Classic.

What was traded from the coast in return for these inland goods? Our excavations in Punta Ycacos Lagoon indicate that workshops produced salt, which would have been in demand by the inland Maya as a basic, biological necessity. Other marine resources, notably stingray spines for ritual bloodletting, conch shells for making trumpets, other sea shells, coral, and seafood were gathered in Port Honduras and would have been the closest source for the nearby inland cities of the Late Classic period. The Late Classic city of Nim Li Punit, with its many carved monuments with hieroglyphic inscriptions accompanying Maya royalty, was located near the headwaters of Golden

Stream, a river that feeds directly into the heart of Port Honduras. Obsidian was traded to Lubaantun and Nim Li Punit but evidently not in the same quantity as to Wild Cane Cay. It appears that obsidian was transported along the coast to Wild Cane Cay from where it was regionally distributed and also exchanged for goods made at inland cites.

Despite the abandonment of inland cites in southern Belize at the end of the Classic period, settlement continued and even expanded in many places in Port Honduras during the succeeding Postclassic period. However, as rising sea levels began to inundate the low-lying land in Port Honduras, some settlements were abandoned. In these instances, the Maya likely relocated to higher, drier coastal locations, such as Wild Cane Cay. Since the Classic deposits lay buried under mangrove peat, we know, for example, that the community on Pelican Cay was deserted. Similarly, the Late Classic salt workshops in Punta Ycacos Lagoon were deserted and at some point inundated.

Participation in the coastal trade of obsidian increased considerably at Wild Cane Cay, with an 800-percent increase in the density of obsidian in Postclassic household refuse deposits.[6] The number of outcrops from which Wild Cane Cay obtained obsidian also increased. In the Late Classic, coastal obsidian trade focused on two major outcrops near Guatemala City, El Chayal and Ixtepeque. The Postclassic obsidian was obtained from six outcrops ranging from distant central Mexico to closer locations in Guatemala and Honduras. Both the amount of trade and the number of trading contacts increased substantially in the Postclassic. Elsewhere I suggest that the Wild Cane Cay Maya were able to shift their allegiances from the southern Maya lowlands during the Late Classic to the northern Maya lowlands during the Postclassic, in line with the changing economic and political arena of the lowland Maya. With the collapse of the southern lowland sites in southern Belize, the nearby Pasion and Petexbatun cities in Guatemala, and Tikal and other cities farther north in the Peten district of Guatemala, the southern lowland Maya market for obsidian disappeared. In its place, Chichen Itza and other cities in the northern Maya lowlands in the modern Mexican Yucatan peninsula emerged as major Maya economic and political powers. Wild Cane Cay was at the southern terminus of the circum-Yucatan coastal canoe trade route. Isla Cerritos served nearby Chichen Itza. Marco Gonzalez and other sites on Ambergris Cay figured in coastal-inland trade with cities in northern Belize, such as Lamanai, which survived the political and economic collapse of the southern cities.

The earliest indication of a European presence in Port Honduras is Spanish olive jar fragments from offshore excavations at Wild Cane Cay. Nineteenth- and early-twentieth-century ceramics are evidence of mahogany and rosewood logging and subsistence fishing at several locations in Port Honduras. The Seven Hills sugar mill and the Confederate settlement at Cattle Landing dramatically increased settlement in the Port Honduras region for a short time. At the same time, subsistence fisherfolk, including the Cabral family, settled in Port Honduras. They survived by fishing, selling coconuts and other tree fruits, and providing transshipment services for workers floating logs down the rivers of Port Honduras. Although much diminished in terms of permanent settlement, even in the twenty-first century Port Honduras hosts a vibrant, albeit illegal, trade in local manatee, Colombian cocaine, refugees, and guns.[7]

PART IV
FRENCHMAN'S CAY, 1994 AND 1997

CHAPTER 15

SETTLEMENT PATTERNS

n 1994, I moved the project base camp to Frenchman's Cay in order to carry out major excavations at that island site. On a map, Frenchman's Cay is much closer to Punta Gorda than Wild Cane Cay, four islands to the north. However, boat travel was more difficult that it had been to Wild Cane Cay since Frenchman's Cay was on the outer range of cays in Port Honduras. Between the inner and outer ranges of cays, strong winds often built up in the waters, forming heavy seas. Wild Cane Cay was at the northern end of Port Honduras, where the inner and outer ranges of cays converged. Although it was possible to travel between these ranges in a direct line between Punta Gorda and Wild Cane Cay, if the seas were rough, we traveled inside the inner range, where the waters were more protected. Traveling to Frenchman's Cay required venturing in the open seas.

I wanted to figure out the relationship of Frenchman's Cay to nearby Wild Cane Cay. Rather than negotiate the rough seas between the two islands on a daily basis, I decided to forgo the relative comforts of Wild Cane Cay for a more primitive existence on Frenchman's Cay. With no house under which to shelter, no cleared campsite, and no deepwater lagoon in which to swim, I found Frenchman's Cay a logistical challenge. I hired the landowners to build us an outhouse and a frame, which we covered with a tarp to become the "S.C.A.B. Lab and Café," referring to the "South Coastal Archaeology in Belize Project." The landowners' teenage children, Lyra and Nathaniel, joined my project as "junior staff." They added the exuberance and curiosity of youth to the team, as well as knowledge about the local environment and culture.

Surrounded by tents, dories in the water in front of the campsite, and settled with students and volunteers, Frenchman's Cay began to feel familiar and even relatively comfortable. Our only luxury was twenty-four-hour radio communication with Punta Gorda, using a two-meter radio powered by car batteries that we charged from a solar panel. We were relatively self-sufficient for weeks at a time, having eliminated trips to town for ice. The frequency of town trips was now determined by the need to replenish our supply of fresh water. When we started getting water at Village Farm on the mainland across from Frenchman's Cay, our trips to town were even less frequent. Frenchman's Cay became our home.

I had suffered the usual attrition of project staff, except for Melissa. She and another student, Jodi, would be working on graduate research at underwater sites in Port Honduras. Two of my students from a field school on Wild Cane Cay, Rachel and Mirtha, were also staff members. They longed for the luxuries of Wild Cane Cay. To me, the two islands were quite similar in their lack of basic amenities. Together with other student staff members, Brad and Shelly, my junior staff, and our volunteers, we coexisted with the acrid smell of the mangrove swamp, the swarms of mosquitoes and sandflies that descended periodically like smog over a city, and the rain that gradually saturated the ground, our clothes, the excavations, and occasionally our spirits. Unfortunately, there was no way to efficiently carry out fieldwork on Frenchman's Cay other than to live there. It was slim consolation to us that we were living on an ancient Maya site. At other times, we better appreciated our surroundings, which also included rustling coconut palms, mangos and other fruit-bearing trees, a snorkeler's delight, and the peace and solitude of living alone on a deserted Caribbean island. At times, especially when there was a wind to drive away the insect pests, Frenchman's Cay became a paradise.

Rough seas curtailed most of the boat survey work, with the resulting benefit that I was able to turn my attention on Frenchman's Cay. This was surprising to my students, who reminded me more than once that in previous years I was always away from Wild Cane Cay on boat survey. It was true that once I learned how to drive a dory and felt comfortable on the sea, I enjoyed both the challenge of the open water and the search to discover new sites. In the past I had often left students in charge of the mound excavations. Apart from excavations in Punta Ycacos Lagoon and at Pork and Doughboy Point and necessary trips for provisions and volunteers, we stayed on Frenchman's Cay.

The island had three small coral mounds, with a dry-land area marked by a scattering of potsherds, broken obsidian, and chert artifacts at the south-

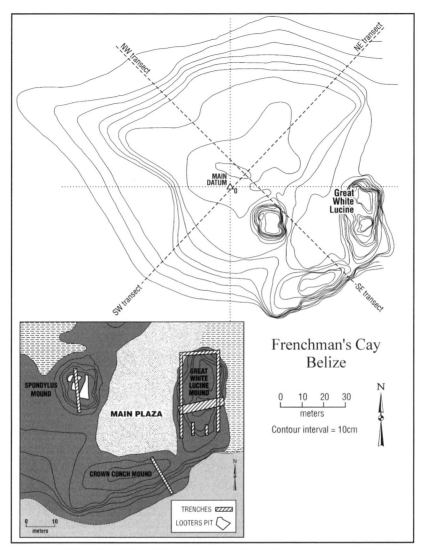

15.1 *Map of Frenchman's Cay with three coral mounds and transect excavations (by Mary Lee Eggart from map by author).*

ern end of a large mangrove cay (figure 15.1). Artifacts on the ground surface indicate that Frenchman's Cay was used from the Late Classic through
the Postclassic periods, overlapping Wild Cane Cay in time. Both El Chayal
and Ixtepeque obsidian were traded to the community on Frenchman's Cay
from highland Guatemala.[1] The limited quantities of green obsidian from
the more distant Pachuca outcrop north of Mexico City provided another

similarity with Wild Cane Cay and indicated far-reaching trading ties. Of course the surface remains did not explain the age of the trade goods or if they had been brought directly to Frenchman's Cay by sea traders or if they arrived at the island site indirectly through local trade with the Maya traders on nearby Wild Cane Cay. I hoped that our excavations would answer these and other questions.

Since my initial visit to Frenchman's Cay in 1981 with King and from brief reports by other archaeologists, there had been a nagging anxiety in my mind about what role Frenchman's Cay played in the local and long-distance economy. Why would there be another coastal trading port so close to Wild Cane Cay? Were the Frenchman's Cay Maya poor in-laws of the more affluent traders on Wild Cane Cay? Did the Maya on Frenchman's Cay pick up the traders who traveled farther offshore, along the outer range of the Port Honduras cays, while the Wild Cane Cay Maya traded with those travelers who plied their wares closer to shore or along the inner range of the Port Honduras cays? Alternatively, was Frenchman's Cay either younger or older than Wild Cane Cay, in which case the islands did not compete for coastal business at the same time? There was also the possibility, of course, that the Maya on Frenchman's Cay did not directly participate in long-distance trade, but instead received a modest amount of obsidian and other exotic materials from the Maya on Wild Cane Cay. I knew the island had structures with coral rock foundations and obsidian on the ground surface, like Wild Cane Cay, but were the islands contemporaneous competitors for coastal trade or occupied at different times, or was Frenchman's Cay not involved in coastal trade?

Having waited many years for the opportunity to carry out fieldwork on Frenchman's Cay, I was excited. My students and volunteers have often remarked on my patience when it comes to excavations. In my long-range plans, I fully expect to excavate many of the sites in Port Honduras when the opportunity and funding are available, based on my developing research questions. As we try to answer these questions about the coastal Maya, others arise, and future field seasons will address them. Archaeological fieldwork, particularly excavations in waterlogged soil in the remote setting of Port Honduras, takes time. Of course, the volunteers normally work on my project for only two weeks, so they cannot personally appreciate my long-range plans. Although some of my students return for several field seasons, they eventually graduate and begin their own careers. I had to wait until I had completed the architectural excavations on Wild Cane Cay and also obtained permission from the owners of Frenchman's Cay. Both took several years to accomplish.

The owners of Frenchman's Cay are an American couple who had decided to live in a secluded part of the rainforest and home-school their children, clearly opting for a degree of solitude and independence from society. One day I decided to visit them at their home, Village Farm, on the mainland in Port Honduras. Over time and coffee we developed a friendship, enhanced by our shared interest in Port Honduras, its archaeology, and preservation of its pristine condition. I also enjoyed their children, Lyra and Nathaniel, who began visiting our project and helping in the research for several days at a time. Despite moans from my field staff about another visit to the sandfly-ridden swamp where the Spang family lived, we visited them often. My staff and volunteers acceded to my choices and sometimes actually enjoyed themselves, as long as they were protected from the sandflies and other insect pests that seasonally descended on Village Farm. One day, Tanya and John Spang asked me whether I might ever be interested in excavating at Frenchman's Cay. I never considered that I might have that opportunity. Suppressing my enthusiasm, I casually responded that I was, in fact, interested and began telling them of my questions about the island's past.

When we arrived at Frenchman's Cay in 1994, the Spang family had cleared some of the vegetation for tent sites, built a frame for our kitchen and lab house, and constructed a wooden walkway with an outhouse over the sea for our use. With the high water table, as at Wild Cane Cay, a land-based outhouse was impossible. Still, the island was overgrown and in places almost impenetrable, with vines, bushes, and trees. With the rainy season still in full force at the time of our arrival, my students thought more of survival than of archaeology. Thankfully, by the time our first group of volunteers arrived, my students had acclimatized themselves to the setting, or at least were thrown into the greater responsibility and preoccupation of taking care of the volunteers and supervising them.

We mapped the dry-land area of Frenchman's Cay and discovered the ancient size of the site by excavations along four transects. As at Wild Cane Cay, our first task was to establish a permanent datum marker for the site by sinking a 4 ft metal rod into the ground and holding it in place with cement. We placed a second datum marker to help locate the orientation of our map and to have a backup datum in case the main one was destroyed by visitors, as had occurred at Wild Cane Cay. Apparently, some local people thought the datum marked the location of special finds, so they dug it up! Since this happened to our main datum at Frenchman's Cay as well, it was fortunate that we had a secondary datum.

Using a surveyor's transit from the main datum, we cleared four transects in cardinal directions for excavations. We placed stakes at 10 m intervals along each transect and excavated at each spot. My graduate assistant, Brad, was in charge of supervising the transect excavations, coordinating teams of two volunteers, and keeping a field journal of who excavated where and when. As usual, I rotated among the excavations, took over for the deepest or messiest ones, partly to show that it was possible, and also because I was the person most interested in the results. Teams excavated in 20 cm levels and shoveled the mud into buckets, carried them to the sea, and water-screened the contents, much as we had done at Wild Cane Cay. The volunteers worked hard, digging in the muddy soil and hauling buckets of mud to the sea, encouraged by the participation of my female staff members in the work, especially Jodi, who evidently seemed frail. Rather than let her carry buckets, an older male volunteer carried hers to the sea. After several days I was not surprised to find Cecil taking a brief, although reluctant, rest in a hammock.

The transect excavations were messy and involved hard labor, but the results allowed me to estimate the size of the ancient site, which was larger than the scatter of artifacts on the ground surface. We continued the transect excavations into the sea to determine whether sea-level rise had submerged part of the ancient site, as it had at Wild Cane Cay. Compared to that island, relatively little of the ancient community was offshore at Frenchman's Cay. As the recovery of artifacts from excavations in the mangroves off the western shore indicated, the site had once extended into the shallow waters where we moored our dories. On the windward shore, coral rock from mound 3 was in the sea, which suggested two possibilities: Either the sea had partially submerged the mound or else rock had been eroded or thrown into the sea. Excavations by one of my graduate students would answer this question in 1997, but in 1994, we merely recorded the observation of the submerged nature of part of the coral mound.

The transect leading into the interior of the island began from the relatively dry ground near the transit to progressively wetter ground and by 80 meters was within the mangrove swamp that formed the greater part of the modern island. There were artifacts in the transect excavations to a distance of 100 meters, which indicated that the land had previously been drier in order to support ancient Maya settlement. The submerged archaeological deposits in virtually all of the transect excavations reinforced this interpretation. Our transect excavations reached the water table at various depths. Along the transect that led to the interior swamp, the water table was at the ground surface. Elsewhere, the ground surface was dry, and we reached the water table between 20 and 50 cm depth. Artifacts were recovered to 100 cm below the ground surface, which was the deepest we were able to dig.

We recovered the artifactual remains of household garbage, including pottery sherds, mainly from utilitarian jars and bowls that would have been used in cooking and storage. The houses were evidently built of perishable materials placed directly on the ground surface. Good evidence of their existence was the associated household waste. We also found broken stone tools, principally from chert, but also some obsidian blades. The waterlogged soil had preserved the seeds from edible palm fruits, corroborating the specialized, tree-cropping island diet at Wild Cane Cay. Identification of the plant remains showed that cohune and coyol palm fruits formed part of the diet.[2] I also identified cohune, coyol, and poknoboy palm fruit remains from household refuse at the ancient island communities at Tiger Mound and Pelican sites.

We plotted the presence and distribution of artifacts in each level of our transect excavations to estimate the distribution of ancient settlement remains. At three acres, the Maya community on Frenchman's Cay was the same size as the modern extent of dry land on Wild Cane Cay, while the ancient community on Wild Cane Cay was much larger. Offshore excavations had revealed it encompassed ten acres.

By excavating in 20 cm levels, we were able to estimate changes over time as well as to correlate these changes with the presence and relative abundance of various artifacts. In addition, years later I correlated the changing species of shells both spatially and by depth in the transect excavations to investigate environmental changes related to the sea-level rise that had impacted Frenchman's Cay as well as the other Port Honduras communities. Using GIS computer technology to spatially display the quantitative data on the habitats of shells we had recovered and identified, I worked with my doctoral student Terry Winemiller and showed that the island was initially much drier and that only later did shells that had adapted to mangrove environments encroach on the community.[3]

In the evenings after supper, we gathered by the water's edge to catch any available breeze and to discuss the day's fieldwork, which often evolved into broader discussions of the ancient Maya. Although I was always prepared to talk about the collapse of the Classic Maya civilization or Maya sea trade, questions about the size of ancient Maya communities, particularly their population size, were more difficult, but just as popular among my volunteers and students. How many people had lived on Frenchman's Cay or Wild Cane Cay in ancient times? I usually deflected such questions back to the student or volunteer who asked them, but they asked me because they wanted my expert opinion. It is a sad commentary on archaeology that population estimates are difficult to make.

Maya archaeologists typically count the number of *house mounds* — low mounds that are believed to have been residential in nature — and multiply the number by 5.6, the average number of people in a modern Maya household.[4] Adjustments are made for the likelihood that not all house mounds were contemporary, that some served other functions, and that some houses may not be represented by mounded remains. That the Maya built houses that today lack mounded remains is clearly the case at many locations in Port Honduras, where there were artifacts but no mounds. The ancient community on Pelican Cay, buried under mangrove peat and submerged below the water table, had abundant household garbage represented by broken artifacts and plant food remains, but no mounds.

The mound-count method of population estimating would indicate a zero population for Pelican Cay. The ancient community on Tiger Mound, with a single, low earthen mound, was much larger than a single household of 5.6 people, as indicated by abundant artifacts we recovered from excavations along four transects. The ancient population at Frenchman's Cay must have been more than the 17 people calculated by multiplying the three mounds by 5.6 people. The density of artifacts in our transect excavations in areas where there were no mounds was good evidence for settlement. Similarly, there were more people at Wild Cane Cay than the 34 people indicated by the six mounds. The high density of artifacts on the ground surface and extending to a depth of 2.5 meters below ground over the modern 3.5-acre extent of Wild Cane Cay and into the offshore area, totaling about 10 acres, reinforces my belief that the island was home to more people. Exactly how many Maya lived on Frenchman's Cay or Wild Cane Cay was unclear to me.

It came as no surprise to my students or volunteers when I told them I had used obsidian to provide an alternative way to estimate the ancient population on Wild Cane Cay.[5] In central Mexico, where obsidian was plentiful because of the nearby Pachuca outcrop, it was available to every household. Using reports for that area that the average household used 21 obsidian artifacts for a year (after which they broke and had to be replaced), I estimated that the average Postclassic Maya household at Wild Cane Cay used 10.5 obsidian artifacts a year and 10.5 of the locally available chert artifacts. The ratio of obsidian to chert artifacts was equal on the cay, whereas chert was not available in central Mexico. I used the densities of obsidian in our midden excavations to estimate the total amount of obsidian at the site. Since we had not reached the base of the Classic period deposits in our waterlogged excavations, I restricted my population estimates to the Postclassic. For each excavation I estimated the number of blades, based on the proximal part of a blade, which is the part struck from the core. With an estimated 2,710,700 blades brought to the island or made there during the three hundred years of the Postclassic period (from about A.D. 900 to 1500), this would mean 9,036 blades a year. Using the figure of 5.6 people per household, there were 861 households on Wild Cane Cay at any given time during the Postclassic. This figure seems high considering the relatively small size of the island.

It seems more likely to me that obsidian was used on Wild Cane Cay to produce other goods and that the island's population was significantly greater than the 34 people that the mound count indicates, but lower than the 861 households (or 4,821.6 people) that my obsidian calculations indicate. Based on the high density and depth of artifacts and the variety and quantity of trade goods — from distant and closer sources — Wild Cane Cay was a permanently settled village. The presence of stone architecture at the site using coral rock dredged from the sea or carried from storm beaches and limestone and sandstone available on the adjacent mainland mean the community was an important village in the Port Honduras region. Although the nature of the community is clear, its population count remains enigmatic. I believe that several hundred people lived on Wild Cane Cay and upward of one hundred on Frenchman's Cay.

CHAPTER 16
TARGET PRACTICE

The announcements on the radio not to travel in the coastal waters north of Punta Gorda for the next couple of weeks because of target practice by the British army presented a problem for survey and for getting food and other supplies from town. That the area was virtually unpopulated evidently made it a suitable location for bombing. The few occupants of the coastal area naturally had a different opinion. The sounds and sight of ammunition from the offshore ship falling short of their land targets were unsettling. If people didn't listen carefully for the radio announcements of target practice, they were taken by surprise at sea. This is what happened early one morning on our way to town from Frenchman's Cay in the summer of 1994.

The sea was calm. The early morning fog lifted off the sea with the increasing warmth of the sun. Melissa and I savored the opportunity to sit back and motor to town with little effort. The boom of an explosion shattered the morning calm. The sound arched in the sky overhead and fell with a flash into the waters toward shore, sending out ripples where it landed. Instantly alert, I looked behind, beyond Moho Cay, where a battleship emerged from the mist. We were between the ship and their target, the Seven Hills Estate, north of the Rio Grande. The land was privately owned but was leased to the British army. The area represented a nagging gap in my survey coverage of the Port Honduras area. I was hesitant to explore there in case the stories of unexploded ammunition were true. Moreover, I had no interest in being a real target in a simulated war. Brief sojourns to the area — with the landowners' permission — had substantiated my fears. The ancient activity represented by a scatter of pottery sherds along a deserted stretch of beach was more enigmatic than the abandoned army vehicle pocked with holes. We called this site "Target Practice." When we heard gunfire while following a winding creek behind Pork and Doughboy Point, I decided to survey elsewhere. I heard stories that undetonated ordnance lay scattered around. Regardless of whether the stories were true, the area was protected from occasional visitors like our archaeological team.

However, I considered that the sea was my territory and I had a right to be there. Therefore, when I saw the British ship, I asked Jodi, who was in the bow of the dory, to send a flare to let the British navy know of our presence. She reached under the bow and opened the fluorescent orange box that we carried everywhere but normally used only on Christmas, New Year's, or the fourth of July. This practice kept the flares tested and made me replace them periodically. One Christmas one of the volunteers had decided to stop taking his insulin — for the first time in his life. It may have been the rum and coconut water we had been drinking to celebrate the holiday. Whatever the cause, when Joe wandered back to his tent early, I noticed that he still had the flare in his pocket. I asked one of my field assistants to go to his tent and check. The assistant said he wasn't going to stick his hand in a man's pocket.

I turned to a volunteer, Gerald Cole, a retired U.S. Navy Seal commander. I figured he would help me out if I asked correctly. Gerald — we called him Gerry — was always looking for challenges. What he really wanted was a machete and a swath of mangroves to be cut down. He told us stories of his days with the Seals — stories of dropping his group by helicopter in the darkness in the sea with instructions that he'd pick them up at 0700 in six days at a specified location, following completion of their mission. His wife, on the other hand, liked Holiday Inn vacations, sitting around the pool sipping martinis, and although Gerry said that was a perfectly fine way of spending a vacation, he also needed something more. My project was that something. With this knowledge, I turned to him and said I had something dangerous that needed to be done. He looked at me with complete attention. I began to tell him about the flare, but Gerry was gone before I could complete the sentence, returning in a very short time, having rushed to Joe's tent, opened the zipper, rustled around for a second, and returned holding the flare up for us to see. I decided to watch the testing of flares more carefully.

I was glad that we periodically tested the flares, as at times like these, in the middle of an apparent attack by the British navy, Jodi had successfully set off a bright orange flare into the sky above us. It worked. Almost immediately, a

British army helicopter was hovering above us. I turned on the two-meter radio to see whether we could open a line of communication with the helicopter pilot who was, in fact, on his radio, but I found that the British army, unlike everyone else in the south, did not monitor the Texaco PG channel.[1]

Tanya was on the radio talking about the target practice with Max at the Texaco station in Punta Gorda. From their conversation I learned that the helicopter had been flying over and around Village Farm for the last hour. They were missing their target at Seven Hills property quite regularly. I guessed that's why they needed to practice. When I joined the conversation, Max told me that the army base outside of Punta Gorda didn't seem to know what was going on at sea.

Out of danger, we were still being observed by the hovering helicopter. It was clear to me and to the other boatload of "American women" that the pilot was having a good look at us. We had all put on T-shirts and shorts over our bathing suits before the helicopter arrived — everyone except Jean, who was in the bow of Melissa's dory. When she finally turned around to see the rest of us, she put on her shirt, too. The radio conversation continued for a while, and the helicopter finally left.

In February, 1995, the British army closed their base near Punta Gorda as part of the departure of the British troops from Belize. The British had patrolled the border with Guatemala and maintained a force of Harrier jets, Gurkhas, and SAS troops in response to the fear that the Guatemalans would invade Belize. Belize was still shown on the maps of Guatemala as a province of that country, and Guatemala never recognized Belize's independence. That the Maya Indians might also have a prior claim to both Guatemala and Belize has not been discussed. When the Spaniards arrived in the sixteenth century, they claimed what is now Mexico, Guatemala, Honduras, and beyond. When Pope Paul III declared that the native Americans were human and therefore to be converted to Catholicism, he also drew a line through the Americas, giving Brazil to Portugal.

The boundary trouble for Belize began when the Spaniards allowed the British to enter Belize for logging, but not to settle or to practice agriculture. In a glorious defense of the British colonial capital on St. George's Cay, off present-day Belize City, the British settlers drove off a Spanish ship attack in 1798.[2] This battle has symbolized the independence of the British colony. However, when Spain granted independence to Mexico and Guatemala in the nineteenth century, the Guatemalans included the present territory of Belize in their new country. Efforts to resolve the dispute have been various and unsuccessful. It seems that the Guatemalans want greater access to the Caribbean than they have with the narrow coastal strip between Belize and Honduras.

Old Inez Cabral was not timid in her expression of distaste for the Guatemalans who were on the Sapodilla Cays, at the southern end of the Belize barrier reef, some 25 miles off shore from Punta Gorda. That was in 1982, during the Falklands crisis. We listened daily to the international news on Frank's old radio. The fear in Punta Gorda was that if the British lost the Falkland's dispute, the "Guats" would invade Belize.

Miss Inez told me she was born and raised on Lime Cay, a tiny, sand-covered island on the Belizean barrier reef. The island was one of a cluster of the Sapodilla Cays where the Cabrals lived. Frank and Adel's grandparents moved from the reef to Wild Cane Cay in search of new land for an expanding lineage. I had never been to the reef since I felt it was too far off shore to go in our dories. The local fishermen went in much smaller dories, including Orlando, who ventured off to Hunting Cay in a twenty-foot dory without a motor. Someday I'll go there and hopefully will not encounter "Sapodilla Tom," the shark that allegedly can crack a dory in half with a single bite.

Miss Inez told me that her husband wanted to live in Punta Gorda instead of on Lime Cay, so they dismantled their two-story frame house and moved it into town, where it stood on Front Street across from the police station. The Guatemalans used the Sapodilla Cays for recreation. The Honduran government also claimed the sandy cays as part of their territory. Miss Inez was audibly upset by the presence of the Guatemalans on the Sapodilla Cays, often cursing them as "those damn Guats." As Frank was uninterested in my lengthy conversations with Miss Inez and since he was my boat captain, I left her house when he did. The British won the Falklands war, so everyone in Belize was relieved, except old Inez Cabral who continued to blast the "Guats'" presence there.

In a concession to the Guatemalans to win their acceptance of Belize's independence, the Belizean government entertained the idea of reducing Belize's offshore coastal zone in the south. Although relatively few Belizeans visit the south, this compromise was met with distaste by the people there. With public knowledge of the possible agreement in both Belize and Guatemala, people in Punta Gorda woke up one day to Guatemalan military boats within view of town. I too preferred to carry out archaeological research in Belize and was relieved that my survey zone, including Wild Cane Cay, remained Belizean territory.

With the change from colony to independent country in 1981 and the departure of the British army in 1995, there have been significant financial losses to Belize.[3] As a colony, the country was depleted of timber resources for the logwood dye industry and subsequently for the mahogany and rosewood furniture industry of Victorian England and America. The extractive economy was continued into this century with large, often foreign-owned, land holdings planted in citrus, bananas, sugarcane, and mangos.[4] Belize gained its independence virtually without an industrial base. There was excitement with the opening of the Toucan match factory outside of Belmopan and local T-shirt makers. Belize has not regained its strength from its colonial heritage.

The days when a British Harrier jet flying at tree level over Wild Cane Cay or bombing us on the southern highway have become a fond memory. In the south, the British military provided an important boost to the Punta Gorda economy, protection along the border with Guatemala, and some comic relief with their scary, yet apparently harmless, target practices in the coastal waters north of Punta Gorda. I heard that the West Indian Fleet occasionally sends a ship to southern Belize for target practice, so I decided to keep the flares ready when we were at sea.

CHAPTER 17

ROUGH SEAS, SUBMERGED SITES

ince there were no insurance agencies in Punta Gorda, I inquired in Belize City about getting insurance for the dories. This request seemed quite reasonable to me. However, it was met with a polite smile by the insurance agent, who told me that they didn't insure dories in Belize. If I had a skiff, I could apply for boat insurance. I thanked him and departed. Later I explained to my granting agency that although dories were not insured in Belize, we were very careful on the sea.

I had three main strategies for survival. First, we had an extensive inventory of safety equipment that we loaded into the dories before each trip. I wrote the inventory of standard equipment on the inside of the *Adel 2* near the stern, so that I could call out a checklist before departing. The inventory included two tents, extra food and pots, extra water, regular food and water, boat first-aid kit, snakebite kit, boat-repair kit, anchors and ropes for both stern and bow, boat flashlight, radio, two paddles, tank of gas, spare full gas can, empty gas cans if going to town, empty water bags if going to Village Farm, and everyone's life jacket and personal items in their packs. Personal items included sunscreen, sun hat, raincoat, insect repellent, long pants and long-sleeved shirt, and flashlight. This equipment was in addition to the shovels, excavation screens, cameras, video camera, transit, tripod, stadia rod, bags, and other equipment and supplies needed to do archaeology, which was, once we got beyond dealing with the sea, the main purpose of the entire project.

Having radio contact from the boat was my second safety measure, but it was not until 1994, when I invested in two-meter radios (radio for transmitting on a ham radio frequency) that it was reliable and there was anyone to contact. I had tried a variety of CB and marine CB radios variously in use by local people, but they rarely worked. It was a surprise to me that one of the volunteers thought we were in constant radio communication with the British army from Wild Cane Cay. It was no consolation to him when I said our radio hardly worked, so I had stopped using it. When I learned that the Texaco station in Punta Gorda had a two-meter radio and the Spang family and others had begun using it to communicate with the station, I purchased a radio for our field camp and another for the boat. In 1994, I was connected to the outside world for the first time.

My best safety precaution was to travel with both the *Adel 2* and the *Seirrita*. Taking two dories on every boat trip was expensive and required more trips to Punta Gorda for gas. However, we had nobody to rely on for assistance if we ran into trouble at sea. The coast guard and police boats were rarely serviceable enough to venture out to sea for emergency assistance. There were few other boats in the coastal waters of Port Honduras except at night, and with these I had no contact.

Some years before, driving into town from Wild Cane Cay with Orlando at the helm, I noticed what appeared to be a drifting dory. I called Wild Cane Cay on the CB radio to convey this information and to asked them to stay on the radio as we approached the other boat. The occupants were raising their paddles, but I wasn't sure whether it was because they were in distress or because they were a danger to us. Fortunately we were only several hundred meters from the cay so that radio communication was possible.

The sea was calm, and the hot sun pierced our eyes and glistened against the sea. As we approached the dory and slowed down, the air shimmered with the sun's glare. The occupants were people I knew from Punta Negra, including the school principal, the teacher, and others. I called on the radio and let the island know that we were safe and would help the drifting dory, which had engine trouble. Since there was no one else out at sea, even on this market day, it was lucky that we had left so late for town and had noticed them. They had few survival aids beyond a couple of paddles. They were taking the teacher into town for a doctor's appointment since she was eight months pregnant. Orlando removed the cover from their engine and discussed the spilling gas with the boat driver. When he pulled the throttle, the engine ignited, so he threw water on the fire to extinguish it. The engine surely wouldn't start after water had been poured on it, but it had been necessary to put out the fire. We drifted and decided to tow their much-larger dory into town. The expedition took much longer than our usual two-hour trip, but it seemed like the only solution. In precarious situations at sea, people helped each other.

Sometimes, however, nobody noticed. I had launched a new dory and set off to sea late one afternoon at the beginning of the 1990 field season, having waited for three volunteers who had arrived late. In the open water along the coast to Punta Gorda Point (north of town), the first part of the trip was rough, so I stayed near the shore. When we rounded the point and passed the mouth of the Rio Grande to enter the protected waters of the Mangrove Cays, the daylight and my sense of direction began to fade. Everyone in the dory relied on me, so I picked a course, checking my memory for the route to Wild Cane Cay. Not having driven a dory myself at that point, I now had a view from my seat at the stern that was different from when I had been a passenger. Despite my boating and water skills, I knew that driving a dory in the open sea was different from paddling a canoe or sailing a boat.

I told the volunteers to put on their life jackets, hiding my fear as the propane tank rolled gently with the waves against the dory. I couldn't let my fear or anxiety about being lost — which I technically was since I didn't recognize anything — be known to the crew. It was dark.

We passed an open stretch of sea that I remembered past the Mangrove Cays and should have come across Wild Cane Cay. However, we did not. I remembered that the cay was difficult to find at night. In 1982, the Maya workers had taken the boat fishing up the adjacent Deep River one evening after supper. Lying in my tent, I could hear the engine approaching and getting louder, but then it faded into the distance. When the engine noise became clearer again and then dissipated once more into the silence of the night, I realized they were lost. When the engine noise stopped altogether, it was apparent they had run out of gas. The rising moon had finally guided them back to the cay by paddling. I now hoped for moonlight, too.

Instead, the engine hit a rock and bounced right off the stern. Before the engine could sink into the sea, I was in the water and holding on to the head, which had cut out. I placed the Mariner 15 hp — all 75 lbs were much lighter in the water — back on the stern and clamped it down. I prayed for it to start, but it didn't. We drifted in the darkness alongside a mangrove cay. I guided the dory to a sandy shore. I had no idea where we were.

We nestled under the tarps and emergency reflective "space blankets" from the first-aid kit, ate survival food, and called on the radio until the battery discharged. Although I saw a boat in the distance, with a light shimmering against the dark water, nobody came nearby.

At dawn we walked around the island and managed to flag down a passing skiff. The man and woman who stopped said that they did not stop the first time they saw us because they thought we were just drying laundry. In fact, we were trying to get his attention by waving the foil blankets and fluorescent life jackets. I found the laundry interpretation difficult to believe since, although I wasn't sure where we were, I knew the area was uninhabited. I found out later that Steve was just visiting Punta Gorda to see his friend Anna, so he was unfamiliar with the coastal area. They towed us to Wild Cane Cay, which was just on the other side of a mangrove cay. I know exactly where we were then, having spent more time at the helm of the *Adel 2* in calm seas, rough water, heavy rains, tropical storms, during "small craft advisories," during the day and at night, under moonlight, and shrouded in darkness. Seeing that cay humbles me even today.

By 1994, I had more experience with the sea and respect for both my abilities and limitations. I also took safety equipment and a portable two-meter radio and often traveled with two dories, a practice I called "taking our insurance policy with us." I've used my boat insurance on several occasions, including the night we spent on Pork and Doughboy Point. When a house in Punta Gorda became available, I moved the project to town for the last Earthwatch team of the 1994 field season for an easier living situation. We left Punta Gorda early in the morning to pick up Lyra and Nathaniel at Village Farm en route to Punta Ycacos Lagoon. We spent the day excavating at two salt-making sites in the lagoon. Excavations at the David Westby site, named after a local fisherman who originally discovered it, would form the basis of Melissa's master's thesis. I would work on material from the other site, Orlando's Jewfish, a site discovered while Orlando and I were taking a break from survey to fish and discovered artifacts on the seafloor. After a pleasant, although exhausting, day of underwater excavations, we relaxed in the *Adel 2* on our way back to Village Farm to return Lyra and Nathaniel. Tanya invited us to stay overnight there, but I hesitated to impose on them again, even though I enjoyed their company and wanted to stay. What made up my mind was that one of the volunteers, Mike, was not feeling well. In fact, he had been vomiting over the side of the dory. I felt we should take him back to town. As we soon learned, he would have had a more comfortable night at Village Farm.

I had time to think about the day's excavations in Punta Ycacos Lagoon while driving the dory. The roar of the engine precluded any extended conversations. In addition, I kept a close watch on the sea and the sky. After we were some distance from the Village Farm dock on our way back to Frenchman's Cay, the breeze started to pick up. My crew turned to face me with their backs into the wind, so they did not see the approaching storm clouds. There was nothing unusual about our appearances. Like the others, I had taken off my boots and clothes, except for my bathing suit. I wore my raincoat to protect myself against the sea spray and the wind. I had my raincoat on backward to fend off the wind, with my life jacket on for warmth, and the brim of my hat pulled forward over my eyes to deflect the salt spray. Our clothes were kept dry in plastic bags inside our backpacks. My passengers were chatting.

It was not the wind, which was getting stronger, that worried me: A bank of dark clouds was approaching us that raised my anxiety level. I told everyone to put on their life jackets. They immediately followed instructions. Putting on life jackets was a normal response to any choppy conditions in our daily lives at sea. However, my passengers did not notice the rougher seas or see the menacing clouds that were nearing us. The sky and sea had been clear when we had set off from Village Farm. We were approaching Pork and Doughboy Point, the first point after Village Farm. One of my students, Jodi Brandehoff, would base her master's thesis on work we had recently done at the site.[1] I looked down and spoke to Melissa, who was sitting nearby and, like the others, did not see the impending storm. Did she think we should stop at Pork and Doughboy?

Melissa turned around from the relative calm of the setting sun and faced the front of the dory and the ominous clouds. In the few seconds that took her to respond in the affirmative, I had already decided to land because the tempest was now almost upon us. In a loud, stern voice, I told the others to put on their boots and prepare to land.

Suddenly we were mere meters from land, the sky was dark, and the sea was increasingly rough. The waves hit the side of the dory broadside and splashed into the boat as we approached the clearing in the mangroves that was normally protected. The bow scraped against the mangroves. Melissa leaped out of the boat into the sea with the bow line. She scrambled to tie the dory to some mangrove roots. The waves again crashed against the side of the dory and pushed us into the mangroves. We had landed, but we were not safe. I threw the stern anchor seaward, which helped to keep the boat away from the trees, but the waves continued to splash into it. I cut the engine and tilted the propeller out of the water. I grabbed a bucket and bailed. Melissa bailed. The volunteers bailed. It seemed like the sea was determined to overpower the dory, but we were not going to give up easily.

The strong winds and rough sea finally subsided enough for us to stop bailing. We had been standing in the water and were soaking wet. We sat on the bank and watched the lightning and thunder dance across the sky. Our radio batteries were getting low, and I could not reach our base camp. I called Village Farm and asked Nathaniel to call the cay to let them know that we were safe and that we were waiting for the storm to subside before leaving. Neither Melissa nor I were interested in prolonging our stay at Pork and Doughboy Point any longer than was necessary. However, we were all tired. The lightning and thunder had persisted for several hours and showed no signs of stopping.

Nathaniel stayed by the radio at Village Farm, periodically updating us on his conversations with Frenchman's Cay. We could hear them, but our batteries were too weak to transmit to the cay.

We ate special "survival food," which was just more special "survey food," including spicy chicken Vienna sausage, cheese whiz, and a variety of Mexican cookies, which were among the unusual foods I had found in Punta Gorda. I had given in to the volunteers' request to put up a tent, and they retired around 9 P.M. The radio signal was breaking up, so I told Nathaniel we had set up a tent and might spend the night. Melissa and I were still hoping to return to Frenchman's Cay. We stayed up chatting with a young volunteer who was interested in adventure. We watched the sky, hoping that the storm would pass.

I told them about our excavations at the site — or rather offshore. Although I had visited the site many times while traveling along the coastline to and from Wild Cane Cay, either to take a rest from the seas or to look for temporally distinctive stone tools or pottery sherds brought to the surface by the pounding waves that hit the point of land, it was not until 1994 that we mapped and excavated the site for the first time. Artifacts from the surface indicate a Late Classic period use of the site, making it contemporaneous with Wild Cane Cay, Frenchman's Cay, the Punta Ycacos salt workshops, and many other smaller communities in the Port Honduras region. The site's location provides seafarers today, as in the past, a place to take refuge from storms or to spend the night. Pork and Doughboy Point forms the southern boundary of the Port Honduras bight, with Seven Hills Creek to the north and the Rio Grande to the south.

For her thesis, Jodi supervised an underwater excavation off the point at Pork and Doughboy to find out whether the artifacts in the offshore area were in situ — as their presence below the seafloor would indicate — or whether they had just been washed away from the land by waves instead. Several years later, in 2003, I returned with a graduate student, Kevin Pemberton, to excavate on the land and map that part of the site. Jodi set out a one-by-one-meter test unit in an area with a concentration of pottery sherds on the seafloor and began excavating using shovels and screens, with the help of volunteers. In contrast to the calm waters of Punta Ycacos Lagoon, Jodi and her crew had to contend with the force of the Caribbean. They excavated two layers, each measuring 10 cm, and recovered abundant artifactual remains.

Once the offshore excavations were under way, I set up the transit on the dry land to make a map of the site. I was assisted by two Earthwatch volunteers, who took the stadia rod and 100 meter tape. We measured Jodi's excavation at 22 meters offshore. Since most of the site is submerged and now off shore, the volunteers got wet. We mapped in rays: Every 2 meters from the stadia rod I took a depth reading and called to the volunteers to examine the seafloor for artifacts. The system began to break down when they didn't seem to be able to hear me. They were more than 100 meters off shore, proceeding an additional 2 meters with each reading I took through the transit (figure 17.1). I called out for them to go another 2 meters and was surprised when they said they couldn't. Then I looked at them through the transit and saw they were floating. The water was above their heads. I called them back to shore. We had mapped far enough and certainly beyond the shallow area off three sides of the point where the artifacts — and ancient site — were concentrated.

We recovered quantities of pottery sherds, charcoal, other botanical remains, and stone artifacts from each of the two 10 cm layers that we eventually excavated. Later in the lab we concluded that the pottery styles indicated the deposits were Late Classic. An experiment in a wave tank at the university suggested that the deposits were in situ rather than having been washed from the land. Jodi and I placed charcoal in sand in the bottom of the wave tank. When the machine was turned on, the charcoal floated away. This experiment suggested that, had the artifacts eroded from the land, the charcoal would

17.1 *Using a stadia rod and 100 meter steel tape to map the depths and the distribution of artifacts offshore. Photo is taken from the transit on land.*

have floated away instead of staying in the deposits as it did in our offshore excavations. Certainly the presence and depth of the offshore archaeological deposits at Pork and Doughboy Point were similar to the situation at Wild Cane Cay and the underwater sites.

As I continued my story, I glanced at the sky, which was still full of lightning, and realized that we would have to spend the night there. After endless gazing out to sea and attempts by my volunteers to tell life stories, I decided to take out my contacts and stay overnight. It was 11:30 P.M. The radio was dead. We were tired. We put up the remaining tent. It was cold and uncomfortable, but at least the sandflies were outside. It didn't seem that I slept until I woke up to the stillness of early morning light. In the silence I could hear the insects outside and hoped that we could break camp quickly. I woke Melissa and called out to the volunteers. They were already awake and chatting. We were loaded into the dory surprisingly quickly and ready to leave. The sandflies expedited our departure.

I put my foot on the stern seat, attached the gas line, pumped, turned the throttle, and pulled out the choke. Then I readied myself and pulled the cord, which came off in my hand, accompanied by a rattle of loose parts inside the engine.

It was 5 A.M. The volunteers were looking at me, realizing that the starter cord in my hand meant that we were going nowhere. With a sinking feeling, I looked up over the broken engine toward Village Farm. The sea was flat. We could paddle to Village Farm, and I could ask John for help. John had repaired my engines so often that the last time he made me repair the 20 hp motor on the *Adel 2*. We had backed the dory up to the cement wharf at Village Farm. We had hauled the motor out of the water, up to the boathouse, and onto a sawhorse. John told me he was tired of engine repairs, that everything was always breaking down. He told me I'd have to fix the engine, starting with taking it apart and cleaning everything. I knew nothing about engine repair. I knew how to take off the engine hood, which I proceeded to do. Then John told me to take off the carburetor and clean both it and the tank. I didn't know which part was the carburetor. He showed me and told me to hurry up.

I had come on a very bad day, but I was still grateful. After hours of cleaning engine parts in gasoline, fumbling with nuts and bolts, and receiving coffee from Tanya, we finished the job by flashlight. Although some of the mystery faded when the engine started in the barrel of water, it was John's cursing that made me realize how precarious a life we all led. When I acknowledged to him that I should be able to fix the engine, he told me I couldn't do everything.

I was caught off guard. That wasn't the response I had expected from John — a man who had taken his family to live in the jungle, where they had to be self-sufficient in a host of day-to-day activities. He said he was tired of being a jack-of-all-trades and spending his life repairing. Everything eventually broke. We agreed, but I realized it wasn't my entire life. I reminded John that it was just on bad days that he seemed to spend all his time repairing things. However, we both knew that this was life in Belize.

I shifted my gaze away from Village Farm and memories of engine repairs and back to the dory and the immediate problem. I, too, was tired of things breaking down, especially the engines, and tired of having to ask for help and taking up John's time. I had just enough pride in my ability to captain the dory that I decided to attempt to repair the engine. I asked for the tool kit. They passed down the plastic container with the boat manuals, which I knew would be of no use since I really knew very little about engines. I asked for the other tool kit. It was delivered to me with haste.

Everyone sat quietly as I pried off the engine hood and looked inside. I looked around for anything conspicuously out of place or dangling. Apart from the starter cord, the distributor cap was loose, so I removed it. A bolt had come off the main part of the engine and was trapped in a gutter in the engine housing. I removed the bolt and put it in my pocket. I looked around the engine, tightened bolts, and checked parts. Then I wrapped the starter cord in position. I looked up for a moment toward Village Farm and sighed. When I pulled the cord, the engine started. I let it idle for a while and then replaced the engine hood.

With greater relief than I could remember ever having felt, I reversed the engine and drove the dory away from Pork and Doughboy Point. I switched the engine into forward gear and headed for Punta Gorda. Only later did my volunteers tell me they were impressed with my engine-repair skills, especially when the bolt in my pocket was never replaced in the engine. We had a relaxing trip since the sea was calm and the sky was clear.

I called Village Farm from the Texaco PG to let them know we were safe and to thank Nathaniel for staying up to monitor the radio. We talked about the pros and cons of various batteries for my radios and getting another car battery from Texaco. We had a successful day's excavation, with a boatload of sacks of broken artifacts from the salt-making sites. It was a surprise to me that the volunteers who had stayed in town were jealous that they had missed the adventure. I was just relieved to be home and to have negotiated the sea.

CHAPTER 18
CORAL ARCHITECTURE

n January, 1997, I returned to live on Frenchman's Cay for six months during my sabbatical, taking a team of field assistants for large-scale excavations of the coral architecture. I was excited to be working in the dry season and to have a long time to horizontally expose the island's stone architecture, the associated burials, and figure out the relationship of the island's elite, who used the stone buildings with the elite Maya traders on Wild Cane Cay. Why were there two trading ports so near to one another?

We arrived in the driving rain, wielded machetes to clear an opening in the dense undergrowth that had reclaimed the island since our departure, and found ourselves ankle deep in water. Evidently the dry season had not yet arrived. Because we planned an extended stay on the island, we had brought more equipment and supplies than usual, so I had hired Julio Requena to haul our tables, benches, three-hundred-pound army surplus tent, and other heavy and unwieldy supplies in his skiff. The dories were loaded with my staff, our gear, and food. Since the site looked more like a refugee camp than an idyllic Caribbean island, I wondered whether my Vietnamese field assistant was remembering her childhood escape from Vietnam by boat with her family. After unloading, we set up our tents in standing water, with heavy sheets of plastic carefully placed over the tent floors and up the sides like a dish to keep the water out. Huddled under a tarp strung between trees, eating sausages and crackers, with swarms of sandflies and mosquitoes descending with the setting sun, my focus was on the basics of food and shelter. The idea of excavating the nearby coral mounds seemed remote.

We didn't have much time to acclimate to our new home since I had to pick up our first team of Earthwatch volunteers from Punta Gorda the next day. As I left the next morning in the *Adel 2* with one of my field assistants, I hoped the others would be able to establish at least a semblance of our archaeological field station. Tents needed to be put up for each of the volunteers, and the assistants also needed to set up the water tank, radio tower, propane stove, and unload the food and other equipment. Most difficult would be the task of assembling the kitchen and lab tent we'd hauled on the plane, bus, and Requena's skiff before Mai and I returned with the volunteers. The tent, which was 18 by 36 feet with a 10 foot ceiling, would provide the only public space under which to shelter, cook, read, and store our equipment, food, supplies, and artifacts. On my return with the volunteers later that day, we were greeted by a group of enthusiastic young women in rubber boots carrying machetes. They waded into the water to catch the dory. My field staff had managed not only to set up the big tent but also to carve a field station out of the underbrush. We were ready to begin the excavations.

My objective was for the field staff and volunteers to survive and enjoy their experience as they helped excavate. The difficult living conditions could easily drive volunteers away, but they could also bring the group together, working as a team in adversity. Unlike the popular television shows of the early-twenty-first century, notably "Survivor," where a participant was periodically voted off the tropical island, my goal was for everyone to survive. The field staff worked hard to make this happen.

Excavations in the three mounds at Frenchman's Cay were designed to piece together the role of the ancient community in sea trade, especially its relationship to the major trading port on Wild Cane Cay.[1] Was the same coral construction style used at the two island sites? Were they contemporaneous? In 1994, we excavated a 3 by 1 meter trench in two of the three mounds at Frenchman's Cay, exposing finger coral and coral rock, as at Wild Cane Cay. We returned in 1997 to aerially expose the earthen floors and stone foundations of ancient buildings, look for associated burials with grave goods — especially pottery vessels — to help date the structures, and figure out the relationship between the two island sites. Two of my graduate students would supervise excavations in two of the mounds, while I would supervise the other mound excavations. Rachel would excavate mound 1, which we called Spondylus Mound, in order to investigate the coral rock construction in relation to other Maya communities. Aline's excavations were in the partially submerged mound 3, which we called Crown Conch. Her focus would be on the relationship between the construction of the mound and sea-level rise. She would carefully excavate to find out whether the coral rocks we saw in the sea were thrown or washed off shore or whether they represented intact construction that had been submerged in the sea. Assisted by Mai, another graduate student, Shannon, and Nathaniel, my excavations in the largest mound, Great White Lucine, would include trenching across the mound and opening up a larger horizontal area to look for evidence of construction and use of the building and hopefully to uncover burials that would inform us of the ancient people who used the structures and the age of the buildings by the age of the grave goods.

We placed a 16 m trench across the width of each of the three mounds to discover the construction techniques and to locate any structures contained within the mounded coral rubble. By excavating a larger area in Great White Lucine, I hoped to also be able to estimate the size and shape of the buildings.

The trench in Spondylus Mound revealed that there were two construction episodes and that the first coral rock foundation was placed on an earlier midden. Examination of the profiles of the excavation walls showed where large pits had been dug into the mound and filled with loose coral rock in the past. Intact areas of the mound uncovered in the trench showed a basal layer of large coral boulders with a thin layer of loose finger coral on top. Traces of red clay on the finger coral may have been the remains of a structure floor as in Fighting Conch mound at Wild Cane Cay. A load of large coral rocks was placed on top of this first foundation. This was the first layer we encountered. Any subfloor or clay floor had eroded in the past.

Aline's trench in Crown Conch cut across the mound from the main plaza to the sea (figure 18.1). The base of the coral construction was 80 cm below the water table, indicating a change in sea level since the initial construction (figure 18.2). The construction was a coral platform made of staghorn coral, brain coral, and star coral rocks (figure 18.3). Shells from the coral from Crown Conch suggest that coral rock was gathered from storm beaches since the shells are from multiple habitats that would have become commingled in such a location. Finger coral was placed on top of the coral rock layer to serve as a subfloor for a dirt floor. Coral rocks placed above the floor are the remains of a subsequent building, which again was the first layer we encountered. In addition to the basic coral foundations in Crown Conch, a pit had been dug into the upper coral foundation. The pit contained a fragmentary bowl with

18.1 *One-meter-wide trench from main plaza to the sea across Crown Conch mound.*

18.2 *Inundated trench in Crown Conch mound.*

18.3 *Using trowels to expose coral rock foundation in trench 1 of Crown Conch mound.*

markedly incurved sides. A midden with conch and other shells was uncovered above the coral rock construction. On our last day of excavations, I suggested to Aline that she excavate the 1 × 1 m unit adjacent to the sea to provide a more complete profile of the mound from the land into the sea. In doing so, she exposed the fragmentary and waterlogged remains of two people, the only burials during the entire field season. Below the coral rock construction is a layer of sandy clay, with mangrove mud below.

The recovery of Late Classic pottery sherds from the coral rock foundations of Spondylus and Crown Conch mounds indicates they were constructed no earlier than the Late Classic period, between A.D. 600 and 900. Quite a few pottery sherds were recovered from Crown Conch in contrast to the virtual absence of any from Spondylus Mound. Many of the sherds from Crown Conch were decorated, which enabled me to later assign ages by comparing the styles with pottery from stratified midden deposits discovered in the transect excavations (figures 18.4–18.6) In addition, I used cross-dating with pottery of known dates from other sites in the Port Honduras region and beyond.[2]

18.4 *Pottery sherds from coral rock foundation of Crown Conch mound assigned to the Polonio polychrome pottery type, dated to the Late Classic (A.D. 600–900).*

In Great White Lucine, we reopened a 1 × 3 m trench where we had uncovered sandstone slabs on our last day of the 1994 field season (figure 18.7). For the last two and a half years we had patiently waited to learn whether the slabs marked a burial or wall. We expanded the trench 16 meters across the mound and 3 meters in width to find the exterior walls and to fully expose the slabs. We did find the exterior walls, which were really a façade on a coral rock platform. The slabs I had anticipated would mark a burial were instead

18.5 *Pottery sherds from coral rock foundation of Crown Conch mound assigned to the Cattle Landing pottery type, dated to the Late Classic (A.D. 600–900).*

an interior wall. Although this was certainly an anticlimactic ending to our 1994 trench excavations, we expected to find burials during the months ahead, as had been the case in Fighting Conch mound at Wild Cane Cay.

We exposed a layer of coral rocks below the modern ground surface. These would have been the foundation for a platform with a floor above that has not survived the centuries. After each rock was drawn on graph paper (figure 18.8), we removed the rock layer and discovered a floor. This dirt floor rested on a subfloor of finger coral that was supported by a coral rock foundation. The foundation continued a meter below the water table. Below the mound construction, we found a midden — rich in plant and animal

18.6 *Clay figurine whistle fragments from coral rock foundation of Crown Conch mound assigned to the Village Farm mold-made pottery type, dated to the Late Classic (A.D. 600–900).*

18.7 *Great White Lucine mound from the main plaza.*

18.8 *Drawing the coral rocks of a foundation in Great White Lucine using a string grid frame.*

remains — that predates the coral architecture. Below this midden layer was mangrove mud devoid of artifacts.

Perhaps the most exciting discovery in 1997 was a limestone wall on three sides of Great White Lucine (figure 18.9). The wall was first recognized during surface clearing on the western periphery in an area with a scattering of limestone slabs. Three courses of limestone slabs were exposed along a six-meter section of the wall facing the plaza. The slabs formed a smooth façade. Between the slab veneer and the coral rock masonry platform, we discovered loose finger coral. The slabs were set into this bed of finger coral, which served as backing masonry for the coral rock platform. Naturally, the façade was the most appealing aspect of our excavations to visitors, who found it more recognizable than layers of coral rock and dirt floors.

Similar building construction is found at inland Maya cities, where sandstone or limestone was used as foundation material instead of coral rock. At the nearby inland city of Lubaantun, small, cut-sandstone slabs form a building façade over rubble fill — also composed of sandstone.[3] At sites farther north, such as Lamanai, Altun Ha, Caracol, or Tikal, located on limestone bedrock, limestone was used for construction fill and building facades.[4] At Frenchman's Cay, we followed the wall along three sides of Great White

18.9 *Cut limestone façade facing coral rock platform of Great White Lucine.*

18.10 *Using a transit to map Great White Lucine mound.*

Lucine. No traces remained on the seaward side, where either natural erosion or human intervention had removed the wall. The wall was submerged in the swamp that abutted the mound on the eastern side, so it was not apparent except to touch. In order to map the wall along that edge, Nathaniel lay in the swamp water locating the edges of each slab and holding the base of the stadia rod so we could map the rocks (figure 18.10). Photos reveal the water but not the odor or feel of the mangrove swamp. Either subsidence or sea-level rise or both were responsible for the present, submerged location of the wall and the lower foundation of Great White Lucine.

Large-scale excavation of stone architecture was a departure from my survey and excavation of the more common submerged sites in Port Honduras. The coral rock platforms faced with limestone were known only from three island sites in Port Honduras, so these buildings must have been designated for the coastal elite. I wanted to understand the labor investment involved in the construction of the buildings, their age by pottery from associated burials, and the size and age of the coral buildings at the three island sites. While Fighting Conch at Wild Cane Cay was packed with burials, enabling me to assign ages to the six construction episodes, the lack of burials with pots in our excavations at Frenchman's Cay meant I had to rely on pottery from the construction of the buildings. I assumed that the pottery came from nearby household garbage and became incorporated into the foundations as fill. The emerging picture of coral architecture in Port Honduras places Frenchman's Cay as a Late Classic coastal power, with Wild Cane Cay dominating in the Terminal Classic and Early Postclassic, coincident with the rise of Chichen Itza. At that time, Frenchman Cay's power waned, although there was still more modest habitation on the island, just not using coral rock foundations. The age of Green Vine Snake's coral buildings and the island's place in the power struggle in Port Honduras remain undetermined. With no dry land except for the mounds themselves, Green Vine Snake presents even more of a challenge to extensively excavate than camping on Frenchman's Cay.

tied the stern to the dock, put on my boots and hat, and climbed out of the *Adel 2* onto the new cement dock at the Texaco station in Punta Gorda. A couple of people stayed with the boat to keep it from smashing against either the cement dock or the chicken wire that covers the rocks underneath the dock. The rest of us carried empty gas containers and empty Coke bottles. As a woman arriving from the sea, wearing boots, shorts, and a wide-brim hat — and wet and salty — I was an object of curiosity for people who had stopped their cars and trucks for gas. Women dory drivers were rare in Belize. Apart from Anna and Tanya, I was the only female driving a dory, until I had Melissa and Andrea drive the *Seirrita*. Anna fished in the coastal waters of Port Honduras and sold her fish in Punta Gorda. Tanya drove her dory from Village Farm to sell produce and buy provisions in Punta Gorda. My students and I became known in Punta Gorda and the coastal waters of Port Honduras as the women of Frenchman's Cay. There was a local mystique about a group of American women living in a sandfly-infested swamp on Frenchman's Cay, wielding pick axes and driving dories. Unlike many stories, this one was actually true.

I placed the empty gas containers between the gas pumps and opened them. I looked toward Felix and asked him to fill them up with mixed gas, with half a pint of lube in each container. The rich mixture helped prolong the life of the dory engines, which were at the mercy of the saltwater.

I took off my hat as I entered the Texaco station. I swung my backpack off my shoulder and onto the black counter in front of me. I pushed open the top of the soft drink cooler to my left and gazed inside for the day's contents. I removed a Coke, opened it with the built-in opener by my side, took a straw from the box on the counter, and began to suck the contents into my salt-drenched body. Then I turned my attention to the young woman in front of me across the counter. When Sylvia had finished with the other customers, I said hello, and she smiled and greeted me in response. I returned some empties and asked her whether I could use the radio to call the cay.

Miss Sylvia smiled and motioned permission. I walked around the counter, aware that I was dressed differently from the way she was. She wore a polyester dress and town shoes. There was no point in dwelling on these differences. As a female and driving a dory, I was different from her other customers. I was always polite and took off my hat as I entered the gas station, but I was different. I walked over to the radio to make a call.

We monitored the Texaco PG channel on the two-meter radio like everyone else, although we could switch to our own frequency for more privacy. After years of experimenting with other radio systems, we were happy that the two-meter radios had suddenly given us permanent and reliable communication with the town and our friends at Village Farm, who also monitored Texaco PG during their waking hours. When I first went to Wild Cane Cay, I had no radio, no ice, or any other luxuries. However, once I had finished my dissertation and had the relative wealth that came with research grants and Earthwatch volunteers who stayed for a short time, I added luxuries to my field project: radios, ice, meat from town, pressure lanterns instead of the flickering light from kerosene hurricane lanterns, and what seemed to me an incredible diversity of food items — at much greater cost and energy to procure. The volunteers were surprised by the primitive conditions under which they thought we lived and were shocked when I told them about earlier conditions.

I picked up the handheld microphone. I waited for the current conversation to stop. Then I called Frenchman's Cay and let them know we had arrived and would be leaving town soon. I thanked Miss Sylvia and walked a few hundred feet down Front Street to the newly installed phone booth in front of the government buildings at the center of Punta Gorda. I found it convenient to make phone calls before the government phone office opened at 8 A.M. As I made my call, I became aware that I was alone in the early morning at the phone booth. I glanced over my shoulder to see the Belizean government archaeologists from the Department of Archaeology. I smiled, nodded my head in recognition, and hoped that they would wait until I finished my call. They waited.

They had come to Punta Gorda on their regular visits to the government caretakers at Lubaantun, Nim Li Punit, and Uxbenka. They had also been assigned to visit my project, which pleased me immensely, since it was seldom that anyone from the government visited my sites. When they discovered that I was driving the dory, they decided to ask the coast guard for a ride to visit us on Frenchman's Cay the next day. I don't know if it was the dory ride, that we would be stopping at Village Farm on the way, or the fact that I was driving that prompted their decision. I considered that they preferred to ride in a skiff.

We returned to the Texaco dock, with our dories laden with volunteers. I stepped into the *Adel 2,* swung my backpack off my shoulder and into the dory beside the gas, and wedged my Coke between them. I looked up and saw that everyone was back in the dory. We traveled in calm seas along the coast, stopping at Village Farm for coffee, conversation, and drinking water. Late in the afternoon we left Village Farm heading directly out to sea to Frenchman's Cay.

I realized the sun was setting and the sky would be dark soon. There was little time between day and night on the Belizean seas. The sun glistened across the horizon until the moment it appeared to drop off the edge of the world. We'd spent most of the day visiting at Village Farm, where we picked up 80 gallons of water in our water sacks, along with Lyra and Nathaniel to work at the cay with us.

We were barely 500 meters from the dock when the *Serreita*'s engine stopped. After endless attempts to restart it, my student driver was not having any luck. I asked her whether she wanted to go back to Village Farm or wanted me to tow her. It would be dark, but the sea was calm. The sky was clear, and there would be a full moon. She wanted us to tow her, so I brought the *Adel 2* alongside the *Seirrita*. The kids were excited. Their eyes danced in the late afternoon sun: To them, there was always a story when they went with the archaeologists.

I searched the horizon, realizing we were headed straight out to sea. We would not have the security of the coastline as a guide in the darkness. I checked our direction on my compass and kept the *Adel 2* on course by flashlight. The route was logged in the GPS, handheld, waterproof unit that we carried along to locate sites. I turned on the depth sounder and checked that the lighted screen on the seat beside me was working. I never relaxed completely. Still, I enjoyed the journey, acutely aware of the sea's power. This is where I belonged.

Since I liked fish and fishing, I had learned to compromise in estimating the best route between Village Farm and Frenchman's Cay. At first, driving with Orlando, I was on the side of getting to our destination. Later, driving the dory myself, I began to divert to fish without any discussion with my passengers.

I felt comfortable and even enjoyed the pressure of driving and working with the sea. Instead of small outlines in Port Honduras, I began to experience the ancient Maya sites in their setting — their physical landscape, with water distance measured by sea conditions, view, and position along a coastal trading route. With Wild Cane Cay on the north, Frenchman's Cay on the outer range of cays, and Green Vine Snake on the inner range, the coastal Maya could have controlled access to the coastal waters and have forced travelers to stop at their communities. Otherwise, the only canoe route was beyond the outer range of Port Honduras cays, where the swells kept us away.

The weight of 80 gallons of water in bags stabilized the *Adel 2* in the water and helped us glide out to sea toward Frenchman's Cay. We trolled for fish on the way and caught a small barracuda, which we cut for bait. Rounding a point on the inner range of cays, I leaned back and increased the throttle. The wind, afternoon sun, and choppy seas coming across the bow made for a relaxing ride.

Suddenly something was on the line. I slowed the engine, keeping pressure on the line, and started slowly hauling it in. An enormous barracuda emerged from the sea by my side. For a moment I could feel its power and strength and almost taste it in the cast-iron frying pan sizzling in coconut oil. Sleek, with water sliding off its body as I drew it toward me, the fish slowly bit through the 150 lb test line and disappeared silently into the water. The biggest barracuda I had ever seen was gone.

I knew we had to get that fish. It was almost in the boat, and it had taken my best lure. I had my crew search the dory for hooks and spoons, but they found none. I conceded temporary defeat, with the private knowledge of returning to get the barracuda who taunted me but also gave such passion to the sea.

In the familiar noise of the roaring engine, I considered the progress of the fieldwork. We were almost finished with the excavations of the three mounds on Frenchman's Cay. Despite extensive looting, we had found what appeared to be undisturbed coral foundations similar to those at nearby Wild Cane Cay. We had horizontally exposed the coral layers at Frenchman's Cay, as we had done at Wild Cane Cay, in order to investigate the buildings shrouded inside

19.1 Seirrita *tied to shore at Frenchman's Cay.*

the mounds. The smaller size of the site on Frenchman's Cay, the smaller number of mounds, and the lower density of artifacts on the surface compared to Wild Cane Cay suggested that Frenchman's Cay was a subsidiary trading community. The Maya on the two islands were probably related by marriage, providing a blood tie that strengthened their hold on coastal trade through Port Honduras.

Subsequent study of the Frenchman's Cay artifacts during several trips to Punta Gorda, where I had stored the material, led me to believe that the two islands were trading ports at different times. Frenchman's Cay controlled coastal trade during the Late Classic, whereas Wild Cane Cay became dominant during the Postclassic. This view is based on the dating of the coral architecture — a sign of the wealth of each community. In addition, obsidian is more common during the Late Classic at Frenchman's Cay, whereas at Wild Cane Cay, this exotic material is abundant in the Postclassic deposits. Exactly what that relationship was and how Green Vine Snake figured in the control of sea trade through Port Honduras coastal waters would have to wait for another year's fieldwork.

I figured that one or two of my staff members might be able to keep up with me in future seas. Andrea had gone to law school. Melissa was working in contract archaeology. My hopes were focused on Rachel, Aline, and Shannon, but more realistically I would find a new crop of undergraduates from my Introduction to Archaeology class. As long as I had questions to answer about the ancient Maya and the sea, I hoped to return. I knew as I checked the depth sounder on the seat beside me that the sea would never let me become complacent.

A couple of hours later, under the glimmer of many flashlights, we approached the kerosene lantern set by the seaside on Frenchman's Cay. The crew radioed to Village Farm that we had arrived safely. While the rising moon illuminated the sky and sent shimmers across the waves, we let the line slacken on the *Seirrita*. The dories drifted to shore together (figure 19.1).

NOTES

1. Sixteenth-century Spanish explorers had disrupted a thriving coastal canoe trade around the Yucatan, extending even beyond the Maya area to the Gulfs of Mexico and Honduras (see Sabloff and Rathje 1975). Was sea trade also characteristic of the earlier Classic Period, when great city-states rose to prominence in the southern Maya lowlands of Guatemala and Belize between A.D. 300 and 900? Alternatively, did trade take place by overland trails and rivers at that time, and did sea trade develop only after the collapse of the southern city-states and the rise of Chichen Itza and other cities in the northern Maya lowlands? I hoped to investigate the timing and importance of sea trade and its relationship to the inland cities, particularly those in southern Belize: Lubaantun, Nim Li Punit, Uxbenka, and Pusilha.

   The royal and other wealthy Maya at cities in the interior of the Yucatan peninsula imported exotic materials such as jade, obsidian, mercury, and painted pots as status markers for use in public feasting, bloodletting, and other ceremonies and as gifts to help cement good relations with rulers in other lowland city-states (Culbert 1991; Inomata and Houston 2001; Masson and Freidel 2002; Reents-Budet 1994). The inland elite also desired resources from the sea, including stingray spines for bloodletting; fish and salt for food; conch shells for musical instruments; manatee bones for carving figurines; and coral and other items from the sea for food, ritual, and perhaps utilitarian uses (McKillop 2002, 2004a, 2004b).

   From my previous fieldwork at Moho Cay and also because the inland Maya desired resources from the sea as well as from more distant areas, my impression was that sea trade was important in the Classic period. Certainly coastal-inland trade was a feature of this era, but whether this was integrated with sea trade would be determined by my research (see also McKillop and Healy 1989 for other research on the coastal Maya).

   For my Master's thesis research at Trent University, I had carried out excavations at Moho Cay, a Classic Maya trading port located in the mouth of the Belize River. The river provided access to important Maya cities, such as Tikal, in the central Maya area of the Peten district of Guatemala and to closer sites in the upper Belize valley of western Belize, such as Xunantunich, Baking Pot, and Cahal Pech. See McKillop (1980, 1984, 1985, and 2004a) and Healy et al. (1984) for publications on the Moho Cay excavations. When the site was destroyed for tourism development, I decided to look for a more remote area for Ph.D. fieldwork. I took advantage of my stay in Belize in 1981, when I taught a course on Maya archaeology to the guides of the public archaeological sites in Belize through a Canadian International Development Agency (CIDA) grant to my former M.A. advisor, Paul Healy. After the course, I investigated the coastal area in the far south of Belize, about which I'd read reports by early adventurers, travelers, and archaeologists in a general review of the literature on everything I could find on the coastal Maya.

2. Lubaantun had drawn much public attention in the wake of reports of a crystal skull allegedly found at the base of a mound by Anna Mitchell-Hedges on her sixteenth birthday, when she accompanied her father, Frederick Mitchell-Hedges (1931), on a British Museum expedition to southern Belize. The British Museum's work, together with excavations in 1970 by Norman Hammond (1975) indicated that Lubaantun was a Late Classic city with impressive public buildings faced with local sandstone. The lack of carved monuments, *stelae,* commemorating with hieroglyphs various events by the city's leaders is perplexing, considering the city's large size and its evident political and economic importance in the region. Work by Richard Leventhal (1990) at nearby Nim Li Punit and Uxbenka — smaller cities with carved stelae — may reveal the political economy of the region. Pusilha was explored by the British Museum in the 1920s and again, beginning in 2002, by Geoffrey Braswell.

3. The earliest excavations on Wild Cane Cay were by Thomas W. F. Gann, the medical officer to the then colony of British Honduras. Excavating in mounds in 1908 and 1909 and again in 1911 and 1917 (Gann 1911, 1917, 1918, 135–36), Gann determined that they were constructed of coral and mainland stone and contained human burials. In 1914 Herbert Spinden made subsequent investigations (Kidder 1954). Frederick Mitchell-Hedges, Lady Richmond Brown, and Thomas Gann excavated in one mound in 1924, which was mentioned briefly in a fishing travelogue book, along with the insects that drove the visitors away and prompted Mitchell-Hedges (1931, 21–22) to remark, "a more damnable place it would be hard to find. . . . I should like to change the name to 'Misery Island.'" The British Museum's expedition to British Honduras, led by Thomas Joyce, Captain E. L. Gruning, and Robert Ashton, excavated for a day at Wild Cane Cay in 1929 (Joyce 1929, 440). In their quest for carved monuments suitable for museum display, Joyce's team concluded that the site was worth another look — but by someone else. That Lubaantun too was abandoned in favor of the stelae at Pusilha places Wild Cane Cay in a more favorable light. In fact, carved monuments were transported from Pusilha to the British Museum.

In 1931, Junius Bird was permitted by his project director, Boekelman, to map and briefly excavate at Wild Cane Cay during Boekelman's shell-heap expedition to Central America (Bird 1931, and personal communication, 1982). Bird produced a remarkably accurate map of the island (Hammond 1975, figure 106). He also visited and mapped two mounds on nearby Frenchman's Cay (Bird 1931). Hammond (1975, 278) examined Bird's excavated material in the Museum of Natural History in New York and ascertained that the material contained Late Classic ceramics. Following a visit there with Alfred Kidder and Gustav Stomsvik, Gordon Ekholm (1950) reported that a landowner, P. Cabral, possessed a surface collection that included a carved conch shell (Dockstader 1964, figure 66) and a Tohil plumbate effigy toad vessel. Kidder (1954) illustrated these items in subsequent publications.

Widespread academic attention focused on Wild Cane Cay following Kidder's publication of the plumbate vessel, distinctive "unit-stamped" pottery, and several copper artifacts, as well as publications of Gann's and Bird's material housed in museums. Unfortunately, the plumbate vessel is now in a private collection in the United States (see McKillop and Healy 1989, cover illustration; Bray 1970, plate 27). The only plumbate pottery from Belize recorded in Anna O. Shepard's (1948, 112) seminal treatise was a turkey-head fragment from Wild Cane Cay from the American Museum of Natural History's collections. Warwick Bray (1977, figures 2:13, 7:6, 7:11, 14:1–2, 15) reports copper bells, rings, and lost-wax, cast-copper masks from Gann's (1918, 135), Kidder's (1954, 14), and others' collections. Samuel Lothrop (1952, 26, table XVII) found traces of silver in copper artifacts from Gann's work at Wild Cane Cay.

Many others have visited Wild Cane Cay, collected artifacts, or excavated. For example, in 1973, Jack Lean (personal communication, 1990), accompanied by the then owner of the cay, Mary Cabral, traveled there to excavate an area about 4 meters square and 1.5 meters in depth near the house. They found a skeleton with a shattered vessel and covered it up. When they returned the next year to reexcavate the burial, they discovered that someone else had preceded them. In another report, Junius Bird (1931) mentions that the crown prince of Sweden visited the cay and purchased artifacts from the then owner, P. Cabral. The fact that the island was settled by Europeans from the nineteenth century, figured in the mahogany business, and was a regular stopping point for the coastal mail boat (which started in 1886; Eric King 1986) meant the island was accessible and visited by many people who were naturally curious about the abundant artifacts on the surface and those that could be found by digging. It was only in 1971, in fact, that the government of Belize began to control and license the search for sites, their excavation, and the removal and export of artifacts.

Hammond visited Wild Cane Cay in 1970, interpreting the site as a Late Classic to Postclassic fishing and trading community. From the island's surface he also collected obsidian, which he send to the Lawrence-Berkeley Laboratory for chemical analysis, the results of which figure in Hammond's (1972) model of Maya obsidian trade. With this and more casual work by others at Wild Cane Cay, it became clear that the islanders had participated in sea trade, but the timing and extent of the trade and its role in the island's settlement history were still undetermined.

4. See Taylor (1951) for a discussion of the Black Carib (Garifuna) village of Barranco, south of Punta Gorda; see Davidson (1984) for an overview of the Garifuna in Belize and elsewhere in Central America.

5. Cayetano (1992, 38–40) recounts that when the Honduraneans — in their quest for independence — defeated Spain, the Black Caribs, who had sided with Spain, were hunted and killed. Some escaped from Roatan to Belize in November, 1832, where they received grants to settle land at Stann Creek Town. However, Burdon (1931, vol. 2, 60–61) reports that in a magistrates' meeting of the settlement in 1802, it was noted that Black Caribs were in the settlement and were not welcome since they were considered to be unruly. Cayetano (1992, 43) reports that they made a series of landings in Belize in 1802. Davidson (1984) reports that from the time of the initial settlement in Roatan, the Garifuna were traveling in their dories to fish in Belizean waters, but that permanent settlement did not occur until later. Even in the late-twentieth century Garifuna women from Punta Gorda regularly paddled dories across to Puerto Barrios in Guatemala, suggesting the likelihood of early canoe travel (Iris Vernon, personal communication, 2003). Not until after the initial, official settlement in Stann Creek in 1832 did the attitude of the British settlers become more accepting of the Black Caribs, who were regarded as a cheap source of labor (Cayetano 1992, 45). Currently there are Black Carib communities in Stann Creek (Dangriga), Hopkins, Georgetown, Seine Bight, Monkey River, Punta Negra, Punta Gorda, and Barranco (Davidson 1984). The village of Hopkins is the most recent and was settled in 1937 by Black Caribs who survived a massacre by the army of their village of San Juan, Honduras (Cayetano 1992, 39–40). John Lloyd Stephens (1841, 27–32) describes stopping at "Puenta Gorda" for a few hours in October, 1839, en route from Belize City to the Rio Dulce and seeing a Carib community of thatched huts of about five hundred people who spoke Spanish and had fled Honduras. A priest with Stephens baptized many but was unable to marry them since most of the men were away cutting mahogany or elsewhere. Apparently priests rarely came to the village.

6. I had three volunteers who had paid their air travel to Belize and were willing to live in tents and eat not much more than rice, beans, and whatever fish they caught in exchange for the opportunity to excavate at an ancient Maya site.

7. Kekchi Maya from the Alta Verapaz region of Guatemala began settling the Toledo district in the mid-nineteenth century. Immigration increased after 1877, when precolonial native land titles were voided and forced labor for Indians was instituted in the Alta Verapaz. These changes were a result of the boom in coffee production principally by Germans (Cambranes 1985; A. King 1974; McCreery 1983, 12–18; Wilk 1987, 34). With the lengthening of work duty from 30 to 45 days in 1892 and the erosion of other rights, the Kekchi left the area and moved to Punta Gorda (Cambranes 1985, 199; Wilk 1987, 36).

The Mopan Maya, whom the Spaniards had converted to Catholicism with varying success in the late 1600s in central Belize and Guatemala, made an initial settlement in the Toledo district in 1886. They were escaping taxation and forced labor in San Luis, Guatemala, where the government had begun a railway (Gregory 1972, 14–15; Thompson 1930, 41; Wilk 1987, 39). When Guatemala claimed their initial settlement near modern Pueblo Viejo as Guatemalan territory, the Mopan Maya moved their community in 1889 to San Antonio, west of modern Punta Gorda (Wilk 1987, 39).

Indian reserves were created in 1924, and each recognized Maya village was assigned land. The alcaldes (mayors) were supposed to collect taxes from land distribution within the reserve. With the shifting land-tenure patterns related to swidden agriculture and the lack of assigned reserve land to smaller Maya communities — alquilos consisting of three to ten households — land tenure problems continued (Wilk 1987, 44).

8. The original inhabitants of Port Honduras were Maya, linguistically known as the Manche Chol. The few early records for southern Belize, as discussed by Wilk (1987), J. Eric S. Thompson (1972), and Doris Stone (1932), indicate that at the time of European contact, the Maya were dispersed in the rainforest. However, few records exist of what were likely frequent travels in the area by Europeans. Certainly the presence of early Spanish artifacts, such as an olive jar fragment that dates between 1570 and 1770 that we excavated from Wild Cane Cay attest to greater European presence in the coastal waters of Port Honduras than archival sources suggest. Moreover, recent research by Grant Jones (1989) and others (Bolland 1977; Grant 1976; Shoman 1994) in northern Belize indicates that many indigenous Maya actively resisted European intrusions. These recent findings contrast sharply to earlier views of Belize as virtually unoccupied at the time of the European conquest and the later arrival of the British (Clegern 1967). Thompson (1972) reports that by 1700 southern Belize was unpopulated by Maya, who had initially been difficult to control by the Spaniards, who had eventually deported most to Guatemala. Clearly, more archival and archaeological work needs to be carried out in southern Belize to discover the use of the area by Maya and Europeans.

As well as the Spaniards, British buccaneers, or corsairs, who plied the coastal waters along the Caribbean coast of Belize, encountered Maya, and some of these accounts were recorded. For example, the famous pirate Bartholomew Sharp captured a Spanish Dominican friar, Fr. Joseph Delgado, and several Indians along the Moho River, south of Punta Gorda in 1677. This account was translated from Delgado's original documents in the National Library in Paris by J. Eric S. Thompson (1972, 22–29). The account includes Delgado's visits to several dispersed homesteads from the Moho River north.

In a separate account by General Francisco de Ayeta in 1687, three Franciscans and a lay brother were sacrificed at Paliac, identified by Thompson (ibid., 21) as the Rio Grande, while trying to convert Indians. Thompson (ibid., 29) identifies the locations of these two accounts, on the Moho River and Rio Grande, respectively, from a 1775 map by British cartographer Thomas Jeffreys, noting that the map is the best of the area in the eighteenth century. Jeffreys's map is from *Thomas Jeffreys' West Indies Atlas,* published in London in 1775.

The British were cutting logwood and mahogany in Port Honduras by at least 1800 (Humphries 1961, 15). In 1786 a treaty with Spain had set the limits of the British settlement as between the Rio Hondo and Sibun River (ibid., 6). Not until 1837 were the first land grants made outside that area. Among them were parcels on the Deep River, Golden Stream, Rio Grande in Port Honduras, and the Moho and Sarstoon rivers farther south (ibid., 24). Humphries's (ibid., 15) search of correspondence from settlers and the settlement's superintendent to Britain, now housed in the Colonial Office in London and the Belize archives in Belmopan, indicates that cutters were on the Rio Grande, Golden Stream, and Deep River by 1806. Furthermore, the loggers had occupied the Deep River from 1799 or 1800 and had been shipping cargo on a regular basis. In 1814, the settlers reported that cutting extended to the Moho River (ibid.). By 1825, the Sarstoon was regarded as the southern boundary of the British settlement (ibid., 21; see also map in Burdon 1931, vol. 2, 292).

By 1869, a sugar estate with a steam engine was in operation at Seven Hills, north of present-day Punta Gorda (Burdon 1934, vol. 3, 314). Settlement of the Sapodilla Cays in 1873 is mentioned (ibid., 332).

My subsequent archaeological work in Port Honduras revealed the remains of several historic settlements related to nineteenth-century logging and the sugar industry, as well as to an earlier Spanish presence in the area. Although the focus of my fieldwork was the ancient Maya, I recorded historic sites we discovered as well, partly because it was surprising to find them. A camp in the swamp or the savanna or on an offshore cay marked by a scattering of broken china or bottles made me wonder what courageous folks had come to the area, what they were doing, and why they had left. Nineteenth-century ceramics were recovered from Wild Cane Cay, Village Farm, and several places up the Deep River, including along Muschamp Creek. Archival evidence of logging has previously been noted.

By 1982, few permanent residents remained in the Port Honduras region. Anna Ramirez Castellanos lived with her children and dogs on a small, unnamed cay near Wild Cane Cay and lived by selling fish in Punta Gorda caught from a small dory with a 10-horsepower engine. Two families of expatriate Americans included Charlie Carson, his wife, and two children at New Haven, on the mainland north of Wild Cane Cay. On their small farm they grew coconuts, pineapples, and other produce and operated a makeshift drydock for hauling yachts using old railway ties salvaged from the nineteenth-century, logging railroad. John Spang and Tanya Russ lived on an organic farm with their two children, Lyra and Nathaniel, on the mainland between Seven Hills and Middle River. Although the Carsons and Anna Ramirez frequently came to Wild Cane Cay to visit Frank and Adel, I don't remember meeting John and Tanya until long after Frank Cabral had died. John, Frank, and others, including Albert King and Bobbie Polonio, had variously lived on nearby Frenchman's Cay with an expatriate American, Dick Moore, a retired military explosive operator who raised pigs on the cay until his death in the 1970s.

In addition to these few permanent residents, many boats passed through the area, particularly at night. Some were local fisherfolk. Others, I suspect, were involved in importing and exporting drugs — initially locally grown marijuana, but increasingly cocaine from Colombia brought by small plane or speedboat to the reef and dropped for pickup by local skiffs. I had no contact with them, although their activities were well known by the Belize Coast Guard and the American Drug Enforcement Agency, both of whom periodically visited us and other coastal residents. I included myself as a resident since my field team was recorded in the Belizean census by an evidently desperate group of census takers who arrived at Wild Cane Cay one day by boat.

9. During the 1930s, J. Eric S. Thompson worked in southern Belize, and in 1970 Norman Hammond carried out excavations at Lubaantun.

10. Interviews with Frank and Adel Cabral were conducted and, along with personal observations, form the basis of this chapter's discussion about the Cabral family.

11. Coconut palms, *Cocos nucifera,* are not indigenous to tropical America but quickly dominated production, replacing native palms, which have much smaller fruits (McKillop 1994a, 1996b).

12. The presence of breadfruit as well as mango, citrus, and banana on Wild Cane Cay (McKillop 1998b) are characteristic of European, particularly British, settlement in Central America (William V. Davidson, personal communication, 1998).

13. See McKillop (1996b) for an overview of ancient Maya use of native palms, with a discussion of their dietary and other uses from ethnographic and ethnobotanical studies.

CHAPTER 2

1. For descriptions and recipes for Belizean food, see E. L. Burns's *What's Cooking in Belizean Kitchens?* (n.d., Graphics One Ltd., Belize).

2. Obsidian is a volcanic glass that outcrops in the volcanic regions of Mexico and Central America but not in Belize. Because it enables researchers to chemically fingerprint artifacts found at lowland Maya sites in Belize and elsewhere with their highland outcrops, obsidian has been widely used to trace ancient Maya trade routes (Andrews et al. 1989; Guderjan et al. 1989a; Hammond 1972; Healy et al. 1984; McKillop 1989b, 1995b; McKillop et al. 1988; Rice 1984). Obsidian was usually traded from volcanic highland regions in the form of cylindrical cores (figure 2.1), from which 125 or more sharp-edged blades were made by striking the flat surface of the core at the edge (Sheets 1975).

3. Stelae (carved monuments with Mayan hieroglyphs placed in front of Maya buildings commemorating historical events of the rulers) at the nearby inland city of Nim Li Punit show offerings of blood dripping from fingers on bark paper in a brazier. See also Schele and Freidel (1990); Schele and Miller (1986), and Reents-Budet (1994).

4. For convenience, archaeologists often use an arbitrary *site north* for mapping, or *gridding,* a site for surface collection or excavation. At Wild Cane Cay the site grid was placed to conform with the island's oval shape and to afford a clear line of sight avoiding the hundreds of coconut and other fruit trees. The grid was used for surface collection and for the selection of places to excavate.

5. Classic Maya carved monuments and their hieroglyphic texts, pottery figurines, and pictorial scenes on painted pots indicate that Classic Maya women — at least noble women — enjoyed high status and, variously, political power or influence due to their noble birth (Arden 2002; Joyce 2000; Martin and Grube 2000; Maxwell 1998). Carved monuments meant for public viewing depict royal Maya women assisting in rituals and feasts by holding cloth bundles and pottery vessels containing food or sacrificial paraphernalia and participating in ritual bloodletting (see Reents-Budet 1994 for various illustrations). Hieroglyphic texts on monuments record the importance of royal women in negotiating or solidifying peace through marriage alliances with kings or noblemen in other city-states amid the bellicose climate of the Late Classic period. In addition, some noble women gained prominence, which was recorded, as mothers and spouses of male rulers. Rarely, as at Palenque, are women referred to as rulers, as in the case of references to Pacal's mother.

6. Perhaps they thought that many archaeologists in the United States and Canada were women. Since they had no reference group of Maya archaeologists, this fact may have worked to my advantage. In fact, when I began my research in 1979, there were relatively few female Maya archaeologists directing field projects, in contrast to the many projects that men directed — a fact that I did not consider at the time. In Belize, for example, there were field projects directed by Tom Hester and Harry Shafer at Colha; my M.A. advisor, Paul Healy, in the Maya Mountains; Peter Harrison and Billie Lee Turner at Pulltrouser Swamp; Richard "Scottie" MacNeish at various places in his search for the Preceramic; Norman Hammond at Cuello; David Freidel at Cerros; and David Pendergast at Lamanai, among others.

   Where were my female colleagues? Historically, relatively few women have directed field projects in the Maya lowlands. Olive Ricketson worked with her husband at Uaxactun, where she directed the field lab (Ricketson and Ricketson 1937). Their daughter, Mary Bullard, worked in the Tikal lab, married William Bullard, and carried out excavations with him at Baking Pot, in western Belize (Bullard and Bullard 1965). Mary subsequently directed the field lab at Quirigua in the 1970s (Black 1990, 259). Edith Ricketson and Mary Bullard's work, along with the study of Piedras Negras ceramics by Mary Butler and Tatiana Proskouriakoff's fieldwork with the Carnegie Institution of Washington at Mayapan and Chichen Itza (Pollock et al. 1962), punctuate a long record of fieldwork by men in the Maya area (Black 1990).

   By the 1970s, however, women were directing independent field projects for their doctoral research in the Maya lowlands. These women included Elizabeth Graham (1983, 1994) in the Stann Creek district of Belize, Diane Chase (1982) at Santa Rita

Corozal in Belize, and Anabel Ford (1981, 1986) with her survey between Tikal and Yaxha, as well as my master's thesis work at Moho Cay (McKillop 1980). Other women were carrying out fieldwork as part of larger projects, including K. Anne Pyburn (1988) at Nohmul, Wendy Ashmore (1981a) at Quirigua, and Patricia McAnany (1986) at Pulltrouser Swamp. The 1980s and 1990s witnessed a further increase in fieldwork directed by women such as Marilyn Masson (2000), Shirley Mock (1994), and Rosemary Joyce (1991) in the Maya lowlands. In addition, important work was carried out in artifact collections, epigraphy, and hieroglyphs by Joyce Marcus (1976), Linda Schele (Schele and Miller 1986), Mary Miller, Dorie Reents-Budet (1994), Barbara MacLeod (see Reents-Budet 1994), and others.

Leading an expedition into uninhabited territory out at sea seemed to me the obvious way to follow my research interests in Maya sea trade. My professors at Trent University and the University of California at Santa Barbara encouraged me, and I received a scholarship and grant to carry out the fieldwork. My background in canoeing and camping had prepared me for leading wilderness canoe trips in Canada (see Trudeau 1970). Venturing out to sea in motorized canoes, carving campsites in the swamps, and camping for several months at a time were familiar activities that I enjoyed. Certainly working in small, remote sites away from the big Maya cities may have facilitated my research, but it also marginalized my work, according to my colleagues. The absence of other archaeologists in Port Honduras or elsewhere in southern Belize meant that the local people in Punta Gorda and the surrounding Maya and other communities accepted that I was not only an archaeologist, but also the *only* archaeologist. The fact that I am a woman was not questioned since I was foreign, spent money in Punta Gorda, and went to sea, the last of which was uncommon for anyone.

7. Details of the mapping and sampling are given in my dissertation (McKillop 1987), as well as McKillop (1989a).

CHAPTER 3

1. Grant (1976); Humphries (1961).
2. Starting in 1867, there was an influx of settlers from the southern United States with a land request at Punta Ycacos (Burdon 1934, vol. 3, 281, 285, 291, 248). The Toledo settlement was established in 1868 by 66 U.S. immigrants and 45 Spanish laborers, women, and children (ibid., 314; Camille 1986a, 1986b).
3. Camille (1986a, 1986b).

CHAPTER 4

1. Detailed descriptions of the excavations are given in McKillop (1987), with summary descriptions in McKillop (1989a, 1996a, 1998b, and 2002).
2. McKillop (1994a, 1996b).
3. Emory King Sr. (1991).

4. Further descriptions and illustrations of the plant food remains from Wild Cane Cay and the nearby sites on Frenchman's Cay, Pelican Cay, Tiger Mound, and Orlando's Jewfish are found in McKillop (1994a, 1996b, 1995c, 1995a, 1998b, and 2002). The large size, abundance, and good preservation of the plant food remains are attributable to their recovery from permanently waterlogged soil. Plant food remains have been recovered from a number of other Maya sites, but not in any great quantity or similarity in size to those from Wild Cane Cay and other Port Honduras sites; moreover, they are not as well preserved. Normally, special techniques, such as flotation, are used to recover plant remains, which are identified microscopically, rather than macroscopically, as at Wild Cane Cay. In addition to those from Port Honduras, plant food remains have been reported from Cuello, Colha, Copan, Cerros, Pulltrouser Swamp, Albion Island, Cihuatan, Ceren, Rio Azul, Dos Pilas, and Santa Leticia. Much of the research on ancient Maya plant food was initially carried out by Charlie Miksicek (see Turner and Miksicek 1984, for example) and more recently by David Lentz (1999), Cathy Crane (Cliff and Crane 1989), and the author.

5. McKillop (1984, 1985). In 1994, I discovered a fresh manatee kill in Paynes Creek National Park and videotaped the remains of the slaughter. Attracted to the location by buzzards swarming overhead, I noted that the flesh was so fresh there was no odor. We had just passed a skiff leaving the area. Interviews (on tape) of local fishermen in 1982 indicated that at that time Belizeans still hunted manatee for meat in the belief that these animals were not scarce. Popular belief in 1997 and 1998 was that foreigners — usually from Guatemala or Honduras — hunted the manatee.

6. McKillop (1987). See McKillop and Winemiller (2004) for a discussion of shells recovered from nearby Frenchman's Cay.

7. Fishing weights. See McKillop (1984, 1987) for illustrations.

8. Michael Spence (1987) analyzed the burials from the 1982 excavations.

9. McKillop (1987, 2001). See also Ensor and McKillop (2002).

CHAPTER 5

1. Other researchers independently found the visual identification of the geological sources of Maya obsidian artifacts to be accurate, with blind tests comparing visual and chemical identification carried out by Geoffrey Braswell, John Clark, Kazuo Ayoama, and me (Braswell et al. 2000). Visual identification, is controversial, although the high accuracy reported by the main Maya obsidian specialists lends promise to this technique. Because visual identification is cheaper than chemical sourcing, Braswell et al. (ibid.) argue that more obsidian artifacts can be connected with their sources through visual identification. I found that small samples of fewer than ten obsidian items do not show the diversity of sources used at a Maya site that is evident in larger samples (McKillop 1987; McKillop and Jackson 1988). Sourcing a large number of obsidian samples is important in order to accurately reconstruct ancient obsidian trade routes.

2. Sheets and Muto (1972) introduced the "cutting edge to mass" (ce/m) ratio. Irwin Rovner (1976) introduced the comparison of blade widths.

3. Hattula Moholy-Nagy et al. (1984) discuss obsidian from Tikal.

4. McKillop et al. (1988).

5. For the Late Classic, the number and percentage (in brackets) of obsidian chemically identified (except for Pachuca, which is based on visual identification of its green color) with different sources are as follows: 12 (41 percent) from El Chayal, 15 (52 percent) from Ixtepeque, none from Rio Pixcaya, and 2 (7 percent) from unknown Source Z. For the Early Postclassic, the number and percentage are as follows: 6 (9 percent) from El Chayal, 63 (89 percent) from Ixtepeque, 1 (1 percent) from Rio Pixcaya, and 1 (1 percent) from unknown Source Z. The detailed report is in McKillop et al. (ibid.).

6. Ucareo obsidian is found at only a few lowland Maya sites, including Isla Cerritos (Andrews et al. 1989), Lubaantun (Stross et al. 1978), and Wild Cane Cay (McKillop et al. 1988).

   Wild Cane Cay seems to be the northernmost distribution point for La Esperanza obsidian, which is better distributed outside the Maya area in lower Central America (Sheets et al. 1990).

7. Braswell et al. (2000) and McKillop (1995b); Raymond Sidrys (1977) used this method, although at Wild Cane Cay I restricted the analysis to midden contexts.

8. The average density of obsidian from different areas of domestic refuse at Wild Cane Cay was 136 items per cubic meter (134.4 g per cubic meter) during the Early Postclassic and 17.1 items per cubic meter (16.8 g per cubic meter) during the Late Classic. For more details on the obsidian densities at Wild Cane Cay, see McKillop (1989a).

9. A complete surface collection of all obsidian in each of 191 grid areas, each measuring 10 by 10 meters, was carried out in 1982 (McKillop 1989a). I subsequently entered the data on a computer and incorporated them into a GIS, which allowed me to investigate many combinations of surface obsidian patterning (McKillop, Winemiller, and Jones 2000).

10. Sheets (1975).

11. Sheets and Muto (1972) and Rovner (1976) found that as the distance from the obsidian outcrops increases, the ce/m ratio increases and the blade width decreases, reflecting conservation of a scarce resource.

12. The Pachuca outcrop, north of Mexico City, is the only known source of the distinctive "bottle green" obsidian in Mesoamerica. The obsidian is typically free of imperfections (banding or inclusions), which makes it of superior quality for tool manufacture.

13. Coastal transportation of Ixtepeque obsidian is reported by Healy et al. (1984) for Moho Cay and McKillop et al. (1988) for Wild Cane Cay. Chemical identification of Lubaantun obsidian is reported by Stross et al. (1978). Hammond graciously lent

me the Lubaantun obsidian, which, from visual inspection, contains no Ixtepeque material.

14. See Healy et al. (1984); McKillop (2004a).
15. McKillop (2002).
16. McKillop (1989a, 1996a).
17. Andrews et al. (1989); Guderjan and Garber (1995), Guderjan et al. (1989a, 1989b), and McKillop (1995b) for Ambergris Caye obsidian; Graham and Pendergast (1989); Graham (1994); MacKinnon (1989a,1989b).
18. See Anna O. Shepard (1948) for the definitive description of the pottery, as well as Hector Neff (1989) for more recent analyses.
19. Sanders (1960). McKillop (2001) describes ceramics from Wild Cane Cay resembling Tulum Red.

CHAPTER 6

1. Bird (1931) and personal communication (1982); Hammond (1975, figure 10).

   The description of the excavations of Fighting Conch mound and its structures and burials are reported here for the first time, so detailed illustrations accompany the text. Readers who are more interested in summary comments can find them at the end of the chapter.

2. Ricketson (1925); Graham and Pendergast (1989).

3. Generally, the best speculations of sex are made from observing a variety of features from an entire skeleton. In the absence of a complete skeleton, sexual dimorphism is greatest in the hip bone because of the skeletal consequences of human birth by females. The hip bones are fragile and often not well preserved at archaeological sites. A number of features of the skull and mandible are also indicators of sexual dimorphism. For burial 10, the field observations included some of the strongest indicators of sex from the hip bones and skull. The angle of the mandible is the corner of the jar on each side, which in males tends to be closer to 90 degrees, whereas in females it tends to be less angled. The sciatic notch is located on the side of each hip bone. In females, the notch is wider because of the larger pelvic cavity. Similarly, the subpubic angle, formed where the two sides of the hip bone join at the front, tends to be a wider angle in females than in males. Maya skeletal remains from burials have been identified to age, sex, and health status from a variety of sites, notably Seibal, Lubaantun, Tancah, and Cuello by Frank Saul and Mary Saul (Saul 1972, 1975, 1982; Saul and Saul 1991), among others (see Whittington and Reed 1997; White 1999). Keith Jacobi (2000) carried out a genetic study of historic Maya teeth from 518 burials in and around a Spanish church at Tipu, Belize. He examined dental traits, such as Carabelli's cusp and other extra cusps and shovel-shaped incisors, which are inherited. He also measured teeth since their shape and size show genetic relationships among individuals.

4. For the locations of Maya burials, see McAnany (1995); McKillop (1980, 2004a) for Moho Cay; Healy et al. (1998) for Caledonia; Pendergast (1979) for Altun Ha; Hammond et al. (1975) for Lubaantun; Robin (1989) for Cuello; Chase and Chase (1996) for Caracol; and Welsh (1988) for a general summary of Maya burials.

5. See Sanders (1960) for illustrations of Tulum Red pottery from the Tulum site.

6. The radiocarbon dates are reported at two standard deviations, which means there is a 95 percent likelihood that the age is within the reported range.

7. McKillop (1994b,1996a,1998a, 2002); McKillop et al. (2004).

8. McKillop (1996a).

9. Burial 4 at Moho Cay included two stingray spines and three obsidian blades, with a late Early Classic/early Late Classic pottery vessel (McKillop 2004a).

10. The part of Moho Cay that contains the archaeological site was dredged to create a harbor for a marina. Although I had a permit to carry out the archaeological work, another branch of the Belizean government granted a permit to build the marina, destroying the site (McKillop 1984).

11. Chase and Chase (1989); Miller (1977).

12. Freidel (1975).

13. Freidel (1981).

14. Andrews and Andrews (1975); Miller 1977.

15. McKillop (1989a).

CHAPTER 8

1. McKillop (2002) also describes the offshore excavations at Wild Cane Cay. We excavated *shovel tests* — holes that are the width and diameter of a shovel — in order to locate artifacts beyond the modern island, both in the swamp and the shallow, offshore area in the water. The shovel tests were set out 10 meters apart and excavated by arbitrary 20 cm levels to sterile soil or to a maximum depth of 100 cm. Beyond that depth, digging was impossible. The purpose was to find the extent of the buried cultural remains and hence to determine the ancient site size. The technique of shovel testing is not common in the Maya area but is well suited to waterlogged or offshore areas where more extensive excavations are unfeasible. Shovel testing is common in North American archaeology, particularly with government-mandated archaeological assessments carried out prior to land development to check for the presence of archaeological sites.

CHAPTER 10

1. McKillop (1994b, 1995a, 1995d, 1996a, 2002); Steiner (1994).

2. Further discussion of sites mentioned in this chapter, together with a summary of the cultural history of Port Honduras, including the use of obsidian over time, are found in other publications (McKillop 1994b; 1996a; 2002). Sites mentioned in this

chapter are marked in figure 10.6 in chapter 10. See McKillop and Herrmann (n.d.) on chemical sourcing of obsidian from Port Honduras sites.

3. McKillop (1995d, 1996a, 1998a, 2002). As at Wild Cane Cay, I named the coral mounds after the common names of shell species found in the area.

4. In 1994, the government of Belize designated Punta Ycacos Lagoon and the surrounding land as Paynes Creek National Park.

5. McKillop (1995c, 1998a, 2002).

CHAPTER 11

1. I hired Orlando off and on until he was involved in a gun fight, charged with attempted murder, went into hiding in the bush for a couple of years, finally turned himself in to the Punta Gorda police, and spent some time in jail. Even before then I had grown tired of his habit of cursing my students, talking to spirits, and threatening to have the queen of England arrest us. Having said that, I keep in touch with Orlando and respect his knowledge of the sea and the bush. The site, Orlando's Jewfish, is named after the discovery of the site, when Orlando and I were taking a break from boat survey in Punta Ycacos Lagoon. We stumbled onto artifacts on the sea floor as we tried unsuccessfully to catch a jewfish as it left its underground burrow.

CHAPTER 13

1. Braud 1996; McKillop 1995b, 2002.

2. Details of the excavations of Stingray Lagoon and the analysis of salt-making artifacts from Stingray Lagoon, Killer Bee, David Westby, and Orlando's Jewfish sites are in McKillop (2002).

CHAPTER 14

1. McKillop (2002).

2. McKillop (1994a, 1996b).

3. McKillop (2002).

4. Ibid.

5. Interested readers can find additional details in other publications on the Maya prehistory of Port Honduras (McKillop, 1994b, 1996a).

6. The remarkable increase in coastal trade involving Wild Cane Cay is discussed in more detail elsewhere (McKillop 1989a).

7. In the summer of 2000, the Punta Gorda ferry was hijacked on its daily return trip from Puerto Barrios, the boat was stolen, and most of the passengers and the owner's son, Julio Requena Jr., were murdered. These and other unsolved boating accidents add a measure of humility and caution to my adventures in coastal Maya archaeology.

CHAPTER 15

1. Stross et al. (1978) chemically identified obsidian blades that Norman Hammond had surface collected on his survey of the Port Honduras cays (see Hammond 1975). McKillop and Herrmann (n.d.) chemically identified blades from my research on Frenchman's Cay.

2. McKillop (1996b).

3. McKillop and Winemiller (2004).

4. D. Chase (1990); Pyburn (1990).

5. McKillop 1989a.

CHAPTER 16

1. In 2001, I was disturbed to hear a report of an American missionary plane that had been shot down in Peru because it was suspected of being involved in drug smuggling. As ABC news reported, the pilot of the missionaries' plane "tried to radio the Peruvian air force and . . . was in contact with the air traffic control tower in the city of Iquitos. The calls were apparently fruitless because Donaldson (the pilot) was communicating over a civilian radio channel to airport officials 50 miles away, while the attacking Peruvian jet communicated solely on a military channel" (ABCNews .com, April 23, 2001, "Planning Purposes: American Missionary Organization Says Pilot Filed Flight Plan").

2. Emory King Sr. (1991).

3. Shoman (1994); Grant (1976).

4. Moberg (1996). See Moberg (1992) for a discussion of the citrus industry in southern Belize.

CHAPTER 17

1. Brandehoff-Pracht (1995); The offshore excavations and mapping are also discussed in McKillop (1996a, 2002).

CHAPTER 18

1. Magnoni (1999); McKillop (1997); McKillop and Winemiller (2004); McKillop et al. (2004); Watson (1999).

2. See McKillop (2001) for further descriptions of the Frenchman's Cay ceramics and other pottery from Port Honduras.

3. Hammond (1975).

4. For Lamanai, see Pendergast (1981). For Caracol, see Chase and Chase (1994). For Altun Ha, see Pendergast (1979). For Tikal, see Coe (1967) and Harrison (1999).

REFERENCES

Andrews, E. Wyllys IV, and Anthony P. Andrews. 1975. A Preliminary Study of the Ruins of Xcaret, Quintana Roo, Mexico. *Middle American Research Institute Publication* 40. New Orleans: Tulane University.

Andrews, Anthony P., Frank Asaro, Helen V. Michel, Fred H. Stross, and Pura Cervera Rivero. 1989. The Obsidian Trade at Isla Cerritos, Yucatan, Mexico. *Journal of Field Archaeology* 16: 355–63.

Arden, Tracie, ed. 2002. *Ancient Maya Women.* New York: Altamira Press.

Ashmore, Wendy. 1981a. Precolumbian Occupation at Quirigua, Guatemala: Settlement Patterns in a Classic Maya Center. Ph.D. diss., Department of Anthropology, University of Pennsylvania.

———, ed. 1981b. *Lowland Maya Settlement Patterns.* Albuquerque: University of New Mexico Press.

Bird, Junius. 1931. Boekelman Shell-Heap Expedition, 1931. Manuscript in files of American Museum of Natural History, New York.

Black, Stephen. 1990. The Carnegie Uaxactun Project and the Development of Maya Archaeology. *Ancient Mesoamerica* 1: 257–76.

Bolland, O. Nigel. 1977. The Maya and the Colonization of Belize in the Nineteenth Century. In *Anthropology and History in Yucatan,* ed. Grant D. Jones, 69–99. Austin: University of Texas Press.

Brandehoff-Pracht, Jodi. 1995. Test Excavation at Pork and Doughboy Point, Belize. Master's thesis, Department of Geography and Anthropology, Louisiana State University, Baton Rouge.

Braswell, Geoffrey E., John E. Clark, Kazuo Aoyama, and Heather I. McKillop. 2000. Determining the Geological Provenance of Obsidian Artifacts from the Maya Region: A Test of Efficacy of Visual Sourcing. *Latin American Antiquity* 11: 269–82.

Braud, Melissa R. 1996. Evidence for Salt Production at the Inundated David Westby Site, South Coastal Belize. Master's thesis, Department of Geography and Anthropology, Louisiana State University, Baton Rouge.

Bray, Warwick. 1970. Ancient Mesoamerica: Precolumbian Mexican and Maya Art (Exhibition of Material from Private Collections in Great Britain). Birmingham: Birmingham Museum and Art Gallery.

———. 1977. Maya Metalwork and Its External Connections. In *Social Process in Maya Prehistory,* ed. Norman Hammond, 365–403. Austin: University of Texas Press.

Bullard, William R., Jr., and Mary Ricketson Bullard. 1965. *Late Classic Finds at Baking Pot, British Honduras.* Occasional Paper 8. Toronto: Royal Ontario Museum.

Burdon, John A. 1931–1934. *Archives of British Honduras,* vols. 1–3. London: Sifton Praed.

Burns, E. L. n.d. *What's Cooking in Belizean Kitchens?* Belize City: Graphics One Ltd.

Cambranes, J. C. 1985. *Coffee and Peasants in Guatemala.* Stockholm: Plumsock Foundation.

Camille, Michael. 1986a. Historical Geography of Toledo Settlement, Belize, 1868–1985: A Transition from Confederate to East Indian Landscape. Master's thesis, Department of Geography and Anthropology, Louisiana State University, Baton Rouge.

———. 1986b. Historical Geography of the U.S. Confederate Settlement at Toledo, Belize, 1868–1930. *Belcast Journal of Belizean Affairs* 3(1–2): 39–46.

Cayetano, Sebastian. 1992. *Garifuna History, Language, and Culture of Belize, Central America and the Caribbean.* Belize City: Angelus Press.

Chase, Diane Z. 1982. Spatial and Temporal Variability in Postclassic Northern Belize. Ph.D. diss., Department of Anthropology, University of Pennsylvania.

———. 1990. The Invisible Maya: Population History and Archaeology at Santa Rita Corozal. In *Precolumbian Population History in the Maya Lowlands,* ed. T. Patrick Culbert and Don S. Rice, 199-213. Albuquerque: University of New Mexico Press.

Chase, Diane Z., and Arlen F. Chase. 1989. Routes of Trade and Communication and the Integration of Maya Society: The Vista from Santa Rita Corozal, Belize. In *Coastal Maya Trade,* ed. Heather McKillop and Paul F. Healy, 19–32. Occasional Papers in Anthropology 8. Peterborough, Ont.: Trent University, Department of Anthropology

———. 1996. Maya Multiples: Individuals, Entries, and Tombs in Structure A34 at Caracol. *Latin American Antiquity* 7: 61–79.

———, eds. 1994. *Studies in the Archaeology of Caracol, Belize.* Monograph 7. San Francisco: Pre-Columbian Art Research Institute.

Clegern, Wayne M. 1967. *British Honduras: Colonial Dead End, 1859–1900.* Baton Rouge: Louisiana State University Press.

Cliff, Maynard, and Cathy Crane. 1989. Changing Subsistence Economy at a Late Preclassic Maya Community. In *Research in Economic Anthropology: Prehistoric Maya Economies of Belize,* supplement 4, ed. Patricia A. McAnany and Barry Isaac, 295–324. Greenwich, Conn.: JAI Press.

Coe, William. 1967. *Tikal: A Handbook of the Ancient Maya Ruins.* Philadelphia: University Museum, University of Pennsylvania.

Culbert, T. Patrick, ed. 1991. *Classic Maya Political History.* New York: Cambridge University Press.

Davidson, William V. 1984. The Garifuna in Central America: Ethnohistorical and Geographical Foundations. In *Black Caribs: A Case Study in Biocultural Adaptations,* ed. Michael Crawford, 13–35. Current Developments in Anthropological Genetics. New York: Plenum Press.

Dockstader, Frederick J. 1964. *Indian Art of Middle America*. New York: American Museum of Natural History.

Ekholm, Gordon. 1950. Personal diary. On file in the American Museum of Natural History, New York.

Ensor, Bradley E., and Heather McKillop. 2002. Morphological and Technological Suitability of Postclassic Maya Ceramics from Wild Cane Cay, Belize. Unpublished manuscript.

Fedick, Scott L., ed. 1996. *The Managed Mosaic: Ancient Maya Agriculture and Resource Use*. Salt Lake City: University of Utah Press.

Ford, Anabel. 1981. Conditions for the Evolution of Complex Societies: The Development of the Southern Maya Lowlands. Ph.D. diss., Department of Anthropology, University of California at Santa Barbara.

———. 1986. Population Growth and Social Complexity: An Examination of Settlement and Environment in the Central Maya Lowlands. Anthropological Research Paper 35. Tempe: Arizona State University.

Freidel, David A. 1975. The Ix Chel Shrine and Other Temples of Talking Idols. In *A Study of Changing Pre-Columbian Commercial Systems,* ed. Jeremy A. Sabloff and William L. Rathje, 107–13. Monographs of the Peabody Museum of Archaeology and Ethnology 3. Cambridge: Harvard University Press, 1975.

———. 1981. The Political Economics of Residential Dispersion among the Lowland Maya. In *Lowland Maya Settlement Patterns,* ed. Wendy Ashmore, 371–82. Albuquerque: University of New Mexico Press.

Gann, Thomas W. F. 1911. Explorations Carried Out in British Honduras during 1908 and 1909. *Annals of Archaeology and Ethnology* 4 (1911): 72–87.

———. 1917. Result of Excavations at Indian Church, Kendal, Wild Cane Cay, Vaca, and Corozal in the Colony of British Honduras. Manuscript, Saville files, American Museum of Natural History, New York.

———. 1918. The Maya Indians of Southern Yucatan and Northern British Honduras. *Bureau of American Ethnology Bulletin* 64. Washington, D.C.: Smithsonian Institution.

Graham, Elizabeth. 1983. The Highlands of the Lowlands: Environment and Archaeology in the Stann Creek District, Belize, Central America. Ph.D. diss., University of Cambridge.

———. 1994. *The Highlands of the Lowlands: Environment and Archaeology in the Stann Creek District, Belize, Central America*. Monographs in World Archaeology 19. Madison: Prehistory Press.

———, and David M. Pendergast. 1989. Excavations at the Marco Gonzalez Site, Ambergris Cay, Belize, 1986. *Journal of Field Archaeology* 16: 1–16.

Grant, Cedric H. 1976. *The Making of Modern Belize: Politics, Society, and British Colonialism in Central America*. New York: Cambridge University Press.

Gregory, James R. 1972. Pioneers on a Cultural Frontier: The Mopan Maya of British Honduras. Ph.D. diss., Department of Anthropology, University of Pittsburgh.

Guderjan, Thomas H., and James F. Garber, eds. 1995. *Maya Maritime Trade, Settlement, and Population on Ambergris Caye, Belize*. Culver City, Calif.: Labyrinthos Press.

Guderjan, Thomas H., James F. Garber, Herman A. Smith. 1989. Maritime Trade on Ambergris Caye, Belize. In *Coastal Maya Trade*, ed. Heather McKillop and Paul F. Healy, 123–33. Occasional Papers in Anthropology 8. Peterborough, Ont.: Trent University, Department of Anthropology.

Guderjan, Thomas H., James F. Garber, Herman A. Smith, Fred Stross, Helen Michel, and Frank Asaro. 1989. Maya Maritime Trade and Sources of Obsidian at San Juan, Ambergris Cay, Belize. *Journal of Field Archaeology* 16: 363–69.

Hammond, Norman. 1972. Obsidian Trade Routes in the Mayan Area. *Science* 178: 1092–93.

———. 1975. *Lubaantun: A Classic Maya Realm*. Monographs of the Peabody Museum of Archaeology and Ethnology 2. Cambridge: Harvard University Press.

———, Kate Pretty, and Frank P. Saul. 1975. A Classic Maya Family Tomb. *World Archaeology* 7: 51–71.

Harrison, Peter D. 1999. *The Lords of Tikal*. New York: Thames and Hudson.

Healy, Paul F., Jaime J. Awe, and Herman Helmuth. 1998. An Ancient Maya Multiple Burial at Caledonia, Cayo District, Belize. *Journal of Field Archaeology* 25: 261–74.

Healy, Paul F., Heather McKillop, and Bernetta Walsh. 1984. Analysis of Obsidian from Moho Cay, Belize: New Evidence on Classic Maya Trade Routes. *Science* 225: 414–17.

Humphries, R. A. 1961. *The Diplomatic History of British Honduras, 1638–1901*. New York: Oxford University Press.

Inomata, Takeshi, and Stephen D. Houston, eds. 2001. *Royal Courts of the Ancient Maya*, 2 vols. Boulder: Westview Press.

Jacobi, Keith. 2000. *Last Rites for the Tipu Maya: Genetic Structuring in a Colonial Cemetery*. Tuscaloosa: University of Alabama Press.

Jeffreys, Thomas. 1775. *Thomas Jeffreys' West India Atlas*. London.

Jones, Grant D. 1989. *Maya Resistance to Spanish Rule: Time and History on a Colonial Frontier*. Albuquerque: University of New Mexico Press.

Joyce, Rosemary A. 1991. *Cerro Palenque: Power and Identity on the Maya Periphery*. Austin: University of Texas Press.

———. 2000. *Gender and Power in Prehispanic Mesoamerica*. Austin: University of Texas Press.

Joyce, Thomas A. 1929. Report on the British Museum Expedition to British Honduras, 1929. *Journal of the Royal Anthropological Institute* 59: 439–59.

Kidder, Alfred V. 1954. Miscellaneous Archaeological Specimens from Mesoamerica. *Notes on Middle American Archaeology and Ethnology.* Carnegie Institution of Washington, Department of Archaeology 117. New York: AMS Press.

King, A. 1974. Coban and Veracruz. *Middle American Research Institute Publication* 37. New Orleans: Tulane University.

King Sr., Emory. 1991. *Belize 1798: The Road to Glory, the Battle of St. George's Caye.* Belize City: Tropical Books.

King, Eric. 1986. The Development of Communications to and within Belize, 1700 to 1950: A Survey. Part 2. *Belcast Journal of Belizean Affairs* 3 (1–2): 31–38.

Lentz, David L. 1999. Plant Resources of the Ancient Maya: The Paleoethnobotanical Evidence. In *Reconstructing Ancient Maya Diet,* ed. Christine D. White, 3–18. Salt Lake City: University of Utah Press, 1999.

Leventhal, Richard. 1990. Southern Belize: An Ancient Maya Region. In *Vision and Revision in Maya Studies,* ed. Peter D. Harrison and Flora S. Clancy, 125–41. Albuquerque: University of New Mexico Press.

Lothrop, Samuel K. Metals from the Cenote of Sacrifice. *Memoirs of the Peabody Museum of Archaeology and Ethnology* 10 (2). Cambridge: Harvard University Press.

MacKinnon, J. Jefferson. 1989a. Coastal Maya Trade Routes in Southern Belize. In *Coastal Maya Trade,* ed. Heather McKillop and Paul F. Healy, 111–22. Occasional Papers in Anthropology 8. Peterborough, Ontario: Department of Anthropology, Trent University.

———. 1989b. Spatial and Temporal Patterns of Prehistoric Maya Settlement, Procurement, and Exchange on the Coast and Cays of Southern Belize. Ph.D. diss., Department of Anthropology, University of Wisconsin.

Magnoni, Aline. 1999. Relative Sea-Level Rise and Excavations at Crown Conch Mound: A Partially Submerged Ancient Maya Mound, Frenchman's Cay, Belize. Master's thesis, Department of Geography and Anthropology, Louisiana State University, Baton Rouge.

Marcus, Joyce. 1976. *Emblem and State in the Classic Maya Lowlands.* Washington, D.C.: Dumbarton Oaks.

———. 1993. Ancient Maya Political Organization. In *Lowland Maya Civilization in the Eighth Century A.D.,* ed. Jeremy A. Sabloff and John S. Henderson, 111–83. Washington, D.C.: Dumbarton Oaks.

Martin, Simon, and Nicholai Grube. 2000. *Chronicles of Maya Kings and Queens.* New York: Thames and Hudson.

Masson, Marilyn A. 2000. *In the Realm of Nachan Kan: Postclassic Maya Archaeology at Laguna de On, Belize.* Boulder: University Press of Colorado.

———, and David A. Freidel, eds. 2002. *Ancient Maya Political Economies.* New York: Altamira Press.

Maxwell, Diane D. 1998. Classic Period Royal Maya Women: A Feminist Analysis. Master's thesis, Department of Anthropology, Trent University, Peterborough, Ontario.

McAnany, Patricia A. 1986. Lithic Technology and Exchange among Maya Lowland Farmers in the Eastern Maya Lowlands. Ph.D. diss., Department of Anthropology, University of New Mexico, Albuquerque.

———. 1995. *Living with the Ancestors: Kinship and Kingship in Ancient Maya Society.* Austin: University of Texas Press.

McCreery, David. 1983. *Development and the State in Reforma, Guatemala, 1871–1885.* Latin American monograph 10. Athens: Ohio University, Center for International Studies.

McKillop, Heather. 1980. Moho Cay, Belize: Preliminary Investigations of Trade, Settlement, and Marine Resource Exploitation. Master's thesis, Department of Anthropology, Trent University, Peterborough, Ontario.

———. 1984. Ancient Maya Reliance on Marine Resources: Analysis of a Midden from Moho Cay, Belize. *Journal of Field Archaeology* 11 (1984): 25–35.

———. 1985. Prehistoric Exploitation of the Manatee in the Maya and Circum-Caribbean Areas. *World Archaeology* 16: 338–53.

———. 1987. Wild Cane Cay: An Insular Classic Period to Postclassic Period Maya Trading Station. Ph.D. diss., Department of Anthropology, University of California at Santa Barbara.

———. 1989a. Coastal Maya Trade: Obsidian Densities at Wild Cane Cay, Belize. In *Research in Economic Anthropology: Prehistoric Maya Economies of Belize,* supplement 4, ed. Patricia McAnany and Barry Isaac, 19–56. Greenwich, Conn.: JAI Press.

———. 1989b. Development of Coastal Maya Trade: Data, Models, and Issues. In *Coastal Maya Trade,* ed. Heather McKillop and Paul F. Healy, 1–17. Occasional Papers in Anthropology 8. Peterborough, Ont.: Trent University, Department of Anthropology.

———. 1994a. Ancient Maya Tree-Cropping: A Viable Subsistence Adaptation for the Island Maya. *Ancient Mesoamerica* 5: 129–40.

———. 1994b. Traders of the Maya Coast: Five Field Seasons in the Swamps of South Coastal Belize. *Mexicon* 16: 115–19.

———. 1995a. Modeling Classic Maya Settlement and Sea-Level Rise in South-Coastal Belize. Paper presented at the American Anthropological Association meeting, Washington, D.C.

———. 1995b. The Role of Ambergris Caye in Maya Obsidian Trade: Evidence from Visual Sourcing and Blade Technology. In *Maya Maritime Trade, Settlement, and Populations on Ambergris Caye, Belize,* ed. Thomas H. Guderjan and James Garber, 163–74. Culver City, Calif.: Labyrinthos Press.

———. 1995c. Underwater Archaeology, Salt Production, and Coastal Maya Trade at Stingray Lagoon, Belize. *Latin American Antiquity* 6: 214–28.

———. 1995d. The 1994 Field Season in South Coastal Belize. *LSU Maya Archaeology News* 1. http://www.ga.lsu.edu/ArchaeologyNews95.htm.

———. 1996a. Ancient Maya Trading Ports and the Integration of Long-Distance and Regional Economies: Wild Cane Cay in South-Coastal Belize. *Ancient Mesoamerica* 7: 49–62.

———. 1996b. Prehistoric Maya Use of Native Palms: Archaeobotanical and Ethnobotanical Evidence. In *The Managed Mosaic*, ed. Scott L. Fedick, 278–94. Salt Lake City: University of Utah Press.

———. 1997. Excavations in Coral Architecture at Frenchman's Cay, 1997. *LSU Maya Archaeology News* 2. http://www.ga.lsu.edu/ArchaeologyNews97.htm.

———. 1998a. Archaeological Management Plan of Port Honduras, Toledo District, Belize. Report on file, Department of Archaeology, Ministry of Tourism and the Environment, Belmopan, Belize, C.A.

———. 1998b. Archaeological Survey of Wild Cane Cay, Port Honduras, Toledo, Belize: Archaeological Impact Assessment. Report on file, Department of Archaeology, Ministry of Tourism and the Environment, Belmopan, Belize, C.A.

———. 2001. Ancient Maya Pottery from Port Honduras. Unpublished manuscript.

———. 2002. *Salt: White Gold of the Ancient Maya*. Gainesville: University Press of Florida.

———. 2004a. "The Classic Maya Trading Port of Moho Cay." In *The Ancient Maya of the Belize Valley: Half a Century of Archaeological Research*, ed. James F. Garber, 257–72. Gainesville, University Press of Florida.

———. 2004b. *The Ancient Maya: New Perspectives*. Santa Barbara, ABC-Clio.

McKillop, Heather, and Paul F. Healy, eds. 1989. Coastal Maya Trade. Occasional Papers in Anthropology 8. Peterborough, Ont.: Trent University, Department of Anthropology.

McKillop, Heather, and Stuart Herrmann. n.d. Chemical Analysis of Obsidian from South Coastal Belize: A Regional Perspective. Manuscript on file, Department of Geography and Anthropology, Louisiana State University, Baton Rouge.

McKillop, Heather, and L. Jackson. 1988. Ancient Maya Obsidian Sources and Trade Routes. In *Obsidian Dates* 4, ed. Clement Meighan and Janet Scalise, 130–41. Monograph 29. Los Angeles: University of California, Institute of Archaeology.

———, Helen Michel, Fred Stross, and Frank Asaro. 1988. Chemical Source Analysis of Maya Obsidian: New Perspectives from Wild Cane Cay, Belize. In *Archaeometry '88: Proceedings of the Twenty-Sixth International Archaeometry Symposium*, ed. Ron M. Farquhar, Ron G. V. Hancock, and Larry A. Pavlish, 239–44. Toronto: University of Toronto.

McKillop, Heather, Aline Magnoni, Rachel Watson, Shannon Ascher, Terry
    Winemiller, and Bryan Tucker. 2003. The Coral Foundations of Coastal Maya
    Architecture. In *Archaeological Investigations in the Eastern Maya Lowlands*,
    ed. Jamie Awe, John Morris, and Sherilyne Jones, 347–58. Belmopan, Belize:
    Institute of Archaeology.

McKillop, Heather, and Terance Winemiller. 2004. Ancient Maya Environment,
    Settlement, and Diet: Quantitative and GIS Analyses of Mollusca from
    Frenchman's Cay, Belize. In *Maya Zooarchaeology*, ed. Kitty Emery, 57–80.
    Los Angeles: University of California, Institute of Archaeology Publications.

McKillop, Heather, Terance Winemiller, and Farrell Jones. 2000. A GIS Approach to
    Spatial Analysis of Obsidian from Wild Cane Cay. Paper presented at the Society for
    American Archaeology Annual Conference, Philadelphia.

Miller, Arthur. 1977. The Maya and the Sea: Trade and Cult at Tancah and Tulum,
    Quintana Roo, Mexico. In *The Sea in the Pre-Columbian World*, ed. Elizabeth
    Benson, 97–140. Washington, D.C.: Dumbarton Oaks.

Mitchell-Hedges, Frederick. 1931. *Land of Wonder and Fear*. London: Century.

Moberg, Mark. 1992. *Citrus, Strategy, and Class: The Politics of Development in Southern
    Belize*. Iowa City: University of Iowa Press.

———. 1996. Crown Colony as Banana Republic: The United Fruit Company in
    British Honduras, 1900–1920. *Journal of Latin American Studies* 28: 357–82.

Mock, Shirley B. 1994. The Northern River Lagoon Site (NRL): Late-to-Terminal
    Classic Maya Settlement, Salt Making, and Survival on the Northern Belize Coast.
    Ph.D. diss., Department of Anthropology, University of Texas–Austin.

Moholy-Nagy, Hattula, Frank Asaro, and Fred H. Stross. 1984. Tikal Obsidian:
    Sources and Typology. *American Antiquity* 49: 104–17.

Neff, Hector. 1989. Origins of Plumbate Pottery Production. In *Ancient Trade and
    Tribute: Economies of the Soconusco Region of Mesoamerica*, ed. Barbara Voorhies,
    175–93. Salt Lake City: University of Utah Press.

Pendergast, David M. 1979. *Excavations at Altun Ha, Belize, 1964-1970*, vol. 1.
    Toronto: Royal Ontario Museum.

———. 1981. Lamanai, Belize: Summary of Excavations, 1974–1980. *Journal of Field
    Archaeology* 8: 29–53.

Pollock, Harry E. D., Ralph L. Roys, Tatiana Proskouriakoff, and A. Ledyard Smith.
    1962. *Mayapan, Yucatan, Mexico*. Washington, D.C.: Carnegie Institution of
    Washington.

Pyburn, K. Anne. 1988. The Settlement of Nohmul: Development of a Prehispanic
    Maya Community in Northern Belize. Ph.D. diss., Department of Anthropology,
    University of Arizona, Tucson.

———. 1990. Settlement Patterns at Nohmul: Preliminary Results of Four Excavation
    Seasons. In *Precolumbian Population History in the Maya Lowlands*, ed. T. Patrick
    Culbert and Don S. Rice, 183–97. Albuquerque: University of New Mexico Press.

Reents-Budet, Dorie. 1994. *Painting the Maya Universe*. Durham: Duke University Press.

Rice, Prudence. 1984. Obsidian Procurement in the Central Peten Lakes Region, Guatemala. *Journal of Field Archaeology* 11: 181–94.

Ricketson, Oliver. 1925. Burials in the Maya Area. *American Anthropologist* 27: 381–401.

Ricketson, Oliver G., and Edith B. Ricketson. 1937. *Uaxactun, Guatemala, Group E. 1926–1937*. Carnegie Institution of Washington Publication 447. Washington, D.C.: Carnegie Institution of Washington.

Robin, Cynthia. 1989. *Preclassic Maya Burials at Cuello, Belize*. British Archaeological Reports International Series, vol. 480. Oxford.

Rovner, Irwin. 1976. A Method for Determining Obsidian Trade Patterns in the Maya Lowlands. *Katunob* 9 (1): 43–51.

Sabloff, Jeremy A., and William L. Rathje. 1975. *A Study of Changing Pre-Columbian Commercial Systems*. Monographs of the Peabody Museum of Archaeology and Ethnology 3. Cambridge: Harvard University Press.

Sanders, William T. 1960. *Prehistoric Ceramics and Settlement Patterns in Quintana Roo*. Contributions to American Anthropology and History 60. Carnegie Institution of Washington Publication 606. Washington, D.C.: Carnegie Institution of Washington.

Saul, Frank P. 1972. *The Human Skeletal Remains of Altar de Sacrificios, Guatemala: An Osteographic Analysis*. Papers of the Peabody Museum of Archaeology and Ethnology 63 (2). Cambridge: Harvard University Press.

———. 1975. Appendix 8: Human Remains from Lubaantun. In *Lubaantun: A Classic Maya Realm*, by Norman Hammond, 389–410. Monographs of the Peabody Museum of Archaeology and Ethnology 2. Cambridge: Harvard University Press.

———. 1982. Appendix II: The Human Skeletal Remains from Tancah, Mexico. In *On the Edge of the Sea: Mural Painting at Tancah-Tulum, Quintana Roo, Mexico*, by Arthur S. Miller, 115–28. Washington, D.C.: Dumbarton Oaks.

———, and J. Mary Saul. 1991. The Preclassic Population of Cuello. In *Cuello: An Early Maya Community in Belize*, ed. Norman Hammond, 134–58. New York: Cambridge University Press.

Schele, Linda, and David Freidel. 1990. *A Forest of Kings*. New York: William Morrow.

Schele, Linda, and Mary Miller. 1986. *The Blood of Kings*. New York: George Braziller.

Sheets, Payson D. 1975. Behavioral Analysis and the Structure of a Prehistoric Industry. *Current Anthropology* 16: 369–91.

———, Kenneth Hirth, Fred Lange, Fred Stross, Frank Asaro, and Helen Michel. 1990. Obsidian Sources and Elemental Analyses of Artifacts in Southern Mesoamerica and the Northern Intermediate Zone. *American Antiquity* 55: 144–58.

Sheets, Payson, and Guy Muto. 1972. Pressure Blades and Total Cutting Edge. *Science* 175: 632–34.

Shepard, Anna O. 1948. *Plumbate: A Mesoamerican Trade Ware.* Carnegie Institution of Washington Publication 573. Washington, D.C.: Carnegie Institution of Washington.

Shoman, Assad. 1994. *Thirteen Chapters of a History of Belize.* Belize City: Angelus Press.

Sidrys, Raymond V. 1977. Mass-Distance Measures for the Maya Obsidian Trade. In *Exchange Systems in Prehistory,* ed. Timothy K. Earle and Jonathan E. Ericson, 91–107. New York: Academic Press, 1977.

Spence, Michael W. 1987. Report on the Burials of Wild Cane Cay, Belize. *In* Wild Cane Cay: An Insular Classic Period to Postclassic Period Maya Trading Station, by Heather McKillop, 282–95. Ph.D. diss., University of California at Santa Barbara.

Steiner, Edward P. 1994. Prehistoric Maya Settlement along Joe Taylor Creek, Belize. Master's thesis, Department of Geography and Anthropology, Louisiana State University, Baton Rouge.

Stephens, John L. 1841. *Incidents of Travel in Central America, Chiapas, and Yucatan,* vol. 1. New York: Harper and Brothers.

Stone, Doris Z. 1932. Some Spanish Entradas, 1524–1695. *Middle American Research Institute Publication* 4: 209–96. New Orleans: Tulane University.

Stross, F. H., H. R. Bowman, H. V. Michel, F. Asaro, and N. Hammond. 1978. Mayan Obsidian: Source Correlations for Southern Belize Artifacts. *Archaeometry* 20: 83–93.

Taylor, Douglas Macrae. 1951. *The Black Carib of British Honduras.* Viking Fund Publications in Anthropology 17. New York: Wenner-Gren Foundation.

Thompson, J. Eric S. 1930. *Ethnology of the Mayas of Southern and Central British Honduras.* Field Museum of Natural History Anthropology Series 17 (2). Chicago.

———. 1972. *The Maya of Belize: Historical Chapters since Columbus.* Belize City: Benex Press.

Trudeau, Pierre E. 1970. Exhaustion and Fulfillment: The Ascetic in a Canoe. In *Wilderness Canada,* ed. Borden Spears. Toronto: Clarke, Irwin.

Turner, B. L., and Charles H. Miksicek. 1984. Economic Plant Species Associated with Prehistoric Agriculture in the Maya Lowlands. *Economic Botany* 38: 179–93.

Watson, Rachel M. 1999. Excavations of Maya Coral Architecture, Spondylus Mound, Frenchman's Cay, Belize. Master's thesis, Department of Geography and Anthropology, Louisiana State University, Baton Rouge.

Welsh, W. B. M. 1988. *An Analysis of Classic Lowland Maya Burials.* British Archaeological Reports International Series, vol. 409. Oxford.

White, Christine D., ed. 1999. *Reconstructing Ancient Maya Diet.* Salt Lake City: University of Utah Press.

Whittington, Stephen, and David M. Reed, eds. 1997. *Bones of the Maya: Studies in Ancient Skeletons.* Washington, D.C.: Smithsonian Institution Press.

Wilk, Richard R. 1981. Agriculture, Ecology, and Domestic Organization among the Kekchi Maya of Belize. Ph.D. diss., University of Arizona.

———. 1987. The Kekchi and the Settlement of Toledo District. *Belizean Studies* 15 (3): 33–50.

INDEX

Photos and illustrations are indicated with *italic* type.

Muschamp Creek, 110–11
Muto, Guy, 201n11

Nathaniel Spang. *See* Spang, Nathaniel
(junior staff)
Nim Li Punit, 141–42, 192n2, 197n3

obsidian blades: Butterfly Wing site, 141;
coastal areas, 108; fieldwork purposes,
19–20, 41–43; Frenchman's Cay, 148–
50, 188; Hammond's excavations, 192–
93n3; identification techniques, 41, 43–
46, 200n1, 201n12; map of sources, *42;*
Moho Cay site, 87, 202n9; offshore areas, 98; Paleoindian, xi; for population
estimates, 154–55; Tiger Mound site,
122; as trade good, 19, 47–48, 141–42,
197n2, 201n13; uses for, 19–20
obsidian blades, Wild Cane Cay: fieldwork purposes, 19–20, 41–43; household middens, 18–19, 39, 40, 142; pho-
tos/illustrations, *19, 39, 44, 79, 83, 85;*
quantities traded, 46–47, 201n8;
source identifications, 43–46, 201nn5–
6; trade routes, 47–49, 86. *See also*
burial sites
offshore areas, fieldwork: artifacts, 97–98,
134–37; excavation process, 96–98,
108, 133–34, 167, 203n1; mapping/
marking, 94–96, 98, 131–33, 152. *See
also* sea levels, changes
Orlando (dory driver), 92–93, 112, 124–
25, 129, 159, 162–63, 204n1
Orlando's Jewfish site, 140, 204n1

Pachuca obsidian, 47, 67, 86, 149–50,
154, 201n12
Paleoindian people, xi
palm food remains, 35–36, 81, 153
Pasion, 141, 142
Paul III (pope), 158

Pelican Cay, 138–39, 140, 142, 154
Pemberton, Kevin, 167
Pepito (Julio Requena, Jr.), 92, 204n7
Peru, 205n1 (ch 16)
Petexbatun, Guatemala, 141, 142
pigpen, 54–55
pilgrimage centers, 87–88
Pineapple Grove site, 110
plane-table alidade, 21
plant food remains: overview, 200n4;
Frenchman's Cay, 153; offshore areas,
98; Pork and Doughboy, 167; Sting
Ray Lagoon, 137; Wild Cane Cay, 33–
36, 81
plumbate pottery, 48, 192–93n3
poknoboy seeds, 35–36, 153
Polonio, Bobbie, 124–25, 195–96n8
population estimates, 154–55
Pork and Doughboy site, 35, 138, 165–70
Port Honduras: map, *4;* and rising sea
levels, 137–39, 140; settlement patterns, 141, 142, 143; trade network
overview, 139–42. *See also* coastal fieldwork (Port Honduras); colonial era
pottery artifacts: Clearwater site, 111;
coastal sites, 108, 110; Frenchman's
Cay, 148, 153, 173, 176, *177–79,* 183;
from historic excavations, 192–93n3;
Killer Bee site, 120; offshore areas, 97–
98; Pork and Doughboy, 167; saltwork
sites, 134–36; Tiger Mound site, 121–
22; trade networks, 48, 86, 141; Wild
Cane Cay, 37, 53–54. *See also* Fighting
Conch mound
Preclassic period, overview, xi
Proskouriakoff, Tatiana, 198–99n6
provision trips: Frenchman's Cay, 148,
156–58, 184–89; survival strategies,
161–62; Wild Cane Cay, 6, 8, 90–91,
127–30
pumice, 40